PRAISE FOR *GO BLENDED!*

"Liz Arney has done the hard work of taking her deep experience and making it practical and useful to other school designers. Anyone launching or redesigning a school with blended learning should incorporate the lessons of *Go Blended!*"

—Stacey Childress, CEO, NewSchools Venture Fund

"A practical, must read for any educator who is leveraging technology to meet the instruction needs of all youth."

—John E. Deasy, former Superintendent,
Los Angeles Unified School District

"Principals, teachers, coaches, superintendents, and IT directors—anyone who wants to implement a 'personalized learning program' in a school, district, or charter management organization—take notice!! Liz Arney's book harvests lessons from the best test kitchens and offers practical approaches that spell success for you and your students."

—Don Shalvey, Cofounder, Aspire Public Schools,
Deputy Director of the Bill and Melinda Gates Foundation

"*Go Blended!* is required reading for every teacher, principal, and administrator implementing technology in their classrooms. Read it in book groups; keep it handy on your desk; have a copy on your nightstand. You'll find yourself returning to it over and over for the invaluable lessons it offers and the landmines it will help you avoid."

—Joanne Weiss, Education Consultant and Entrepreneur,
former Director of the Race to the Top Program and
former Chief of Staff to Secretary of Education Arne Duncan

"Liz Arney is the original 'healthy skeptic.' She keeps student learning at the heart of every judgment call and writes with spirit and candor about the choices she helped make at Aspire. This is no 'silver bullet' solution but instead a practical road map to using technology to target instruction directly to student needs. Arney is exactly the guide you should have at your side as you travel this new world of instruction—experienced, thoughtful, and crisp in her advice."

—Betsy Corcoran, CEO and Cofounder, EdSurge

GO BLENDED!

GO BLENDED!

A HANDBOOK FOR BLENDING TECHNOLOGY IN SCHOOLS

LIZ ARNEY

JB JOSSEY-BASS™
A Wiley Brand

Contents

■ ■ ■

To Miles and Quincy

Foreword

When I think about Aspire Public Schools (Aspire), I remember a line from an old song: "I'm a little bit country, and I'm a little bit rock and roll." It's probably more accurate to say we're a little bit country, rock and roll, rap, R&B, and pop—and probably a few other things. When people get to know our school system, no matter what their context, they often see some relevance for their own. In some ways, we look like a medium-sized school district. In other ways, we resemble individual charter schools or traditional schools trying new things for our students, trying to serve them better. Our experience (and our expressed goal to be perceived in this way) made us even more determined to find a way to share what we've learned so far about blended learning—an area that holds tremendous promise for students everywhere. We think the lessons we're learning are applicable in a lot of very different schools and school systems. And we're writing with the hope that everyone can make new mistakes, or at least different versions of the ones we've already made.

From the first days of Aspire, our mission statement has called us to be and do more than "just" serve our students. Although this will always be our first responsibility, our mission also calls us to share successful practices with other educators. We live this piece of our mission in very real ways. We've spun out an EdTech company (Schoolzilla) to make the data tools and practices we've developed at Aspire accessible to other schools. We've trained principals for one of our host districts on our teacher observation rubric and calibration techniques. And when we embarked on our blended learning work, it quickly became clear that this would be another area where we'd find people eager to share with us, learn from one another, and get better together.

When we started this work, we heard a lot about the innovator's dilemma. We still do. I don't think we did a great job of explaining *why* we thought we had a good chance to avoid that dilemma. Put simply, we think our culture is good defense or at least a strong factor in making that dilemma more manageable. As a result we heard, and continue to hear, some version of the following:

"You're doing great on many things . . . so you'll be stuck in your old ways."

"You'll fall behind and stop innovating."

"As you get bigger and better, you have too much to lose, and you're under too much scrutiny (and accountability as a charter) to try new things."

The culture at Aspire is special, and it definitely is not about being better than everyone else. It never has been. It's about a lot of things, and one of which is never being satisfied with how ready our kids are for college. We can always do more, and we must. The opportunity equation for our students is stacked against the students and communities we serve in lots of stubbornly persistent ways. Plain and simple— we can't ever stop getting better.

At Aspire we're determined to avoid getting stuck in our ways or being afraid to try new things. We strive to never stop searching, exploring, and questioning. Our principals and teachers do a great job of keeping that trait alive and well. One of the best parts of our "never satisfied" culture is it forces us to push the envelope and continually improve our practice. Our culture demands from our teachers and leaders both the freedom and the responsibility to purposefully question, argue, experiment, and try new things. For people who join our schools, they sometimes look for the "Aspire way." The "way we do things" sometimes takes on a kind of mystical power until people realize the "Aspire way" involves a healthy, regular dose of change—and trying, always, to get better. Most people quickly realize there are very few things other than our values and this culture that we strive to protect and hold as consistent and sacred as possible.

It takes a little craziness to leave something that's working just fine, armed only with the hope something else will work better. That's exactly what we're trying to do—keep a little crazy in our work. The blended learning work we've done so far is an example of keeping a dose of entrepreneurial "craziness" alive and well at Aspire—just as we hope to do in the future.

Another part of our culture that has served us well in this work is what I call confident humility. There will always be more schools, educators, and organizations that can teach us loads more than we could ever share with them. I think staying confidently humble serves us well: We're confident enough to try new things and not worry too much that we'll be criticized or penalized too harshly for failure or a drop in results. We're confident enough to know we're not experts, but we know some things that position us well to try, learn, fail, and try again. We're confident enough to say, "We're doing this our way, at a pace that fits our culture, and aligned with our mission as an organization." At the same time, we are also humble enough to know we learn every day from other educators, schools, and systems in powerful ways. We're humble enough to sit and learn from (and with) others who are struggling through the same challenges or who are kind enough to help us even when the issues we're struggling to solve are ones they solved long ago.

In doing this work, we've found once again that the really good ideas often come from the same source: teachers. If you want good ideas about how to improve and use technology in the classroom, ask your teachers. They are probably doing more with technology than you know right now. They will have ideas about what will make them better, and I bet they're dreaming right now of a day, place or time when their ideas can become a reality. When we made an internal request for proposals (RFP) for blended ideas and pilots, we found our teachers had lots of ideas. We learned many were already experimenting with technology and trying to see what it could do to improve their instruction.

We have an amazing group of people at Aspire, dedicated to students in ways that amaze me every day. I see the smiles and tears, fatigue and energy, dedication, and occasionally despair, when we succeed and when we fail to achieve what we want for our students. And there is an unwavering commitment to get back up when we fall, to keep serving our students across Aspire and in public schools across our country. I've called our teammates heroes, and I'm told our teachers hear that phrase and sometimes cringe. They cringe not just out of humility but because they are not superhuman. They are not gifted with some special power, but they do tackle this work with huge hearts, coupled with enough determination and grit to tackle a daunting task—getting every student in our country ready for college. It is awe-inspiring.

I could name hundreds of people who deserve the hero merit badge both inside and outside of Aspire. I go to sleep at night hoping all of them know this, and I hope people admire them for what they do every day. Among these people, Liz Arney is a special one. She's the author of this book, which will be the first part of the "Sharing Successful Practices" series. Liz has been with Aspire for more than a decade as a long-time master educator and coach. "Bleeding purple" (our signature color) is defined by Liz Arney. She understands who we are and where we want to be, and has an unwavering commitment not just to our kids, but to all students who need great schools and the future those youngsters deserve.

Liz is a thinker and a critical one, a collaborator, an innovator, and a friend. This combination of qualities is exactly what we needed when we embarked on blended learning. We tapped Liz to lead this work because of those qualities, and she has shouldered the weight of marching into the unknown, armed only with the knowledge of what we do well and what we don't. You'll benefit not just from her willingness to lead this work at Aspire, but from her endless appetite to learn from others, to always question what we think we know, and to see things from someone else's perspective, based on their experiences.

We had a few things in our backpack as Liz led us on this journey, but one of the most important was a very clear goal: We must tap every possible opportunity to increase the effectiveness of the instruction happening in classrooms, and get our kids ready for college. We're thankful for Liz's leadership and to all those who contributed to the emerging lessons captured within this book.

At Aspire Public Schools, our mission calls us to share successful practices. Because we've begun to learn something about what it takes to make blended learning a reality in schools, we're eager to share with others. This book is a proud example of our commitment to students everywhere, especially students who have the opportunity equation stacked against them and their families across the country. We're committed to sharing what we know, learning from others, and making sure we try to make new mistakes and learn new lessons, because of them.

We also have great hope you will take this work further. We deeply hope you make new mistakes, or at least different versions of the mistakes we've made. If you do, we'll all get better together. Happy reading! We look forward to learning from you.

JAMES R. WILLCOX
Chief Executive Officer, Aspire Public Schools

About the Author

Liz Arney is the director of innovative learning at Aspire Public Schools, where she is crafting and running blended learning pilots in order to identify the role of blended learning at Aspire and how best to scale it. As a member of Aspire's Education Team, Liz works closely with teachers, principals, IT teammates, and data and analysis teammates to create supportive structures and processes for increasing classroom technology offerings aligned with Aspire's instructional program and culture. Prior to her work on blended learning, Liz worked at Aspire as a humanities instructional coach, providing professional development, instructional and content support, and induction coaching to grades 6–12 humanities teachers across the organization. She also led the development of curriculum toolkits for English, social studies, science, and math courses in grades 9–12. Before coming to Aspire, Liz taught high-school English in public and private schools in Boston, Seattle, and Taipei, Taiwan, and provided history content coaching to teachers across New England. Liz holds a bachelor's degree in English from the University of California at Berkeley, a master's degree in education from Harvard University, and a master's degree in humanities from the University of Chicago. Visit Liz Arney at www.goblended.com.

About the Contributors

Many teachers, principals, and blended learning leaders informed the contents of this book with their hard work and living examples; I want to call out a few who are quoted throughout the book and who generously gave of their time to bring their ideas and opinions about this work to light. I'm offering additional information about each of them here so readers will know a little more about them.

BLENDED LEARNING DISTRICT AND CHARTER LEADERS

Anirban Bhattacharyya is the digital learning director at KIPP Foundation, a national network of free, open-enrollment, college-preparatory public schools dedicated to preparing students in underserved communities for success in college and in life. Anirban supports KIPP leaders as they create next-generation school models and instructional designs that leverage innovative instructional technology.

Jeanne Chang is the director of technology innovation at E. L. Haynes Public Charter School in Washington, D.C. Jeanne supports school leadership and staff across grades pre-K–12 in developing, implementing, iterating, and evaluating blended learning strategies to better prepare their students for success at the college of their choice.

Jon Deane is the chief information officer for Summit Public Schools, a charter management organization based in California. Jon serves on Summit's leadership team and oversees all data and information systems in Summit's personalized learning model.

Chris Florez is the manager of blended learning for Aspire Public Schools in Memphis, Tennessee. Chris oversees the implementation of blended learning in Aspire's Memphis schools.

Rachel Klein is the director of student advancement in Highline Public Schools, a public district with schools in Seattle, Washington, and surrounding communities. Rachel oversees Highline's efforts to implement blended learning in grades K–12, as well as all of the district's efforts to ensure that students graduate college-ready and have clear pathways into postsecondary education and careers.

Chris Liang-Vergara is the chief of learning at LEAP Innovations, an R&D hub for education innovation that helps foster best practices for personalized learning and technology to accelerate learning. Chris oversees LEAP's Pilot Network to enable educators and schools to pilot new models and products in a highly supportive, collaborative setting with rigorous evaluation.

Nithi Thomas is the blended learning manager for Mastery Charter Schools, a K–12 charter school management organization with schools in Philadelphia, Pennsylvania, and Camden, New Jersey. Nithi oversees Mastery's blended learning initiatives and supports its implementation into the organization's current programming.

Jonathan Tiongco is the director of BLAST implementation for Alliance College-Ready Public Schools, a charter management organization in Los Angeles, California. Jonathan oversees Alliance's portfolio of blended learning schools, which includes blended learning pilots, full-school conversions, and a Next Generation Learning Challenges grantee school.

Caryn Voskuil is in the education studio at IDEO, a design firm in San Francisco. Formerly, she was the manager of school model innovation at Rocketship Education, where she piloted new products and systems across schools.

Tom Willis is the chief executive officer of Cornerstone Charter Schools, a charter management organization in Detroit, Michigan. Tom focuses his energies on three areas: culture, results for kids, and leveraging technology to fundamentally improve learning. His vision is to grow the Cornerstone model so that more children in the city and beyond may experience educational excellence in a safe, structured, and loving environment.

Bryant Wong is the chief technology officer at Summit Public Schools, a charter management organization based in California and Washington. Bryant designs, leads, and manages technology for Summit's organization and schools.

BLENDED LEARNING TEACHERS AND PRINCIPALS

Kim Benaraw is the principal at Aspire Titan Academy, a K–5 charter school in Huntington Park, California.

Lindy Brem is the literacy specialist at Aspire Titan Academy in Huntington Park, California.

Contessa Cannaday is a fifth-grade teacher in a blended learning classroom at Aspire Slauson Academy in Los Angeles, California.

Nancy Castro is a kindergarten teacher in a blended learning classroom at Aspire Titan Academy in Huntington Park, California.

Meredith Dadigan is a fifth-grade teacher in a blended learning classroom at Aspire Titan Academy in Huntington Park, California.

Taleen Dersaroian is a third-grade teacher in a blended learning classroom at Aspire Gateway Academy in Southgate, California.

Freddy Esparza is a second-grade teacher in a blended learning classroom at Aspire Titan Academy in Huntington Park, California.

Raul Gonzalez is a first-grade teacher in a blended learning classroom at Aspire Titan Academy in Huntington Park, California.

Claire Hawley is a first-grade teacher in a blended learning classroom at Aspire ERES Academy in Oakland, California.

Christin Hwang is a third-grade teacher in a blended learning classroom at Aspire Inskeep Academy in Los Angeles, California.

Sandy Jimenez is a first-grade teacher in a blended learning classroom at Aspire Gateway Academy in Southgate, California.

Jennifer Mazawey is a kindergarten teacher in a blended learning classroom at Aspire Titan Academy in Huntington Park, California.

Christian McGrail is a fourth-grade teacher in a blended learning classroom at Aspire Titan Academy in Huntington Park, California.

Lourdes Meraz is a fourth-grade teacher in a blended learning classroom at Aspire Titan Academy in Huntington Park, California.

Allyson Milner is a third-grade teacher in a blended learning classroom at Aspire Titan Academy in Huntington Park, California.

Mark Montero is a second-grade teacher in a blended learning classroom at Aspire Titan Academy in Huntington Park, California.

Carolina Orozco is a third-grade teacher in a blended learning classroom at Aspire Gateway Academy in Southgate, California.

Nancy Pacheco Sanchez is a third-grade teacher in a blended learning classroom at Aspire Titan Academy in Huntington Park, California.

Dennise Reyes-Serpas is a fourth-grade teacher in a blended learning classroom at Aspire Slauson Academy in Los Angeles, California.

Amy Youngman is a humanities instructional coach for Aspire Public Schools in Oakland, California. Previously, Amy was one of Aspire's first blended learning pilot teachers at Aspire ERES Academy in Oakland, where she taught middle-school humanities.

GO BLENDED!

Introduction

At Aspire Public Schools, we embarked on our blended learning journey because we wanted to figure out how technology could increase student achievement given our context, our school culture, and the overall willingness of our teachers to tackle the challenges our students face. We recognized that as adults, our lives are heavily dependent on technology; we also acknowledged that our students, whom we send off to college each year, would be using technology heavily in everything they would do in college. Additionally, we knew that even though our teaching practices were really good, they were not getting all of our students prepared enough to get to and through college; we could see we needed new strategies and tools to increase our students' achievement. Blended learning offered great promise for differentiation, access to content, access to student achievement

---

What Is Blended Learning?

The definition of blended learning is a formal education program in which a student learns:

1. at least in part through online learning, with some element of student control over time, place, path, and/or pace;
2. at least in part in a supervised brick-and-mortar location away from home;
3. and the modalities along each student's learning path within a course or subject are connected to provide an integrated learning experience.

Source: Clayton Christensen Institute.

data, and student engagement. Blended learning was unproven, yes, but we recognized quickly that our schools, teachers, and students would continue to use technology more, not less, and that if we didn't figure out the role technology played in our instructional program, we'd be doomed.

WHY GO BLENDED?

Blended learning offers defined opportunities and spaces for teachers to work with small groups of students to address learning goals (individualization), enhance or extend the curriculum (rigor), or spend time analyzing student data (monitoring). By offering differentiated experiences in both online and in-person contexts, blended learning allows teachers to further focus on individual students as learners and access multiple data points to measure student growth. Additionally, blended learning offers teachers and students opportunities to apply the International Society for Technology in Education (ISTE) standards for students and teachers, the standards for learning, teaching and leading in the digital age (http://www.iste .org/STANDARDS) by providing mechanisms and routines around which students can learn using technology tools.

Our teachers' voices spoke strongly to us about the reasons for going blended after they started piloting the work, as many remarked on how blended changed the work of teaching for them. Nancy Castro, kindergarten teacher at Aspire Titan Academy, shares:

> Since blended learning, I feel my job has been more purposeful. The data that is provided through the software has allowed me to focus more on my guided reading groups and also target my student needs. I feel blended learning has allowed me to use my guided reading and math time more effectively. I get to spend a little more time with my guided reading groups, I get to teach my math lessons during computer time, and I get to pull small groups to work with my low students.

Her colleague, Raul Gonzalez, a first-grade teacher, adds:

> Finding ways to make work sustainable may seem impossible as teachers, but every minute saved is worth it. Blended learning has helped me gain

more time in my day. Let's take workstations for example. Before blended learning, I was preparing stations and organizing their rotations through them for all the students. Now, I don't have to. I prepare only a few stations that students rotate through on any given day, and because of the time allotted on the computers, there isn't a need to make stations that hold students' attention for 45 minutes in a workstation period. In the end, blended learning is an additional resource that I don't just embrace because it's my students working with technology, but also because blended learning has helped make my work as a teacher just a bit more sustainable.

Mark Montero, second-grade teacher at Aspire Titan Academy, states it another way:

What if we don't do blended learning? The students need to know how to use computers, and my students are now well versed with technology and troubleshooting any tech problems that come up. They wouldn't have this daily experience if we didn't do it. I wouldn't have a lot of real-time data to see how they're growing or what they need, especially the more reluctant participants in my class.

Montero also explains that student learning on the computers allow students to experience content they might not otherwise. He states, "Teachers need to change their schedules for blended learning, and then they panic: Is it OK if students learn from another source other than the teacher? Really? Do they always need to learn from just you?"

Christin Hwang, teacher at Aspire Inskeep Academy, explains the benefits of having another partner delivering content to students:

A few weeks ago I taught rounding for the first time this year. Before teaching the lesson I remembered most of the students had already worked on rounding in the math software using number lines, so I was able to make that connection when introducing rounding for the first time. Every year, rounding is a very new and difficult concept for my third-graders, but this year was different! Most students just "got it" so much faster and better. I taught students two different ways of rounding. One was the more conceptual method, using a number line, and the other method was more procedural, a rounding rap. In the previous years, the students lacked a strong conceptual understanding of rounding, so the number line method sometimes confused the students even more. This year, because of the exposure and support from the math software, so many students were able to successfully use the number line and really understand the concept of rounding and its purpose. Some students were even able to automatically round in their heads with the strong conceptual understanding they had developed!

Not only does blended learning support regular classroom teachers, but also literacy specialists. Lindy Brem, Aspire Titan Academy's literacy specialist, shares:

Since we started blended learning, my job has changed in two ways: how I look at reading data and how we structure pulling groups. I definitely think analyzing the data has been the easiest, and structuring groups for the learning center has been the most difficult! I love that I get to add reading software data to our reading spreadsheets each time we have a reading assessment. This information really adds another dimension to the student and figuring out what their strengths and weaknesses are. For example, we have one fourth-grader who is reading at an end-of-first-grade reading level, but scores at Level 3 on her last reading software diagnostic. Her strength was in phonics. So what we were able to determine is that she has skills and is able to identify phonics, she just needs more support with applying those skills to her reading. This new information really helps us support her! Overall, I am really happy that we have had blended learning for the last year, and I think that it has definitely had a positive effect on my job!

We've also been struck by the ways in which blended learning has helped teachers better reach challenging students. Gonzales shares:

Sometimes it's easier to challenge a lower [-skilled] student, and it's harder to challenge an advanced student. I have a first-grader who is a very advanced math student, and he used to get in trouble frequently during lessons because he'd shout out, "I already know this!" Now he's working on third-grade multiplication in the software, and he's helping motivate the class and trying to encourage students to reach higher levels. Because he's now being much more challenged, his behavior has changed, and it's really motivating me as a teacher.

Likewise, some students who struggle have thrived in blended learning classrooms. Montero shares this anecdote:

I have a really quiet student who never participates in lessons. I have difficulty knowing what his strengths are because he isn't vocal. When I started analyzing the software data, I realized that he's the highest achiever in my class in math! And when I checked his reading Lexile, I discovered he's a strong reader. Although he is an English-language learner and very quiet student, I was able to know definitively that he's one of the highest-performing kids in class. This allowed me to celebrate his successes, and when I did, he's built a lot of confidence in class and is starting to talk more!

Blended Learning Is Different from Technology-Enriched Learning

We draw an important distinction between blended learning and technology-enriched learning. Schools that run digital tools are not necessarily blended learning schools. Blended learning is a **model** that puts student learning at the center of it; technology-enriched environments, digital software workstations, and 1:1 implementations all rely on technology for teaching and learning, but the actual model of instruction used with the technology might be strikingly similar to a traditional teaching model.

Anirban Bhattacharyya, digital learning director at the KIPP Foundation and former director of instructional technology at KIPP Chicago, echoes a similar definition of blended learning: "We are working to create 'whole picture' profiles of schools with blended learning models. This will hopefully eliminate the idea that blended learning can be achieved with a hardware/software 'grocery list.'" That is to say, schools that merely choose the same software as blended schools are not necessarily doing blended learning. A model involves more than just the choice of software.

Be a Healthy Skeptic and an Eager Learner

When we began to dip our toe into the pond of blended learning three years ago, we could have been described as "healthy skeptics." By and large, we believed deeply in differentiated and individualized instruction, but we were yet to be sold on the power of technology in our instructional program to increase student achievement. Models hadn't been proven; software had little research behind it. National and family foundations that traditionally funded different teaching and learning initiatives in our schools seemed excited about the potential to change the ways schools are run (including not only the ways in which education could be delivered, but often also the costs of providing that education); that excitement was both a blessing and a cause for concern. Once we started learning from other charter organizations, school districts, and individual schools that were using technology and saw the ways technology could work in our classrooms, we started to believe that technology could hold great promise within our instructional program. In this book, I'll describe our process: learning all we can, going slowly, piloting small, and being thoughtful about what works and what doesn't.

Originally, I was on a team of two, and our job was to figure out the role of blended learning at Aspire. At times during the first six months, I felt that we were the only ones at Aspire who believed that the use of technology for learning could have a significant role in our instructional program; I myself had been far from convinced of that potential when I started out on this journey. (In fact, my title at the time was "Hybrid Learning Champion"—and I was not the most enthusiastic champion at that!) I saw countless schools buy in to the hype around digital learning, make massive technology purchases, and set themselves up for failure. I felt like a cross between a cowgirl on the edge of the untamed prairie and an astronaut on the edge of the universe. It's true that I had a connection back to Aspire: I had to figure a lot out for myself and then convince folks at Aspire that what I'd figured out was great and worth some real time and investment. It's also true that I work for an organization that gave me this amazing opportunity; that took me seriously when I said, "It might work!"; and that functions well enough that all the teams I worked with were mostly (within human limits) willing and got the job done.

In hindsight, people going into this work *should* be healthy skeptics. There's still much to learn, much that's unproven, and much that's bright and shiny without real substance. Despite these reasons for caution, blended learning offers school leaders and teachers a path for making significant changes in schools that favor student learning and can lay the groundwork for 21st-century skill building and the widespread changes technology can bring to learning. We don't believe blended learning is "it"; rather than an end in itself, blended learning is a critical step toward the future of teaching and learning in our schools, whatever that will be, because blended learning sets teachers and students on a trajectory of using technology for student learning that opens up numerous opportunities for change. In short, our work in blended learning has prepared us to continuously adapt and iterate using technology for learning in ways that previous school reforms have not.

Being a healthy skeptic means keeping your mission at the heart of your work: you want to do what's best for your students, which may or may not be the use of technology in every situation. Healthy skepticism means not being enamored with that which is bright and shiny, with devices because they're engaging, with videos because you've never seen instruction quite like that before. Realistically, being a healthy skeptic means not "going blended" because you just think it's a good idea. Rather, you're going blended because you want to figure out how technology can increase student achievement given your context, your school culture, and the overall willingness of your teachers to tackle the challenges your students face. In short, you believe blended learning will help you solve a targeted problem.

This book grew out of our teachers' desire to codify the lessons they learned as more and more of our schools converted to become blended learning schools. The book is both a reflection of teachers' experiences and our experiences getting blended learning off the ground at many of our schools. After countless conversations with school and district leaders interested in how to go blended, we realized that our challenges and the lessons we learned could be applied to a variety of contexts, and this information was better shared than kept within our charter management organization (CMO) and the blended learning community. We hope you'll take the journey and share with us so we can learn from you, too.

Different Contexts, Similar Challenges

Throughout this book, I've included the perspectives of blended learning leaders from across the country managing this work in a variety of contexts. In particular, folks at the KIPP Foundation, Summit Public Schools, Rocketship Education, E. L. Haynes Public Charter School, the Alliance College-Ready Public Schools, Cornerstone Charter Schools, Highline Public Schools (Washington), Mastery Charter Schools, and FirstLine Schools are part of a community of innovative practice whose blended learning leaders have contributed their ideas to the pages that follow.

Part of the culture of schools is that most faculties think they're unique and see their challenges as different from those at other schools. Even within our own organization, in schools with similar demographics, we can show a video of one of our classroom teachers carrying out a lesson, and invariably some teachers will say, "That wouldn't work with my students because my school is different." Yes, all schools are different, and yet we recognize that many of the challenges inherent in getting blended learning off the ground are quite similar, despite differences in context, politics, demographics, teaching population, geographic location, instructional model, and size.

Key Idea

Our blended work with districts and charters across the country has shown us that although many aspects of our programs and blended learning models might be different, our challenges faced and lessons learned are strikingly similar.

Said another way, there isn't one way to go blended; in fact, the proliferation of different models and pilots has created a rich landscape in which to learn how schools can change in service to student achievement. But the DNA of teachers, school leaders, and district administrators is strikingly similar across disparate systems; and common ground includes change management with adults and critical decisions in support of increased technology.

WHAT THIS BOOK IS NOT

Digital Learning Now, Getting Smart, Next Generation Learning Challenges, and other organizations and committees have released excellent handbooks and host dynamic sites for planning and designing blended learning. This book does not aspire to be that kind of guide. Nor does this book include any of the following:

- Specific recommendations for software
- Technical suggestions about hardware and technology infrastructure
- Information about fundraising and paying the ongoing costs of blended learning
- Exploration of or advice about the different blended models
- Ideas for alternative staffing models

Much of this information changes radically from year to year and so is not suitable for this kind of book. Software products continue to develop and change, while some disappear from the market. Hardware and infrastructure specifications evolve even more quickly. Some of the case studies on early blended learning models were published after multiple iterations of the model, to the degree that the case study barely resembled the school's current state. (This is a good thing, as we want a climate in which we continue to learn from our successes and failures!) We also don't believe we have the expertise and best answers for all of these challenges. We recommend you seek out support from organizations focused on offering information related to blended learning when digging into the nitty-gritty of these challenges.

In this book, we've drawn a distinction between technology for *learning* and technology for *teaching*. The former is where we focus our attention: student learning. The latter (SMART Boards, clickers, student apps, open educational resources, flipped classrooms, and so on) are alternate ways of delivering content that rely even more heavily on leaders changing teacher practice but that may or may not have an effect on student achievement.

A Blended Learning Teacher's Journey

While each teacher's journey is different, I've included two of our teachers' journeys in the first year of going blended to capture the multifaceted, complex, and dynamic nature of the process. I hope you'll use these journeys to remind yourself as you read through the book that this work is a journey and that your mind and the minds of your teammates will probably change over time. The first journey is here in the introduction, and the second is in the conclusion.

My Blended Learning Journey

Claire, First-Grade Teacher, Aspire ERES Academy

THE BEGINNING, THE YEAR BEFORE OUR LAUNCH

My story begins the year before we started our pilot. That winter, I met one of the KIPP Empower teachers from Los Angeles. She told me that her school had started a blended learning model that allowed her to meet with all of her students in small groups several times each day. Additionally, she shared that blended learning had made her day-to-day as a kindergarten teacher feel more sustainable. She said she couldn't imagine going back to a model in which she taught most of her lessons whole-class. As an Aspire teacher, I am always trying to find better ways to meet the needs of my students. With computers in the classroom, it sounded as if an entirely new level of differentiation might be possible. I went straight to my principal, Emily, to tell her what I had learned.

NINE MONTHS LATER

Nine months after that fateful conversation, Emily told me that Liz in the Home Office had approached her about the potential of running blended learning pilots in our school. Emily knew I had been excited to try out blended and we suspected that other teachers at our school would be similarly interested.

Liz and I visited KIPP Empower in October and saw kindergarten and first-grade classrooms in action. We observed kids rotating through guided reading groups, a teacher doing a phonics group, and kids engaged on computers. The classrooms felt happy and productive. The teachers appeared calm and focused on their small-group instruction. When I peeked over the shoulders of the students on computers, the programs appeared to be differentiated. It seemed that students were more engaged in the computer programs than they might have been doing other seatwork.

It is always daunting to imagine starting any new program midyear. However, I believed that most of the systems for blended were already in place in our classrooms at Aspire ERES Academy (ERES). We were already doing reading workshop and guided reading. We had a dedicated word work time that involved pulling small groups. We were also teaching guided math lessons during math workshop. With the computers, we would be able to provide students with a high-interest and differentiated option for their independent work time three times throughout the day. Blended learning was beginning to seem increasingly possible.

PRE-LAUNCH OF PILOTS, EARLY NOVEMBER

Come November, the kindergarten, first-, second-, and third-grade teachers at ERES began meeting to discuss how our blended rotations would work. We spent time considering how long we would meet with each group of students, how students would know when to rotate, and how students would know where they were going next. The scheduling of blended proved challenging. We had to account for much longer blocks of small-group instruction. The pilot teachers consulted one another, but were also free to implement blended in whatever way appeared to make most sense for their classroom.

THE LAUNCH, LATE NOVEMBER

After several weeks in November of moving around furniture to make more room for computers, waiting for "single sign-on" (the kid-friendly way for students to access the programs), and creating charts so that students could easily see where to go when, we were ready for the launch. We were not without our share of technology problems at the start!

My first-graders were naturals on the computers. With a fairly minimal amount of instruction, they became quickly fluent with how to navigate through the three programs we were using. As a school, it was the kindergartners who initially needed the most support on how to use the laptops. I found that the most important component of the rotation was signing out of the computers quickly and quietly so that the transition times were minimalized. A class incentive chart was quickly introduced to help students with the transitions.

One of our initial stumbling blocks was that we hadn't figured out how to begin each small group so that there could be a minute or two for the teacher

(*continued*)

(*continued*)

to scan the room and be sure all students were on task. I decided to give students a "Do Now" when they came to meet with me so I could circulate and check on task behavior if necessary.

We teachers learned quickly that there had to be a backup plan for when the Internet went down or when power was out. We taught students to get book boxes and read at their computer if they encountered problems at reading rotations. We made backup packets for students to work on at word work or math if similar problems occurred. When our blended learning teaching assistant, Ms. Furukawa, was present, we taught students appropriate ways to get her attention if they need assistance. Certain students emerged as particularly confident with computers, and we enlisted them to help their friends when necessary.

THE PILOTS, NOVEMBER TO MAY

As the weeks went by, our blended rotations continued to evolve. In my classroom, reading rotations went from being 40 minutes to 60 minutes. Now, we were meeting with each student group for 15 to 20 minutes, and the students not meeting with teachers were able to read independently, listen to books on CD, or use a reading program on the computers. At word work time, I implemented the vocabulary curriculum for students during small groups. Students practiced the class spelling words during their independent time. During math, students were placed in small groups based on pretest data for each unit. Just as in reading and word work, all students were seen each day in guided math groups.

Perhaps one of the greatest changes that I noted after adopting blended was the increased fluidity of the small groups. I was able to assess students more often, and therefore students were moving from group to group more quickly. In guided reading, I was devoting every other Friday to running records. *Words Their Way* was reassessed every 4 to 6 weeks. Math pretest information informed small groups on an almost weekly basis. The progress was not lost on students! They were proud to report their successes to their families!

Because so much of the day was devoted to small-group work, teachers began to notice that their whole-group lesson minutes were shrinking. I taught whole-class lessons for 10 to 15 minutes and would include mostly the connection and modeling. In the small groups, students would participate in the guided and independent practice, discourse, and partner work. Blended learning certainly changes the type of planning that the teacher does. I can't say that it is less work than before, but I *can* say that it is more targeted and efficient in terms of student growth.

CONCLUSION

Blended is no different from any other new academic system that we introduce to students. We emphasize care of materials, focused learning, responsibility, and student independence. I was excited to see how engaged students could be during independent work times on computers. Professionally, I found myself improving the quality and personalization of my small-group teaching. Aspire teachers are natural innovators! I can't wait to see where we can take our students with the blended learning model.

HOW TO USE THIS BOOK

This book is a practical guide to understanding the change management process for school, district, and charter leaders who want to go blended, as well as for classroom teachers going blended. While the process of converting our schools is still quite young, many lessons learned along the way have helped us think differently about how to get blended up and running. These lessons can be applied to district schools and charters alike and are especially timely now that schools in the United States are under increasing pressure to purchase technology as a way of "getting at" the Common Core State Standards and delivering the assessments that accompany them. Blended learning offers a way of thinking about how to use technology purposefully in any classroom, rather than buying technology for its own sake.

I've organized this book into three parts.

Part One explains the fundamental decisions leaders need to make in order to initiate blended learning and lay the foundation for a focused and successful implementation. The four chapters in Part One explore the starting points for all leaders to consider before embarking upon a blended learning initiative: instructional focus, readiness, team building, and planning.

Part Two details the strategic decisions leaders need to make to inform how blended learning will run. These five chapters articulate the questions, concerns, and trade-offs leaders need to make when getting blended learning into place at the school level.

Part Three lays out the on-the-ground steps leaders must take to actually launch blended learning in classrooms and schools.

The content is intended to be read sequentially, as rolling out a complex change management process involves a sequence of steps, mostly in a particular order. That said, we recognize that depending on how your team is configured, whether you're coming at this work as a teacher, department head, school administrator, or district leader, some sections of the guide may feel more applicable to work roles than others. Ideally, your team will comprise school leaders, teachers, and district heads who can work together collaboratively, as going blended is truly a team sport. Because blended learning relies so heavily on critical dependencies and trade-offs, I encourage you to read the book as a whole to better understand how each area affects the others. So while it may seem like a good idea to have folks with an operations focus (rather than teachers, for example) delve deeply into the chapters in Part Two, keep in mind that all the decisions and trade-offs in that section *directly affect teachers and students.* By having all leaders understand the process, your team will be better positioned to make decisions that foster the best outcomes for teaching and learning.

My colleague in Memphis, Tennessee, Chris Florez, manager of digital learning for Aspire, depicts the work as seen in figure I.1.

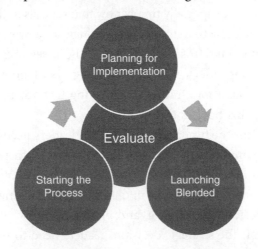

Figure I.1 Blended Learning Implementation Cycle

ARE YOU BRAVE ENOUGH TO TACKLE THIS WORK?

Digital badges have proliferated in many online learning environments to motivate learners and signal achievement, and we want to offer you the same incentives and celebrations in this book. At the end of each chapter you'll find a checklist of what it takes to earn a badge for tackling the work of that chapter as part of your blended learning journey. Check off your accomplishments as you complete them and celebrate your achievement along the way as you learn and do what it takes to go blended in your own school.

GO FOR THE BADGE!

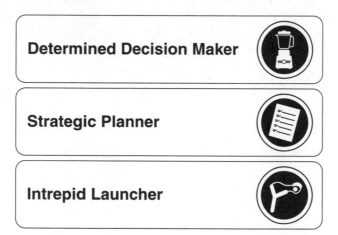

Determined Decision Maker

Strategic Planner

Intrepid Launcher

PART 1

Starting the Process:
The Fundamental Decisions

Frequently I read about districts and schools that start the process of going blended by purchasing a ton of technology first, and then figuring out how to use it second. I can't reiterate enough that this is a fundamentally poor strategy. Whether you're now sitting on a pile of iPads, having realized this fact, or you're on the brink of increasing your technology holdings and are somewhere between terrified and excited about what lies ahead, you have a series of important decisions to make first, in order to set the course of your blended learning journey (and device decisions are not among these fundamental decisions!). The landscape is riddled with mistakes made and lessons learned; in the following chapters, you'll find ways to avoid potential pitfalls and learn from others' mistakes as you start the process.

1

Identifying the Focus and Piloting

Having shared some of my findings about blended learning in recent years, I find that I'm often called on by educators around the nation. School leaders, consultants, instructional technology coaches, and teachers ask for my opinions and advice about going blended and want to tour our blended schools and get copies of documents we've put together. Many principals and teachers within Aspire also call me for technology-related advice. Here's how a typical call might go:

PRINCIPAL: We'd like to get a cart of Chromebooks/iPads/laptops for our students.

ME: Tell me more. How will your teachers plan to use these new devices?

PRINCIPAL: We want students using more technology and figure they can start accessing apps and programs to do their work. We want them to be 21st-century learners, and we know they need to use technology more for learning.

ME: OK, tell me more about your plans. Which teachers? Which apps? Do you have specific outcomes you're aiming for?

PRINCIPAL: I'm not sure. It'll vary from classroom to classroom.

ME: OK. Do you have a plan around who will be responsible for the devices? Train the teachers? Focus your program and app purchasing decisions?

And so it goes on. Usually, at this point, the principal gets a little frustrated with me. These conversations are common in our schools, as that's how technology purchasing has historically happened in our organization and in schools across the country. The problem is that this type of technology procurement for schools, while well-meaning, misses a huge opportunity for school leaders: using technology to solve instructional problems. As tempting as it is, technology shouldn't be used for technology's sake. Getting large-scale technology up and running in a school is incredibly hard work, and it's easy to blame technology when problems arise. However, if school leaders identify the problem they're trying to use technology to help solve, then teachers can focus on solving the problem, rather than focus on the technology itself.

FOCUS ON THE INSTRUCTIONAL PROBLEM YOU'RE TRYING TO SOLVE

Hire technology to help you solve one of your pressing instructional problems, not for technology's sake. Getting schools to identify and focus on a single instructional program is tricky. Schools have many (sometimes competing) priorities.

> Technology is not always the right answer. If there's a better way to solve the problem without technology, then it's probably the wrong problem to hire technology to help you solve. Don't go blended for blended learning's sake, because when times get tough (bandwidth goes down, devices break, software doesn't integrate, or one of the other million things that can go wrong does go wrong), teachers will blame technology, and you'll be stuck. However, when the technology lets you down, ask yourself whether there's a better way to solve your instructional problem. If there isn't, you'll be able to forge ahead through your technology problems with greater resolve.

These are some examples of instructional problems to solve using technology:

• How can we better support teachers to provide more and better small-group differentiated instruction?

- How can we remediate and accelerate the learning of the students on both ends of the curve, whom we're not serving as well as the majority of students?
- How can we improve the ways we're leveraging homework time?
- How can we create more instructional time for a particular topic?
- How can we increase the amount of writing students are doing in all content areas?
- How can we capture over time student work to gauge progress and improve our instructional program?
- How can we identify and help struggling students more quickly and efficiently using data?
- How can we reduce the number of our graduates who need to take remedial math upon entering college?

The problem you're identifying should be measurable and ultimately solvable over time, after which you'll find a new problem to solve. It also should be an instructional problem, as technology does not improve student learning as a highly effective teacher does. **Keep your focus on improving instruction and ultimately student learning using data.**

Sample Problem Technology Might Be Hired to Solve: Lack of consistent school-wide small-group instruction (Aspire Public Schools).

A few months back, I worked with a teacher team who agreed that differentiated, small-group instruction was their most effective means for increasing student achievement, yet some teachers in the school pulled only one or two small guided-reading groups per day, while others couldn't figure out how to manage their classes tightly enough to make any small-group instruction effective.

Solution: Lab rotation to support teachers with small groups.

We arrived at a plan to pull out half the class during reading instruction to utilize computers in a lab for remediation/acceleration in math and English language arts (ELA), while classroom teachers could focus on practicing pulling three small guided-reading groups and managing the remaining students in independent reading. In this way, teachers felt they would be more supported for getting their management and small-group instructional routines in place.

Key Advice: Stay focused on the problem!

21

During the planning session, the teachers were engaged and excited about the new plan. Then, one teacher suggested that she also wanted to teach *just* ELA and social studies, reasoning that if teachers were allowed to specialize, they could do a better job with planning. My response to her was that the school was small, which meant that if teachers specialized in content, they'd probably be teaching that content to three or even four grade levels of students. The teachers were undeterred, as they were already thinking about how much easier their lives would be if they only had to plan for two content areas. So, we revisited the problem: If teachers specialized in teaching content, would this solve their primary instructional problem? That is, would specializing in content allow them to improve the lack of consistent small-group instruction? The answer was no—teachers would have less time with their students in a content-cored classroom (as student schedules would be blocked, instead of being self-contained) and would face the same small-group instructional challenges and barriers they currently faced. Although this exploration was important to the team, having the teacher team that was charged with rolling out blended learning articulate the identified problem helped us stay focused on finding ways to solve it.

Sample Problem Technology Might Be Hired to Solve: Not enough students were reaping the benefits of small-group instruction (Aspire Public Schools).

In one of our schools, we asked teachers how many small differentiated groups they were pulling each day, and then asked the teachers whether they felt student achievement would improve if they pulled more small groups. The teachers all agreed that achievement would improve, but they couldn't figure out how to pull more small groups given all the other demands on their time with their students.

Solution: In-class rotation to support differentiated groups.

We used the data (the number of small groups pulled) to set goals for using blended learning to increase the number of groups pulled each day. Then, midyear, we counted how many small groups teachers were pulling, and the number was double what it was before we started. We still needed to analyze the student achievement data to see whether students were making gains at a greater rate than before, but we were encouraged that we could finally see what increasing group instruction could look like in our classrooms.

Key Advice: Determine ideal schedules that will allow teachers to achieve the goals set.

Originally, we had teachers determine how to structure their time in order to pull additional small groups during blended learning. While some teachers appreciated the autonomy of building their ideal schedules, many struggled with the logistical challenges of having a different instructional schedule. Sometimes, the focus shifted from "How can we pull more groups?" to "How can I squeeze in time for students to be on computers?" If you can't create samples of what you hope to achieve, how can you expect teachers to make your vision of blended learning happen? See appendixes L and M for sample schedules.

Sample Problem Technology Might Be Hired to Solve: Teachers holding students to varying levels of rigor in terms of content acquisition (Summit Public Schools).

Summit Public Schools, a charter management organization (CMO) in the San Francisco Bay Area, wanted to redesign its model to ensure that all graduates had the content knowledge they needed to avoid remedial college courses.

Solution: Summit's teachers created digital content guides for each subject and course as a framework to allow students and parents to see all the content each course encompassed.

For each unit of content, Summit curated an online playlist of open educational resources, then created a short assessment that a student can take on demand through the assessment system. Finally, Summit developed its Personalized Learning Plan (PLP) application, which provides the framework for students to access the curriculum. Jon Deane, Summit's chief information officer, says, "If we want our students to really drive their own learning, and we want to hold them to a high standard for competency in content knowledge, then we knew we had to create the tools to give them access anytime, anywhere. Our students should always be able to see what they know, what they need to know, and have access to the tools to learn it."

Key Advice: Putting into place a competency-based approach requires a great deal of teacher collaboration to articulate the necessary content, a strong assessment system, and, most important, a school-wide culture that supports student-driven learning. Once you have your goals and your assessment system down, you can design the instructional program to support how you want students to learn.

For a quality blended learning implementation, student achievement data should be your focus, as should your plans to scale blended learning across the school or the district. Consider what your students' top needs are and prioritize them to identify the instructional problem you plan to "hire" blended learning to solve. Do students struggle with reading comprehension? Are all students proficient or advanced in math at their grade level? Jon Deane, chief information officer at Summit Public Schools in San Jose, offers this perspective:

> At Summit, we were in the midst of a deep dive into college persistence data as our first high-school class was nearing the end of its fourth year in college. We were getting feedback from our graduates that one of the biggest hurdles to persistence was the requirement to take remedial courses, especially in math. We approached blended learning to help us better prepare students with fundamental math work so that they could avoid the need for remediation in college.

SOLICIT INPUT FROM DIFFERENT STAKEHOLDERS

Chris Liang-Vergara, former director of instructional technology for personalized learning at FirstLine Schools in New Orleans, and now at LEAP Innovations, suggests engaging your school community to build the model and design it for each of the community's different needs: "Create a user-designed experience based off of interviews with school leadership, teachers, support staff, parents, and students. Interview extremes within the organization and create a map to see common needs/ trends. They will come out very organically through conversations with the staff." Different stakeholders provide important contributions and allow you to create buy-in from the very beginning of the process.

ARTICULATE HOW YOU'LL MEASURE SUCCESS

Technology use and time spent on computers are not ways to measure success; consider student achievement, increase in small-group instruction, additional course offerings, growth opportunities for gifted students, and teacher sustainability as some possible viable measurements. Tom Willis, chief executive officer of Cornerstone Charter Schools in Detroit, explains:

> Learning, learning and learning. That should be the focus. Simply put, we wanted to move the needle towards even better learning for our students.

I was always a bit skeptical of virtual/online learning because of its relatively small demand (i.e., only works well for certain kids), but the concept of blended learning made all the sense in the world to us.

Likewise, consider the impact on teachers when calculating success. Caryn Voskuil, former school model innovation manager at Rocketship Education in San Jose, California, shares:

Another way we measure success is in demonstrated lift provided to teachers. Our teachers feel the success of blended learning when the computer does something more efficiently than they could themselves, such as assessment and data collection, as well as "tagging" content to an individual student who may need it most. Our teachers like when alerts are assigned to students, so they can provide on-the-spot intervention or suggested practice items to students identified by the computer.

DON'T BE SEDUCED BY THE TOOLS OR DEVICES

At this point in the process, keep your focus on the learning. It's incredibly easy to be distracted by "bright shiny objects": slick tablets, engaging gaming programs, touch-screen desktops, and beautiful interfaces.

Technology can be incredibly seductive to adults and kids. One need not look further than the proliferation of iPads across schools to recognize the hold that tools have over our imaginations. However, putting in the tools without a plan or problem to solve at best invites experimentation and at worst wastes time and money.

Consider the following scenarios and their underlying problems, which can complicate or undermine your implementation before you even get it off the ground.

Scenario 1: Principal Jones wants to deploy iPads for all seniors to help them become more college ready. Having these mobile devices will allow students to search for content online when researching, submit papers to their teachers, and access any open educational resources their teachers find to supplement the content.

Potential Problem 1: The principal is defining college readiness by the use of technology, but not in any targeted or strategic way. Using technology alone does not make one college ready.

Potential Problem 2: The cart (the iPads) is being put before the horse (the teachers). Without a clear plan for how teachers will use this technology, the implementation will rely strongly on teachers with the greatest skill and putting forth the greatest effort. Success may not be quantifiable, and teachers may be distracted from their core purpose.

Potential Problem #3: Over time, the allure of new technology as engaging wears off, no matter how wonderful the device may seem out of the box. By relying on technology's inherent engagement, school leaders may find themselves in a bind once the magic wears off.

Scenario 2: The math department has suggested that students love math when they use math-based video games for instruction and has asked the principal to purchase math software for all students to use to supplement in-class math instruction.

Potential Problem 1: This scenario sets up a dichotomy between "love of math" (on games) and presumably "no love of math" (from the teacher). Less experienced teachers may abdicate some of their control and authority over the class in the interest of showing kids more love, rather than sharpening the teachers' own skills to leverage students' interest in math and foster a love of math.

Potential Problem 2: The student achievement data may not point to a need for increased math. Deploying technology strategically means looking at the data, identifying the greatest needs and determining whether the costs match the needs. Spending 50 percent of a school's software budget on math gaming software (not to mention the actual devices on which to play the games) may be an unequitable way to focus on your student achievement.

Potential Problem 3: Engagement does not always equal learning. All software is not created equal, and although many products boast Common Core or State Standards alignment, it's worth digging into exactly what "alignment" means. If a product has weak data dashboards or does not articulate the specific standards students are mastering, or if the problems and games don't clearly map to standards themselves, you might be outsourcing valuable instructional time to something that just won't pay off with achievement.

While these scenarios are fictional, the concerns that underpin them are not. In summary, keep in mind the following cautions:

- Use technology to achieve educational outcomes, not as an end to itself.
- Plan your implementation by engaging teachers in the work, then roll out the devices to achieve the work. Don't assume that teachers will or should figure out how the technology should be used after it arrives in the building.
- Technology engagement will wane. Keep teachers focused on how to make their own instruction engaging, rather than relying on the software to engage students.
- Use student achievement data to identify where to best spend your software and hardware dollars.
- Question "alignment," and have someone with deep content knowledge critically examine the content, assessment items or activities, and actual data outputs.

COMMIT TO RUNNING PILOTS

Before you begin, follow this key advice: Run a pilot of the model you plan to use. This work is incredibly complex, yet it offers rich learning opportunities. Some of these lessons are important, but small, and ultimately can be learned in a full rollout. Others are huge, and not understanding them can cripple a full rollout; these lessons and problems are much better learned and solved in a pilot (see table 1.1). In order to run a high-quality blended learning implementation, you'll need to run pilots! Nithi Thomas, blended learning manager at Mastery Charter Schools in Philadelphia, says, "Start small and find a model that is functional before you scale it up." We couldn't agree more. Pilots will save you money in the long run, as you'll make fewer costly mistakes.

In almost every case, the high-impact lessons learned are costly in both time and money and can detract from a school's effectiveness in getting blended off the ground.

Table 1.1 Examples of Lessons Learned in Pilots

Low-Impact Lessons Learned (OK to learn while doing blended on a small or large scale)	High-Impact Lessons Learned (better to learn on a smaller scale first, not during a full rollout)
Teachers take more time than expected to adjust to adaptive learning technology and may initially prefer assigning the majority of work for students to learn online (if the technology allows it).	Some teachers with mediocre classroom management before blended get markedly worse (and more difficult to support) during blended.
The schedule for blended learning does not allow for enough time on the computers to move achievement data.	The school's technology infrastructure (both the network and the bandwidth) is truly inadequate to support the increased number of devices running with blended.
The software reps are unresponsive to the school's needs.	Teachers are unable to create student accounts in bulk and must do them one by one.
Not all teachers or leaders are as "into blended" as originally thought now that their students are on the computers.	The school doesn't have enough tech support for teachers and students on the computers within the current school staff.
Students are not always doing what teachers intend them to be doing on the computers.	The school hasn't put into place adequate acceptable-use policies, cyber-safety policies, and password-security policies.
Teachers cannot figure out how to use the blended learning data and dismiss it.	Students have not adequately learned the routines and procedures for work on the computers.
	It takes longer—a lot longer—than you think it will for students to log in to the computer.

Because running blended is an expensive endeavor, we highly recommend piloting first to better understand your specific school's needs and challenges. Our pilots challenged many of our assumptions about what we thought would work, and we saved countless hours and dollars doing blended on a small scale before rolling it out school-wide—not that we didn't make many mistakes along the way!

Throughout this book, the issues and considerations are the same whether you're running pilots or fully converting a school.

MEASURE THE WORK

In order to measure each pilot, we drafted a rubric (see table 1.2) on which the pilot would be assessed. This is a work in progress but gives teachers and principals a clearer sense of the ways we hope to use a pilot to learn whether or not a blended learning model is right for our schools.

DO YOU NEED A CONSULTANT?

We're assuming you're reading this because you've already decided to go blended. However, read the book, as you'll need to understand the whole process whether or not you engage consultants to help you do this work. Some blended learning consultants provide services like conducting needs assessments and providing professional development for teachers, software integration, data integration, and ongoing support. We used a consultant when we started, and now we work on our own. Think of it this way: Consultants are like wedding planners. If you've never planned a wedding, you might find it incredibly supportive to have the help of a wedding planner every step of the way. Others might have a clear idea of their needs and wants, and the time and capacity to plan their wedding on their own. It's really up to you whether you will need to engage an outside group to help you with this work or can find the capacity within. There's no right answer—in blended learning or in wedding planning, for that matter!

Table 1.2 Decision Criteria Rubric

FIT (How does the content fit with Aspire's instructional program and goals?)

- Implementation of program is aligned with Aspire's instructional methods.
- Program is in alignment with strategies and priorities.
- Data is seamless with Aspire's other data.

ECONOMICS (How do the economics make blended learning an attractive option for Aspire?)

- Program shows potential for savings over time.
- Hardware costs do not extend beyond current budgets or fundraising capabilities.
- Software costs do not extend beyond current budgets or fundraising capabilities.
- Training costs are built into software costs or current professional development budgets.
- Information technology (IT) support costs do not extend beyond current budgets or fundraising capabilities.

STUDENT-TEACHER IMPACT (What needs to be happening in the classroom for us to deem this a success?)

- State of classroom management is tight so that students on computers are 100% on task the whole time, and 100% of students receiving direct instruction are on task.
- 100% of students are engaged while online.
- 80% of students demonstrate engagement online outside of class.
- Teacher checks and uses student data weekly.
- Teacher demonstrates strong confidence in using and supporting the program.
- Student achievement goes up as a result of online performance.
- Pilot shows potential for increased student load or class size because all items above meet or exceed.
- Pilot does all of this without burning out teachers and ideally makes it easier for teachers to teach.

FEASIBILITY (How much do we have to change to make implementation a reality?)

- Steps to implementation and teams involved require minimal impact on existing processes and teams.
- Tech requirements (bandwidth, support, wiring of rooms) are achievable with minimal impact or costs for IT services.
- Facilities requirements (classroom space, storage of tech) are minimal given existing facilities.
- Impact on other classes is minimal given existing master schedule.
- Impact on Aspire as a whole is minimal given existing processes and teams.

GO FOR THE BADGE!

Determined Decision Maker

- Gather your leadership team and identify what instructional problem you want to "hire" technology to help you solve.
  - Describe the problem you want to focus on solving.
  - Identify a measurable outcome with a specific goal that you want to achieve.
- Check your instructional problem against relevant student achievement and teacher data to ensure your problem is aligned with your actual needs.
- Ask yourself and your team the question: Can your instructional problem be better solved in another way that does not involve technology? If so, critically question your choice of problem, and if necessary, revise the problem on which you plan to focus your efforts.
- Document your problem to analyze and reflect on it so your team doesn't lose sight of it during the process.
- Commit to piloting so that you can learn from low-impact mistakes before you scale across a school.

2

Determining School Readiness

We've found at Aspire that not all of our schools are ready to go blended at the same time. In any given year, we might have a new principal, staff turnover, a building move, a rise or dip in student achievement, or some other event that might not make a school quite ready to convert to blended learning. This doesn't mean the school will never be ready—just that the school is not ready *now*. Over the years it has been our principal aim to choose schools really purposefully to get this work off the ground by defining a bunch of conditions that show whether or not a school is ready to convert to blended. In this chapter we'll review ten guiding criteria to help you carefully evaluate your school's readiness for conversion.

CRITERION 1: SCHOOL LEADERSHIP

The most important criterion for deciding whether you're ready to go blended is the readiness of the school leadership, which is why we focus on this criterion first. One of the best ways to assess your school's readiness is by asking key questions like the following:

Is the principal or school leader ready to go blended?
Does your leadership team have the capacity to do this work right now?

Where is the locus of influence in your schools?

Are the influencers and leadership on the same page?

We choose our schools to convert to blended learning based on a variety of criteria, but the criteria we weigh more than others focus on the people in the school. Principal leadership can make or break a blended learning implementation.

> While we strongly believe in teacher leaders, we don't believe that blended learning can be led initially from a classroom, nor that it makes sense for individual teachers to go blended in their schools if the principal is not on board. Blended learning involves so many critical dependencies—especially on the technology team, the school's overall culture of support, and economies of scale with a great impact on costs—that blended learning cannot sustainably be rolled out from a single classroom.

One of our blended learning principals, Kim Benaraw of Aspire Titan Academy, explained the principal's role in a blended learning implementation this way: "If you want to go blended, you have to know that you've got to be totally bought into the idea of a new future for your school. This isn't an add-on, or something you can sort of do." While this advice might be scary to hear initially, it's also important to keep in mind as you embark on this work. We ask school leaders about their interest in going blended (even if they're cautiously interested at first) and find out if they have a strong rapport with their staff and an ability to withstand a major change to their school. We ask them about how blended learning could fit within their current focus for their school. We ask them what excites them about going blended, as well as what scares them. If we suspect that a principal is consumed with other challenges at the school, might lose focus, might struggle keeping teachers focused on instructional change when technology problems arise, or might not completely want to follow the program, we consider that school not ready for blended yet. Strong leadership matters.

Note that a principal's strength using technology is less important. We have principals who use technology, but do not see themselves as "early adopters" or heavy users doing this work. Principals have to want to learn but do not have to have a strong technology background. You will find more about ways of supporting principals with increased technology in chapter 3.

> Blended learning is a big undertaking for any school. Without a strong principal at the helm and staff that have bought into the conversion, this work becomes even more difficult and can easily be undermined at multiple levels.

CRITERION 2: STAFF READINESS

Teachers also matter a great deal in the process of going blended. We look for teachers who are healthy skeptics about the use of technology for learning. Many suggest that younger teachers are more tech savvy; in our experience, this isn't necessarily true. Consider these questions:

Are the teachers ready to go blended? How do you know?
How comfortable are your teachers with ambiguity?
How open is your staff to change?
How focused is your staff on the leadership's priorities?
Do you have early adopters on your staff already trying out tools on their own?

The teachers we attempt to hire are the teachers we want in blended and nonblended classrooms alike: teachers who believe in "College for Certain" (Aspire's motto) for all our students, who are invested in differentiated instruction, and who are open to always learning as professionals. In our schools, teachers already utilize various software programs to take attendance, log disciplinary actions, record grades, administer assessments, analyze student achievement data, identify curriculum resources, and participate in their own professional development and observations. We know that teachers have the capacity to continue to learn new technologies, and it's our responsibility to give them the necessary support to take on new tools.

Interestingly, and somewhat surprisingly for us as we embarked on this work, we found that the teachers most eager to pilot blended learning are not always the best ones to select for pilots. While a school may have an early adopter who has been engaging students with technology and utilizing digital tools for some time, this teacher may not be the best political choice for piloting. (If the teacher's tools or practices haven't already spread across the school over time, then this teacher is probably not the right choice.)

However, we've also found that our most successful blended learning teachers share a willingness to do the following:

- Live in ambiguity and take a few risks
- Function in a restructured environment
- Iterate, within boundaries, to figure out what works best
- Let go of some control
- Create new opportunities for students

In general, all of our pilot teachers possess all of these qualities to a certain degree and really must, as change is hard. Some teachers show signs of these qualities early on in the process of going blended; others learn to be this way over time. We phase in blended learning over a two-year time period in our existing schools converting to blended, with six to eight teachers piloting in the first year and the remaining classrooms in the second year. It's imperative that our first-year converting teachers have these qualities, because they are the ones who transmit the culture over time to the second-year converts.

Anirban Bhattacharyya of the KIPP Foundation offers this perspective:

> A few years ago, we didn't really know how to begin. So we worked with our principals and our strongest teacher leaders to begin a dozen different small pilots in various classrooms. We chose the strongest teachers because we knew that sometimes tech doesn't work, and we needed adults who had a strong command of the classroom when difficulties arose. We worked with principals because we knew that eventually we wanted them to be the owners of the implementations for the entire school.

If you start going blended with teachers who aren't your strongest, and your pilot fails (or is inconclusive), you'll be left wondering whether the teacher or the structure of the pilot was at fault.

CRITERION 3: HISTORY OF STUDENT ACHIEVEMENT

When choosing our first school to go blended, we looked for a school with a history of strong student achievement but room to grow. We believed that if the student achievement data was steadily increasing, the school was stable and capable of taking on what was likely a major disruption. We didn't want to position blended learning as the program to "fix" whatever was wrong in the school with student achievement data, as we felt this attitude might communicate that technology would solve problems that the teachers could not or that technology was some kind of silver bullet that could solve problems on its own. If technology is being brought into a school to accelerate and support what is already going well, technology is set up for success. Technology can't solve problems of school culture, classroom management, or uneven teaching. These are problems the school leadership team needs to take on themselves.

A school's history of student achievement can say a lot about its focus and stability and its potential for success. Consider these questions:

What is the history of student achievement at the school?

In what ways do the leadership and staff demonstrate a focus on student achievement?

How is this year similar to or different from the past few years at the school?

Since our first school conversion, however, we've thought differently about the role of a school's history of student achievement. What matters most is not the school's history per se, but the principal and staff's strong and authentic focus on student achievement. If a school's (or principal's) focus on and urgency about student achievement is sporadic or frequently distracted, that school is not the place for us to go blended yet. If a school continually struggles with school culture or problems that get in the way of focusing on student achievement, then the school is not ready for blended. Since our student achievement isn't optimal at every one of our schools, we knew we had to figure out how to bring blended learning to the schools that were not on a growth trajectory, but whose leadership could be successful and whose students stood to benefit from blended learning.

Our most recent conversion is at a school where the history of student achievement has been mixed for a variety of reasons. With a strong principal now at the helm, we're using blended learning at that school to support the turnaround efforts of the principal and leadership team. Rather than bring the computers into the classroom right away, we're utilizing a lab to provide teachers and students with opportunities for more personalized teaching and learning environments for an hour each day to work on adaptive software—that is, software that adapts to each individual student's understanding based on an initial diagnostic test and ongoing performance. We've split each teacher's class in half to go to the lab; with the remaining students in class, the teacher focuses solely on providing three small-group guided-reading lessons and building the class culture around increased independence during small groups. In this way, we're using blended learning to support and increase teachers' capacity to increase small-group instruction, an instructional strategy that we value greatly and that we consider our greatest lever to differentiate and target instruction and increase student achievement. Small-group instruction allows our teachers to group students and create differentiated lessons based on the group's needs. The instructional problem we're using technology to help us solve is that teachers with a full class of students weren't able to effectively (and efficiently) build their capacity for small-group instruction to increase student achievement. Not all schools share our focus on making small-group instruction work; for them, the instructional problem will be different.

CRITERION 4: STAFF WILLINGNESS

School staff have to want to try out blended learning for a conversion to be successful. Making the change to blended learning for many teachers and principals is an enormous leap of faith and requires significant strength to see how instructional practice will change. Teachers are key partners in any implementation, and without buy-in from them, the effectiveness of your implementation will be compromised. Ask yourself these questions:

Is the staff on board?
Is the school interested in going blended?

Are there teachers on site who are interested in or have experience with blended learning?

Is the principal excited about blended learning?

Are there current initiatives the staff is excited about that could be enhanced or supported by blended learning?

Are there tech-savvy people on site to help implement the pilots?

We didn't expect teachers to want to do this work immediately; on the contrary, I probably would have been a little frightened if teachers were super-eager right away. Collect data on staff understanding of blended learning and interest in going blended as an initial step. Understand staff perceptions and concerns, and assess your ability to address those concerns. Recognize that teachers' and school leaders' minds will change over time, and think strategically about who should be the ones to lead that change. Conduct a kick-off meeting to get everyone on board with the same messages from the very start.

Lesson Learned

Recently, in pursuit of a Race to the Top district grant, the federal Department of Education's competitive grant for digital learning, we approached a group of our principals to be part of the application. We had a small window of time to formulate a blended learning plan and present it to the principals, who would then present it to their teachers. Many principals had not yet heard of blended learning. Some were excited and successfully convinced their teachers that blended was the right way to go. Others were really nervous, were concerned about telling their teachers and hearing their reactions, or felt blended learning was too unproven. Some moved forward and enthusiastically joined the application, having had their staff vote overwhelmingly in favor of going blended, and others did not. Ultimately, we didn't get the grant; if we had, we would have been in a much different position than we were a year later when all of the schools we asked were ready, much more knowledgeable about blended, and really excited to do this work. Now, we begin talking to teachers and principals about their interest in going blended more frequently and ahead of any grant opportunities that may arise, so that principals and teachers can have blended learning in the back of their minds as a potential step down the road and continue to develop their thinking about going blended.

Sometimes when going blended, it makes sense to start really small with a willing population, especially if you're not sure whether going blended is the right decision for your teachers and students. Tom Willis of Cornerstone Charter Schools explains, "We did a small pilot at one of our middle schools in math and English because they were willing to try it and there was a need. A small, well-thought-out pilot is a great way to get started."

Visiting other schools is a low-stakes way to create buy-in and build teacher imagination around what blended learning could look like at your own school. We approached one of our principals about her interest in blended learning, and although she was enthusiastic, she wasn't sure how her teachers would take it. She identified a politically powerful and strong teacher leader who she felt could be a great critic or a great champion, who was interested in blended learning but skeptical about the change in instruction, the number of students in the classroom (thirty compared to her current class size of twenty-two), and what students would be doing on the computers. I took this teacher to visit another blended learning school to see what the model looked like in action, ask teachers questions about our greatest concerns, and wrap our heads around some of the changes we'd need to make to support it in her school. Ultimately, the experience allowed the teacher to have her concerns addressed by teachers and school leaders, so when she returned, she championed the model to her colleagues and got them on board to move forward with the pilot.

Finally, take a look at the staff's ability to function in challenging situations. Are they collaborative? Are they resilient? Has the school leader built a supportive leadership team? Teachers will need the support of leadership and of one another during this process, and you'll want to ensure that you've got adequate supports already among the staff in addition to the support you'll build into the process. Mark Montero, an Aspire Titan teacher in his second year of blended learning, explains, "The reason blended learning works at our school is because of consistency from year to year." His colleague, Raul Gonzalez, adds, "Teachers need to speak the same language and collaborate around blended learning."

CRITERION 5: SCHOOL STABILITY

Many schools change from year to year due to staff turnover, changes in leadership, instructional priorities, and other factors. Stated another way, some years are harder and some are easier to make big changes in a school or lead a new initiative. Often, a stable school is able to make a large-scale change more successfully than a school that is in transition. Consider these questions:

Is the school in transition?

Do you have a core group of teachers who are ready to do this work?

Are you currently focused on bringing new teachers on board?

Is recent staff turnover indicative of a larger problem you'll be focused on solving?

Is your school's culture in transition?

When we ask these questions, the answer usually is yes and no. A school with a high turnover in staff might not be the best place to start this work, as the turnover may indicate a larger problem at the school. We haven't run pilots in the first year with new teachers, as new teachers face a host of challenges, and blended learning can only add to those challenges. We do have resident teachers in blended learning classrooms. Of course, when we opened our new school, we had all new teachers (some of whom were first-year teachers), but when converting schools, we identify the teachers in the building who can most easily shoulder the change process in the first year.

In the second year of conversion, we've had new teachers and beginning teachers start the process with success. The key is to have your strongest team of teachers supporting those who are new through the process.

CRITERION 6: QUALITY OF SCHOOL CULTURE

As an organization, we subscribe to Peter Drucker's saying: "Culture eats strategy for breakfast." Aspire culture is strong throughout our organization and in the other school organizations and districts we have included in this book. In the blended learning context, school culture has a strong influence on our ability to roll out blended learning, so it's worth asking these questions:

How strong is the school's culture?

How positive is the current culture of the school?

What about the school's culture makes it ready for blended learning?

At Aspire, school culture matters greatly on a class level, school level, and organization-wide level. A strong, consistent "College for Certain" school culture allows principals to focus teachers on maximizing student achievement as the top priority. We believe that every student deserves the opportunity to go to college, and it's our job to equip them with the skills to succeed when they get there. Our principals don't spend time "convincing" teachers of priorities, which streamlines decision-making and helps leaders avoid embarking on leading all new (and potentially competing) initiatives each year. A school's culture, not surprisingly, matters tremendously when trying to lead this kind of change with technology.

CRITERION 7: SCHOOL TECHNOLOGY USE

A school's culture concerning technology also matters, as you'll find habits that might need addressing as you increase the amount of technology in your school. Historically, we didn't originally pay much attention to our technology, and in some schools, students and even teachers did not take responsibility for caring for devices in labs or classrooms, resulting in benign neglect. Because our technology was unreliable, teachers were less interested in using technology for teaching and learning. When a device broke, the information technology (IT) team didn't always hear about it, and so the broken devices piled up. Not everyone had read our acceptable-use policy, and as a result, it was enforced only sporadically. Consider these questions:

How do students and teachers currently use and treat technology?

What is the culture of technology use at the school? Is it positive? Equitable?

Who is currently responsible for the technology culture at the school?

What policies do you have in place for technology use?

By taking stock of your tech culture, you'll be able to identify areas of improvement that, if fixed, can have an enormous impact on the success of your work going blended.

CRITERION 8: INFORMATION TECHNOLOGY TEAM AND INFRASTRUCTURE

Because you're going to need to partner with your IT team to do a lot of the technical work necessary to run blended learning, you should take stock of your current infrastructure and relationship with the team and identify areas that need attending to. Some useful questions to ask include these:

Do you have a solid, responsive IT team?

How viable is your technology infrastructure?

Do you have the bandwidth you need?

Do you qualify for the E-rate program (the Schools and Libraries Program of the Universal Service Fund that provides discounts to schools for Internet access), and if so, do you have support for navigating the E-rate process?

Does the site already have devices available to run a blended learning pilot?

Is the school site viable for upgrade to high-speed broadband?

Does the school site have a local network infrastructure that could handle a major increase in activity?

Do you have people to support the increase in technology when it malfunctions?

When we started this work, we had 3 mbps of bandwidth going to and from our schools, which was *considerably* slower than most households had at the time. As I met people embarking on the same journey, I'd ask them what their bandwidth was. If they didn't know, I'd know they were in even more trouble than I was! We knew that our first priority for any technology implementation would have to be for us to upgrade our bandwidth. In addition, we had an IT team whose role had been largely to maintain the network and troubleshoot problems. We didn't have an effective help-desk ticketing system or a clear plan for modernizing our network.

In this way, technology is a team sport, and collaboration with your IT team is critical. When something confusing happens, you'll need them desperately and want them on your side. Likewise, your IT team can find it exciting and fulfilling to have a greater sense of their impact on kids.

My advice: You can't outsource tech support. These folks are your partners on this journey.

Our initial steps toward going blended involved getting a real (and often painful) assessment of the technology infrastructure of each of our schools and of the network as a whole from an IT expert. Our IT team led this charge, but then we sought the help of outside organizations like EducationSuperHighway (a nonprofit focused on ensuring that every K–12 public school has the Internet infrastructure necessary for digital learning) for more expertise around networking. We learned we couldn't upgrade our bandwidth (to increase our speed and run digital learning software) without changing the way our network was configured in classrooms and to the server. In some cases, even after changing the network, we couldn't upgrade the bandwidth of some schools without trenching or putting in towers on neighboring schools to transfer the bandwidth from one school to another. This work was costly, sometimes excruciating, but necessary if we believed we wanted our schools to be able to run whatever technology we ultimately chose.

Key Idea

Understand what your current technology capacities and budget are so you can best identify where to start this work, and strategically plan for both the short term (your blended learning pilot launch) and the long term (a full upgrade of your infrastructure that takes into account your growing technology needs).

Be sure to consider the following:

- What is the current role of your IT team? What is their capacity to support a major increase in technology infrastructure? Do you have an experienced network person on your team?
- What is the actual dollar amount it will cost to upgrade a school or multiple schools? Are any of those upgrades eligible for the E-rate program? If your role

involves you with more than one school site, it's worth exploring if you may get cost efficiencies by upgrading multiple schools at once. For an explanation of the E-rate program, read chapter 9.

You'll need a reliable enterprise wireless network and as much bandwidth as you can get in your schools right away, and if you ramp up for your long-term needs too slowly, you'll pay more in costly work-arounds and painful tech glitches. Do all you can to do the whole upgrade before you begin launching blended. See chapter 9 for more details on technology infrastructure.

CRITERION 9: POTENTIAL FOR GROWTH OR EXPANSION

The number and types of devices you run in pilots might look quite different on a larger scale, and you'll need to keep your eyes on what you can best support in a larger deployment. Consider your current power, space, and storage constraints as you plan now, as you'll want to ensure your ability to scale later. Consider these questions:

Do classrooms have space for permanent laptop carts or desks?
Is there enough room in classrooms to increase class sizes?
Do you have room for a lab?

Running a pilot in a lab may work fine, but scheduling 12 classes through the lab over the course of a week might be completely untenable. Your current circuitry might support your power needs, but adding laptop carts to multiple rooms might necessitate replacing the panel and creating dedicated outlets. If your blended learning model relies on an increase in enrollment to keep costs sustainable, you'll also need to ensure you have space for additional students.

CRITERION 10: OTHER POTENTIALLY COMPETING DEMANDS

In any given year, schools embark on new initiatives based on a variety of interests, demands, and requirements. How you help teachers navigate and prioritize these demands will set the stage for your implementation. Jeanne Chang, director of technology innovation for E. L. Haynes Public Charter School in Washington, D.C., suggests,

> In addition to weighing the pros and cons of individual blended or traditional instructional models, it is critical to take into account all of the proposed initiatives as a whole (online or not) to comprehensively review the feasibility of implementing them all with high fidelity. This is especially important when organizations are first exploring the possibility of transitioning from traditional to blended learning models. The learning curve is steep and can be particularly challenging for all stakeholders—teachers, administrators, students, tech/ops team members, etc.—during the initial launch through even the first few years. Too often a single model's criteria can be met and the checklist complete; however, the combination of four or five initiatives that all tax the same set of resources and staff can dramatically compromise the likelihood of success. Proactively engaging all relevant stakeholders throughout the process instead of after the fact to truly inform decision making is also a crucial factor to consider.

Ask principals and teachers how blended learning could be used to support a key initiative, rather than as an add-on, or prioritize a blended learning implementation for a later time.

While you may never have all ideal conditions in place for a blended learning implementation, when you are armed with the answers to these questions, you'll be able to better plan strategically where you are ready to go blended, and assess what you need to do to get other schools ready, too.

GO FOR THE BADGE!

Determined Decision Maker

Take stock of your readiness to go blended:

- Honestly question leadership's capacity, taking into consideration what they would have to give up or change, to do this work now.
- Identify the locus of greatest influence and engage those individuals in the process.
- Assess your staff's readiness for change and willingness to go blended. Consider staff turnover numbers and trends.
- Examine your student achievement data and what story it tells about the school's readiness.
- Consider the current culture at the school and take stock of what you'll need to put in place.
- Assess your district or organization's capacity to support an increase in technology usage, and identify how you'll ramp up support and increase bandwidth.
- Think carefully about facility constraints and plan now for potential changes when you scale.

3

Building the Team and Creating Buy-in

Having the right leadership and support is imperative to a successful blended learning implementation. In this chapter, we'll determine the necessary teammates to drive this work and explore ways of engaging all stakeholders in the process. Your team should include school leadership, teachers, site-based technology support, district level support, and IT team support.

SCHOOL LEADERSHIP

I cannot state this enough: School leadership matters. As I've mentioned earlier, we choose blended learning schools primarily based on the strength of the school leader. We look for a school leader who is interested in doing this work, has the resiliency to withstand the initial technology speed bumps (or worse!), and can remain focused on the instructional problem they're "hiring" blended learning to help solve. Jon Deane at Summit Public Schools in San Jose describes the critical qualities school leaders must possess this way: "A willingness to confront data and use it to drive decisions, and a desire to rapidly iterate on model designs to promote continuous improvement are two of the most important qualities for a leader doing blended work." Rachel Klein at Highline Public Schools in Seattle adds, "And the savvy to do this without making people mad, as iteration can drive people crazy if they haven't built relationships with each other."

Ways Successful Leaders Make Going Blended Work

- Focus work on instructional problems related to student achievement.
- Stay unemotional (but empathetic) about tech problems.
- Recognize that technology integration is a process.
- Ensure the core components of the program are followed with fidelity; don't allow one-offs.
- Don't throw the baby out with the bathwater when things get tough.
- Be brave in the face of an ever-changing technology landscape.

Make Sure the School Has Some "Skin in the Game"

Blended learning should not be something that happens *to* a school. Rather the school should be part of the process and have some "skin in the game," or vested (monetary) interest, in a successful implementation beyond the abstract desire to do a good job to reach the goal. One lesson we didn't learn quickly enough is that teachers, too, need some skin in the game. Making teachers part of the process has taken many forms for us. Among our more successful approaches have been these:

- Stipend teachers for the additional work they'll need to do to get blended off the ground.
- Draw up a pilot agreement in which you detail what teachers get and what they'll be expected to do for the life of the pilot, and if necessary, return to this agreement if teachers are not holding up their end of the bargain (see appendix D for a sample pilot agreement), and monitor data throughout the year.
- If you've fundraised for the conversion, pay for the infrastructure upgrade first, and phase in the costs that hit the school's budget starting in year one; upgrades and devices are a big cost in the first year, but less so in ongoing years, whereas software licenses are part of ongoing costs. In this way, the school can pay for blended learning over time and make the work sustainable without a big hit to the budget. Ideally, identify for principals line items (like teacher stipends,

bandwidth, and headphones) that they should not try to do without to save money.

TEACHERS

Teachers are the people who actually make blended learning happen in the day to day, so their strengths are your strengths, and their concerns are your concerns—or should be.

- Respect teachers' concerns about classroom space and the fact that changing a classroom environment can be stressful. Communicate sample models for furniture layout and storage of devices to alleviate concerns and save work. See appendix K for a couple of sample layouts we've used in one of our schools.
- Respect teachers' fears about letting go of control of student learning on the computers. For many teachers, letting go of control is a big challenge to overcome; however, by engaging teachers in the student experience on technology, you can create buy-in for new and different avenues for student learning.
- Support master schedule changes by creating "ideal" schedules for blended learning times. We let teachers drive this work and craft their own schedules, but by the end of the year, most came back frustrated from changing their schedules frequently and not feeling great about the trade-offs they made. Now we create "ideal" rotation schedules and work with principals to ensure that all rotations work with the school's master schedule. See appendixes L and M for some sample schedules.
- Support teachers when they're working with competing demands. If you're rolling out the Common Core, implementing a new teacher development system, and going blended, identify the synergies among the three, and work with coaches and other support providers to ensure that teachers clearly understand how each initiative supports the others.
- Build teacher technology use and resiliency over time. Determine what your bare minimums are for technology use each year, and draw a clear line under them. Many teachers will exceed these in the first year. Teachers will vary widely in their motivation and sophistication around technology use, and if you create a

culture of learners among your teachers, they'll all develop at a reasonable pace over time.

- Build in ways of fostering teacher collaboration around blended learning, whether through data talks, classroom visits, common planning time, friendly classroom competitions, teacher-led professional development, or other ways to help teachers learn from teachers.

Mark Montero, second-grade blended teacher at Aspire Titan Academy, explains, "When I did blended learning at first, it was like being a first-year teacher. It's a ton better the second year, and I'm confident it'll be even better next year. As a teacher, I'm constantly growing and trying new things, and I'm excited to see the ways I can continue to improve my practice."

Lesson Learned About Resistant Teachers

We think of resistant teachers as teachers who are not yet ready for blended learning. One reason we roll out blended learning over a two-year period is to give teachers who aren't ready (and who might be resistant) an opportunity to see what blended learning is like with their students in their colleagues' classrooms. In our experience, that year is crucial for less "ready" teachers to make sense of the challenges and benefits of going blended on a slower timeline, without the perceived pressure of changing everything right away. Most teachers become "ready" and even eager before the first year is over, and if not, a strong leader can direct those teachers toward roles that might allow them to maximize their skills without facing the learning curve they might fear or resist.

Sometimes teachers are reluctant to go blended because of a fear of what they might not know. Dennise Reyes-Serpas, a teacher at Aspire Slauson Academy, shares:

> I will be the first to admit that I was very apprehensive to start blended learning. I am not very tech savvy, and the thought of having 16 computers in my classroom was overwhelming. I could picture most of my kids

with their hands up and shouting out my name to troubleshoot their laptops (as was often the case with the four desktops we had before). I tried my best to prepare my students so that the transition to blended learning would go as smoothly as possible. I taught the blended learning lessons and tweaked them for my class. My students were beyond excited, so I jumped on their bandwagon. When we finally started, the transition to having students work on the computers was easier than I thought. Now that we have been doing blended learning for a while, I can't imagine going back to the way my class was before. I love teaching the math lesson twice to half of my class at a time. This allows me to differentiate my instruction according to specific group and individual student needs. My ELA stations are super quiet and this allows me to pull my guided reading groups without interruptions.

SITE-BASED TECHNOLOGY SUPPORT

On-the-ground support for the technology is crucial for the program's success. Mike Kerr, school principal at KIPP Empower in Los Angeles, deserves the credit for this advice. He told me that when they started implementing blended learning, they couldn't live without someone on site to troubleshoot all the technical problems that arose. He was right and still is, and our experience has taught us the same lesson: Vastly increasing the amount of technology in a building requires someone on site to support it. In each of our blended learning schools, we hire a blended learning teaching assistant, someone to call software support lines, help direct kindergartners onto the programs, pull data, save broken laptops, calm teachers when the wireless goes down, identify bugs, capture big and small learnings, identify ways of doing blended better, teach tech lessons when teachers feel unsure, and do a thousand other things that can make or break this work. We know from experience that instructional technology problems create stress for teachers and can discourage them from further integrating technology into their instruction. Raul Gonzalez at Aspire Titan Academy explains, "When you have a blended learning teaching assistant at your school who knows what to do when there's a problem with the technology, that person relieves a ton of stress for the teacher."

BLTAs (blended learning teaching assistants) are the "boots-on-the-ground" champions. We learned quickly that the principal needs to lead the effort and that the BLTA ensures that the effort goes on running. Not only does the BLTA troubleshoot all the technology problems, but he or she is also the one who provides emotional support and sets a steady course. If software is buggy or the bandwidth is spotty, teachers will complain. You need one person in the building who will keep a positive attitude and have a problem-solving mindset to calm the occasional tech drama that will arise. The BLTA needs to be the steady champion of the work, so teachers can focus their energies on teaching, not tech challenges. We originally thought we could have someone do this work part-time for a year; our experience and that of our teachers and principals suggest otherwise. While we've tackled many of our initial challenges with technology infrastructure, problematic devices, software bugs, and teachers' overall resiliency with technology, we need BLTAs to support blended learning data talks, provide extra help with kindergartners and first-graders each year, provide ongoing just-in-time professional development to teachers when needed, and help support software changes from year to year. See appendix B for a sample blended learning teaching assistant job description.

DISTRICT- OR ORGANIZATION-LEVEL LEADERSHIP

Having a position focused on blended learning allows a school or district to concentrate on students and teachers, while the person in the blended learning position concentrates on the logistics of getting everything related to blended off the ground. Someone needs to measure classrooms for furniture, work with electricians and IT teammates on the infrastructure, coordinate the trainings, monitor the budgets, negotiate software contracts, and myriad other (mostly operational) tasks in order for a school to go blended. In my opinion, this effort involves too much for a principal to lead on his or her own. We've met people across the country leading blended learning initiatives who are surprisingly like-minded in their approach and philosophies, yet who are strikingly different in their professional backgrounds. While many of us come from teaching and administrative backgrounds, not all of us consider ourselves technologists, and very few have any formal operations backgrounds.

Chris Liang-Vergara of LEAP Innovations suggests that the lead should be a "person who isn't wrapped up in the day-to-day work but can be agile and free to meet with the wide range of stakeholders, vendors, and others as needed to orchestrate all the moving parts." Highline Public Schools in Seattle, Washington, created a position for a learning technology manager, whose pure focus is to coordinate a lot of the same efforts: piloting, support to schools, support to innovative teachers, informing school leaders about what the potential could be, coordinating with district-level specialists—and, most important, negotiating contracts. Klein says, "This is big, as our principals think they're getting great deals, but frequently they're not." Principals largely don't have time to survey the marketplace and negotiate from the best standpoint.

We've found that leading blended learning entails primary responsibilities that you'll want someone to manage well. In the following section you will find a list that I hope may serve as a good starting point as you consider the type of candidate you need to fill this new role in our schools.

FINDING THE RIGHT NEW TEAM MEMBER

Find someone who has your mission, vision, and instructional program at the heart of his or her work and who empathizes with teachers, as each decision made can directly affect teachers' experiences with blended learning in the classroom. You'll want someone with excellent project management experience who is willing to climb a steep technology learning curve and can build strong relationships with a variety of stakeholders. See appendixes A, B, and C for sample blended learning job descriptions.

The following are key duties that might be part of a blended learning job leader description.

Pilot-Focused Work

1. Synthesize research on the effectiveness of blended learning models, internal best practices, and challenges to design and pilot a blended learning model that aligns with the school's instructional practices, beliefs, and values and that delivers strong student achievement results.

> **Key Idea**
>
> Much of this work can be learned; what is more difficult is the empathy with teachers and principals, the facility with both minutiae (including everything from chair heights, to conflicting badging systems in the software, to subtleties in the instructional program, to unsupportive web browsers) and also the big picture (requiring an ability to work with whole school staffs and think about network needs), as well as the willingness to constantly learn and live in ambiguity. Chances are, you can't hire someone who has got it all; you should hire someone who has teaching and learning as core interests and who is a quick and willing learner of *everything*.

2. Plan and launch blended learning pilot for the coming school year; select sites and teachers, and determine performance metrics.
3. Research, select, and approve content for blended learning pilots and make recommendations for wide-scale launch.
4. Evaluate economic implications of blended learning model for feasibility and short- and long-term cost effectiveness.
5. Partner with cross-functional partners to help determine technology requirements for pilot program.
6. Develop and deliver training program for teachers and principals to execute blended learning model pilot.
7. Manage daily delivery of blended learning model, addressing issues and problems that arise during execution.
8. Evaluate effectiveness of blended learning pilot and distill pilot lessons into planning for wide-scale implementation of blended learning model as appropriate.
9. Work in collaboration with principals, home office, and external consultants to achieve strategic goals.
10. Demonstrate knowledge of and support the school's mission, vision, value statements, standards, policies and procedures, operating instructions, confidentiality standards, and the code of ethical behavior.

Full-Scale Implementation Work

1. Evaluate and curate tools.
2. Develop third-party partnerships.
3. Monitor progress of implementations to ensure success.
4. Work with school leaders to understand their vision and plans within the blended learning implementation.
5. Identify professional development needs and arrange trainings to enable continuous learning and improvement.
6. Understand student impact (engagement and growth) by partnering with school leaders, teachers, data managers, and researchers.
7. Collaborate with IT team around procurement and investments in access, bandwidth, and hardware.
8. Serve as the blended learning expert to provide ongoing support, professional development, and guidance to teachers, school leaders, and other staff.

I can't state it often enough: Someone's got to understand the technology *and* the instruction. As a member of Aspire's education team, I mistakenly thought that our IT team would be the ones who would make all the technology decisions and execute all the plans while I got to figure out what the instruction would look like. Yet, after sitting in many meetings about wireless infrastructure, device specifications, bandwidth, and plug-ins, I quickly learned that in each of those meetings, critical decisions were made that directly affected the teaching and learning environment. Understanding the technology (even the really dry, unromantic parts from an educator standpoint) is critical to your decision making and your success. You just can't outsource technology expertise. Make lots of IT friends— you'll need them!

IT LEADERSHIP

Blended learning can radically affect an IT department by exponentially increasing the amount of work facing an IT team (from procurement to support to infrastructure and network work), potentially without additional personnel or reprioritizing what IT support looks like. In these budget-constrained times, we had to figure out how to do more with the same staff, which meant, in some cases, hiring contractors and temps for short-term work, having blended learning teaching assistants receive additional training in IT support for crunch times, creating more efficient systems around IT support as a whole, and being super-clear about what we could and could not support across the organization.

Ways Successful IT Leadership Works

Your technology team is part of your blended learning team, and you should keep the IT team in the loop. Don't make them feel like blended is being done to them; rather, engage them as partners in this work, as their expertise and participation is critical to your endeavor. Explaining your rationale for everything will save you grief down the road. You're giving the team a ton of work, and they should be engaged as partners in that work. Learn what you can about what it takes on their end (costs, full-time employees, critical decisions they'll make). Learn the jargon and learn the trade-offs. Rachel Klein of Highline Public Schools offers this advice: "Build a better relationship with your IT department and it'll ultimately change the way the school community looks at them. Then, they'll be partners in the instructional process, rather than a (potentially) annoying central office department." Ideally, your IT leadership

- Has short- and long-term vision and plans for network upgrades
- Provides communication on costs—hardware, infrastructure, personnel, and time
- Is able to navigate E-rate, the government program that provides discounts to schools for connectivity
- Is customer-oriented when dealing with district staff, principals. and teachers
- Is resourceful and has a can-do attitude in challenging situations and with limited budgets
- Has a network of professional contacts outside the district or organization to draw upon for helpful advice
- Keeps updated on new devices, network solutions, and so on in order to provide key advice on purchasing decisions

COMMUNICATING YOUR VISION
AND ENGAGING ALL STAKEHOLDERS

When we started this work, we didn't spend a lot of time thinking about how to communicate our intentions. We had a series of informal conversations with principals and teachers, drafted a pilot agreement, and that's about it. (See appendix D for a copy of this document.) After much trial and error, we've learned that having a coherent message and clear plan that engages everyone, not just the early piloting teachers, helps everyone attach to a clear vision. At the time, we didn't truly understand the vision and thought it was better to leave things open so innovation could happen. Lucky for us, some innovation did happen; however, over time we realized that the aspects of the work we intended to be constant weren't always in place in all classrooms.

The more clearly you and your team communicate your message to all stakeholders, the better.

Jeanne Chang of E. L. Haynes Charter School in Washington, D.C., states,

> Having at least one "champion" or "true believer" from each stakeholder group (like school admin, support staff, teacher, student, parent) who's willing to go all out to ensure success and influence others to believe in the model's potential helps tremendously. As the data comes in, leadership teams can use their own student data to convert more constituents over time.

Start with your school leaders as key messengers. Anirban Bhattacharyya of KIPP Foundation offers this advice: "Our strategy was to empower the principals to help implement the systems and procedures around blended learning, so that investment of stakeholders would stay consistent and come from the strongest leaders in our schools." Frequently, we'll support principals' efforts at messaging about blended by bringing them together to share, building presentation decks to keep the messages consistent (and save them work), and sharing great practices from other blended learning schools we run or have visited.

Teachers also have a key role. Chris Liang-Vergara of LEAP Innovations suggests: "Have a full change-management strategy. Lay out the entire staff list and be very clear on how each person will or will not be engaged and which decision they will make, have input on, or simply hear the final decision. Use concrete pilots and hands-on prototyping to drive user adoption and familiarity with the tools/ programs. People can't be engaged and learn and be convinced if you don't give them time and opportunity to." Teachers have a powerful voice in this process, not only with one another, but with other teachers in your district or organization, with students, and with parents. Formal and informal sharing (including class and school tours, presentations, and collaboration time at meetings) allows teachers to share experiences and learn from each other.

We've taken a systematic approach to getting staff buy-in:

1. *Engage principals.* We contact principals we believe are ready, and set up a conversation with them about going blended, the potential benefits and theory of action, and the actual effects on their budget, enrollment, and facility. We expect that principals will need time to consider the idea, talk with other principals, ask questions, and reflect on their staff's readiness to embark on such an endeavor. We tell them that this is an opportunity, and if they're not ready this year, they won't disqualify themselves from another opportunity for funding or a future conversion. If they're not ready, they're not ready, and that's OK—you've planted the seeds for future blended learning conversations.

2. *Have principals engage their leadership teams.* Once principals are engaged, they then approach their leadership teams to gauge their interest. Frequently, engaging the leadership team has involved having the team visit another blended learning school in our organization or outside. Occasionally, the team has put together a series of questions for me that range from "What software will we use?" to "How much time will students be on the computers?" to "What do I cut out to fit this in?" The final question is the question we hear most frequently, and the one we struggle the hardest to respond to, as there's no clear answer. In an ideal world, we'd have math adaptive software that focused on something like fact fluency, and we'd say, "Cut out fact fluency!" Alas, there are no such easy answers.

3. *Decide whether you're moving forward.* Have a conversation focused on a few key questions:
    - What problem are you trying to solve, and how is it connected to the school's goals and to specific student achievement outcomes?

- Is the school committed to piloting the blended model for three years? Is the school committed to covering some blended costs in years 1 and 2, and all costs from year 3 onward?
- What are you most worried about?

We used these questions to determine a school's readiness. If a school is ready and the leadership team wants to move forward, we'll draw up a piloting agreement for teachers and put it in front of the leadership team for feedback. The agreement outlines what we're planning to do and why, as well as what teachers' responsibilities are for the duration of the pilot. Putting parameters in a piloting agreement is critical, not only to meeting the requirements of a grant we've put toward funding the work, but also to ensuring consistency of implementation across the school (see appendix D for a sample piloting agreement). We aim to articulate the nonnegotiable parameters of the pilot and to leave lots of room for teacher iteration to learn what works best.

4. *Engage the rest of the staff and create parameters around the work.* The leadership team then presents the agreement to the teachers the principal has chosen for the first year of the rollout. We ask principals to choose the teachers with whom they'll have the greatest success: teachers who demonstrate strong classroom management, strong student achievement, and strong resiliency, and who are politically positioned to spread this work. In short, if these teachers like blended learning, everyone will. We encourage principals to choose teams of teachers all at the same grade level so they can collaborate with one another. We have drafted a pilot agreement to articulate the expectations to all teachers in the first year. Those who don't want to be in the pilot the first year are allowed to opt out. Those in the pilot the first year receive stipends for their work, as going blended initially creates more work for teachers, and we want to honor that additional work. When we meet with the whole staff, we show a presentation that details:

- The history and context of our decision to go blended
- The definition of blended learning
- Our model
- What instructional problem we want to solve
- What the timeline looked like for pilot teachers and full rollout teachers

We make sure to build in extra time to answer all teachers' questions and take careful notes on their concerns.

ONE PRINCIPAL'S STRATEGY: TAKE THE TEAM
TO VISIT A BLENDED SCHOOL

Kim Benaraw, principal of Aspire Titan Academy, was one of our earliest principals to pilot blended learning. With a strong staff and a history of student achievement, she seemed a likely choice for us as a blended learning leader. Benaraw is an amazing principal who has built a strong staff and student culture in her school. When we approached her with the idea, she was interested, yet had some reservations. She recounts:

> Initially I didn't know what to think about blended learning. I remember as a classroom teacher, kids on the computer were not very productive. I was constantly looking for online computer programs that were free and that were useful. We also only had four computers in the classroom, so having students rotate around them never quite worked . . . Blended learning, when done well, is students working individually on the computer with a specialized program where teachers could monitor progress. In order to execute this well, there needed to be a lot of back work that needed to happen. The school's technology infrastructure needed to be upgraded, we needed to choose and analyze programs, train teachers, and hire a blended learning coordinator to oversee the program at the school. These were all the things that needed to be in place when I was a classroom teacher in order for computers to be a viable learning tool for my students.

Once we had assuaged her concerns about the operational challenges, Benaraw took stock of her staff's reaction and her own concerns about going blended:

> The logistics were manageable and subsequently we handled those, the most important part though was the people aspect. I needed to introduce

blended learning to the staff. Prior to having this formal conversation with the staff, I asked a few people what they thought about students on the computers for 15 percent of the day. The first person I asked was my husband, who happens to be in the computer arts industry. I wanted to know how school would have been for him if he had that different type of instruction. He actually told me that if he was in school he would have appreciated that. He thought school was boring and he was always tired of the same old worksheets that teachers passed out to him. I then asked one of my most veteran teachers, and she initially was very against blended learning. She felt that incorporating computers would take away from student engagement with each other as well as discourse. She brought up valid points that I didn't have the answer for.

We worked with her to identify solutions and create a plan to foster buy-in with her staff.

A few weeks later, I talked to my staff whole group about the transition. I shared what blended learning is and what it would look like for our students. I also told them that I and three teachers would fly up to Oakland and visit Aspire ERES Academy, an Aspire school that transitioned to blended learning. After the visit we would follow up and share what we learned. The three teachers that were selected represented all grade levels, experience levels, and I even took one of our teachers who perhaps was most hesitant.

The visit to ERES answered a lot of questions for us. When we got to ERES, we saw that blended learning was not overwhelming and a big monster of uncertainty, but rather students on the computer for two 30-minute blocks. Everything else mimicked what we do every day. The main difference is that students were working on the computer where we could track their progress, unlike traditional workstations where it was harder to track and differentiate for students. When meeting with the teachers, we liked that students were able to learn in a different medium, and that the classrooms were much quieter and students that weren't on the computer were able to have good discussion and group work and hear what each other had to say. We had to see it, and then we were sold.

ENGAGING PARENTS

Going blended offers great opportunities for deepening engagement with parents because blended learning allows the school to share more student achievement data with families, creates additional resources for students to access at home, and provides a mechanism for the school to demonstrate real leadership around technology use for education's sake. Initially, we hadn't given much thought to how we'd roll out blended learning with families. Allyson Milner, Aspire Titan Academy teacher, explains,

> The students go home all the time and tell their parents about a lesson they had in one program and a funny book they read in another program. While we have told the parents previously that their child will be using the computer as part of their learning day, we never fully explained each program, what it looks like, and what the benefits are.

In the second year of rolling out blended learning, Aspire Titan Academy teachers engaged parents by holding an information session for parents about the blended learning software. Teacher Freddy Esparza explains,

> We played demos of the software students are using daily and explained how they rotate on and off the computers. We also discussed how we track their progress very regularly and use this data to guide our next steps with blended learning. The parents had many great questions about what exactly the kids see, how long they are on, how can they monitor their progress, and can they use the programs at home.

Allyson Milner adds,

> The parents loved the explanation about blended learning being a mix of computer lessons and traditional learning. They understood the value that the computer plays in targeting lessons specifically at their child's need. Overall, I think it increased parent buy-in in our blended learning program. Also, it laid the foundation for future discussions about their child's academic growth and behavior related to both the traditional classroom and the computer programs.

Teachers can also use conferences with parents to engage them in blended learning. Taleen Dersaroian, a teacher at Aspire Gateway Academy, shares:

> For this round of student-led conferences (what we call parent-teacher conferences), my third-grade team and I added a blended learning station! For this station, students took their parents to their computer and told them why we do blended learning. Then, students had parents put on their headphones while they log in to the programs and showed them around each program (we made sure to emphasize to the students to not let the parents answer any questions so as not to skew the data). Additionally, for each program students made sure to tell their parents *why* we do it. I overheard a student telling his mom, "We do blended learning to become better readers, writers, and mathematicians." It's so cool to see students taking ownership of blended learning and explaining it to their parents. A lot of parents didn't even realize blended learning was happening in the classrooms or what it even looked like! The parental response has been positive so far. They especially like when I tell them that blended learning is adaptive to each student's needs. I will definitely implement this station again!

At Alliance College-Ready Public Schools in Los Angeles, Jonathan Tiongco explains their program is even more far-reaching in engaging parents around digital learning: "We run parent training and meetings specifically focused on blended learning education and 1-to-1 learning. We offer parent-education classes on Internet safety and digital citizenship, and also engage parents through blended learning showcase days."

Finally, blended learning is a team sport, requiring a great deal of collaboration and communication. In order to ensure we're all working together effectively and efficiently:

- We encourage weekly blog posts from teachers to collect feedback.
- We have weekly check-ins with principals to build their ownership of blended learning and answer their questions.
- We have weekly check-ins with each of the BLTAs.

- We have weekly check-ins between the blended learning team, the IT team, and the data team.
- BLTAs, principals, or both have bimonthly data talks with teachers to review software data and troubleshoot any problems related to blended learning.
- We survey teachers and students each semester to identify outstanding challenges and inform leadership of areas for improvement. You'll find an example of our end-of-year survey in appendix H.

In these ways, we're able to keep our finger on the pulse of new challenges as they arise.

GO FOR THE BADGE!

Determined Decision Maker

- Identify who is best suited to lead this work at the school level and ensure they're committed to the vision.
- Create "skin in the game" at the classroom and school levels so that all constituencies have a vested interest in a successful implementation.
- Hire tech support at the classroom level so that teachers can focus on teaching, not technology challenges.
- Hire or develop blended learning leadership who can oversee and troubleshoot pilots and implementations from an operational and educational viewpoint.
- Engage IT leadership as partners in this work.
- Coordinate and communicate your work among all teams.
- Create a systematic process for engaging school leaders and teachers in this work.
- Be disciplined in identifying where your strengths and weaknesses lie in the plan, and decide to move forward if you've weighed the costs.
- Create a plan for engaging parents and helping them learn about the work their students are doing.
- Build relationships with your technology team. Share your biggest challenges and define your roles.
- Identify who should be responsible for ensuring overall effective communication among all stakeholders in this process, including parents and students.

4

Recognizing and Planning for the Learning Curve

The learning curve for getting blended learning off the ground can be steep at times but, with careful planning, is surmountable. This chapter looks at creating a tight scope of work, getting support and ideas from others who are going blended, learning from teachers, learning from your mistakes, making important trade-offs, looking for golden opportunities, and phasing in the work over time.

START SMALL AND SMART

Choose schools, principals, and teachers who are ready to do this work and will be invested in its success. Consider your ideal conditions for implementation: school leadership, school culture, teacher capacity, and technology infrastructure. Think about which aspect of student achievement you're aiming to move, and put forward your best way to move it instructionally combined with the technology. With all that in mind, keep it simple—manage the work tightly but give teachers and principals lots of space to innovate. Keep things simple, as there will be plenty of complexity when you are planning to go blended. I've talked to folks who are opening blended schools, who also want students to take home their devices, and also intend to radically change the way their teachers provide instruction. Trying to do so many things at once is not starting small and is a recipe for a really tough year

66

ahead. We piloted blended learning at one school in Year 1, and in Year 3, we were running blended at four full schools, and had started pilots in four more schools. You can scale quickly once you know what you're doing, but first you will need to build systems to get the work done. See a sample project plan in appendix E.

WHO NEEDS BLENDED LEARNING FRIENDS? YOU DO!

Having spent the bulk of my career in education, I've learned one thing about the culture of educators: They may be collaborators and sharers in their own teaching communities (*may* being the operative word), but rarely do schools get together with one another to share practices, troubleshoot challenges, or swap resources. I don't know whether it's a culture of competition among teachers; a fear of judgment by others; a suspicion that one's students or circumstances are unique and unlike those at other schools; or, more innocently, just a lack of time to really find out what's going on at other schools.

At Aspire Public Schools, collaboration is one of our core values pervading our work within schools and across schools. We work in all sorts of different teams together: grade level, subject area, school-wide, cross-school, role-alike, cross-disciplinary, and many others. In my role as the director of innovative learning, I'm responsible for figuring out the role of digital learning in our instructional program. I can't do my work without collaborating with our IT team for hardware and infrastructure decisions, with our data integration team (we call it "Godzilla") for data and visualizations, with our finance team for budgeting, with the ed team and teachers and principals for instructional decisions, with the advancement team for fundraising. No worries on my becoming siloed in my work, as I wouldn't be able to get much done in the day-to-day without my colleagues!

What's interesting to me, however, is that collaboration with my role-alike colleagues at other schools, districts, and charter management organizations (CMOs) has also become completely central to my ability to do blended learning work. When I first began this work, I reached out to folks at Rocketship Education to learn about what they knew, and asked if they'd point me in the direction of others doing this work. From there, I created a small network of friends I called to learn from, ask advice of, and swap stories with. While our models and ideas and schools were very different, we were all trying to figure out blended learning in our schools, at a time when there was little out there in terms of resources focused on schools.

Initially, these relationships were supportive because we didn't feel that we were the only ones doing this work: we were no longer alone. Then, they became resources for venting ("Oh, why can't I get high-speed Internet access in the middle of Los Angeles in this day and age?!?") and sharing of victories. But over time, these relationships have become something much deeper: a network of people all working on very different parts of this complex puzzle, figuring out how to maximize digital learning in a rapidly changing education landscape.

Within the work I'm currently doing and the size of my team, I can't run iPad pilots, or test out gaming programs, or pilot 20 different software programs. I'm not ready to create mastery-based progressions in our high schools, nor do I want to work with 100 students in the same room. I don't have the capacity or the funding, and those efforts would not fit with how Aspire currently sees blended learning. However, I can pick up the phone with friends across the country who are doing those things, and doing them deeply, and who will share with me their lessons every step of the way (many of which can be found in the pages of this book). While the contexts may be different, having a friend who will tell me that classroom management changes significantly with 10 iPads in the room, or that grit and tenacity are big issues for kids new to creating their own educational playlists, this information is invaluable to me and helps inform each step I take as we move forward with blended learning at Aspire. I call some friends for advice on really technical issues I can barely understand involving infrastructure and device concerns, others for advice on software, others about student incentives, still others just to vent, and most of them just to get their latest thinking on this work. I can't even begin to acquire all the expertise I need to do this job effectively; my background is in education and teaching, but I've had a steep curve with regard to wireless access points, plug-ins, bandwidth, and other tech topics I never imagined I'd have to care about, much less discuss on a regular basis. I can't begin to test out all the K–5 math programs on the market, but I know folks I trust whom I can call for an opinion on how they're working with their students, what the challenges are, and, in many cases, what the pricing is. This book is a token of my gratitude for the community I'm a part of and another step in my journey to expand this knowledge-sharing network and to invite others.

I often tell colleagues, "I didn't have a KIPP friend until I started working in blended learning, and now I have KIPP friends all across the country." I'm grateful to be in education and in particular, blended learning, at a time when the culture is shifting and collaboration outside one's school or organization is becoming the norm. I very much appreciate that folks from the Oakland Unified School District who have come to tour and learn from our blended learning charter school in Oakland, California, and in return, they've shared with us much of what they've learned from their experiences to date.

There are online communities devoted to blended learning, communities of practice like the one my blended learning friends and I started, grant-driven communities, and informal communities built at conferences and through thought-leaders. People doing the work—colleagues in and outside your schools and funders cross-pollinating the work across the country—are valuable resources. These days, I also check online resources like EdSurge, Mind/Shift, and the ASCD SmartBrief to keep on top of changes. Like the teachers and school leaders with whom I work, I'm also on a learning curve and experience readiness for the next technology ideas on my own schedule. These resources expose me to the latest in the field and allow me to seek additional information when I'm ready to learn more. This work is too difficult and changing too quickly to do it alone. If you're doing blended learning work, start making friends also doing this work wherever you find them—no matter what their model, geography, or organization, whether they are at a public, private, or charter school— as you'll need them every step of the way. And they'll probably need you, too.

Key Idea

Perhaps the most important lesson we've learned is to make blended learning friends. Everything we know now we learned from others doing this work, and we are grateful. Despite differences in CMOs, school models, geographies, student populations, missions, and pilots, the people doing this work offer a wealth of information and are, frankly, really a fun community of people. All the experiments and implementations of blended learning going on now, even ones that you'd never have the stomach to do yourself, offer interesting ways to push your thinking around this work.

When possible, visit other blended learning implementations. You don't have to follow others' models; you just need to be open to how their work can inform your thinking about your work. Seeing other blended models allows you to see what "sacred cows" the school has chosen to slay, whether the master schedule, grade-level progressions, teacher lectures, or something else, and gives you the space to imagine what that looks like without having to try it! In the process, you can gather up great ideas and practices to bring back and deepen your own work.

LEARN ALL THE TIME FROM TEACHERS

Capture information from teachers formally (through surveys and interviews) and informally, or anecdotally. We figured that the easiest way we could capture aha moments and concerns was to put all the piloting teachers in a locked-down, nonpublic blog. Then we sent gentle reminders to blog every week. We wanted to capture teachers' thinking in real time, and our end-of-semester surveys felt like the wrong forum. And e-mail seemed too random and difficult to manage; e-mail also wouldn't allow teachers to share with one another. Tom Willis of Cornerstone Charter Schools in Detroit suggests, "Create the space and time to allow teachers to watch and learn (and ask lots of questions) of others doing this work." Teachers learn most from other teachers doing similar work, and we wanted to create opportunities for teachers to understand this work together.

We created a simple blog and locked it down so that only the blended team, principal, teachers, and blended learning teaching assistants could read and contribute to it. In the accompanying box, I've shared an example kick-off post for one of these blogs.

Kicking Off Our Work

Welcome to the Blog, Aspire Titan Teachers!

The Project Buzz Learning Blog is a place for us to really capture our thoughts, questions, rants, and concerns as we learn what blended learning might look like at Aspire. A few pointers:

- This blog is not public to funders, the outside world, or Aspire at large. It's a place for us to privately share what we're thinking about, wrestling with, concerned over, love, and hate.
- This blog is public to those of us on the team who are trying to learn from blended learning: the pilot teachers and principals, the Home Office Blended Learning Team, and a few other Home Office folks who are interested in such things. It's our hope that by making this blog mostly private, you'll feel comfortable sharing your thoughts and ideas without concerns of being judged. This is a grand experiment and we want to learn from you!
- This blog is not a place to put in HelpDesk tickets, nor get responses from IT or Godzilla [our data integration team]. You'll still need to use proper channels for getting that kind of support.

Overall, we're running these pilots this year to learn from them, and I suspect that most of our lessons learned will be millions of small ones (naming conventions and passwords, establishing rotation routines, effective content assigning). It's imperative for all of us to document these so we actually learn from them, and it's my greatest hope that this is the easiest, lowest-stakes way to capture your learning along the way! So join in the conversation!

We wanted teachers to vent, and they did! They also shared concerns, aha moments, insights, and good ideas with us and with each other. The blog allowed us to identify and fix problems we might otherwise not be aware of and to cross-pollinate what was working.

LEARN FROM YOUR MISTAKES

Remember, the failures may teach you more than the successes. Keep a laser-like focus on what works, and get rid of what doesn't. Some of our pilots worked markedly better than others, and I felt pretty terrible when one didn't go as planned. However, I learned some huge, hairy, important lessons that have informed all the work I've done moving forward. (Spoiler alert: Classroom management matters greatly!)

This work is both rapidly changing and often maddeningly slow. Chris Liang-Vergara of LEAP Innovation's advice is this: "Share realistic expectations from the start; be clear about the challenges that will be experienced." The technology shifts constantly, with increasing numbers of new products and services on the market, upgrades, updates—the list goes on and on—yet the work of getting the technology infrastructure upgraded and in place can be extremely challenging and frustrating in older buildings and with limited funding.

Despite that difficulty, our blended learning implementations look different with each year as we continue to improve and iterate on this work. Jennifer Mazawey, Aspire Titan Academy kindergarten teacher, explains,

> Over the last year, I feel that I have really gained more knowledge of how to use blended learning more effectively in my classroom. I think some things at first were more trial and error but now I feel like I am using it more deliberately and making blended learning student independent time complement the time that I spend in small groups with my students. I use the lessons more effectively by adding extra lessons to those that need help in certain areas, for example high-frequency words or letter and letter sound practice. Now with Common Core, I have added book sets to the digital book collection to go with our current units. It's really great when the students tell me they have connections to what we learn in class and to what they have learned on the computers.

Even our schools in their third year of implementation are still changing and improving on their practice. We switch software; we begin to privilege some instructional strategies we previously were less inclined to use; we look more deeply at online learning data; and we consider new routines for making our rotations more efficient. Freddy Esparza, second-grade teacher at Aspire Titan Academy, reflects,

> After piloting blended learning last year, I remember thinking back, "How can I make students more involved, reflective of their time on the computers, and understand the purpose of their work in blended learning?" This caused me to make great changes to how I run blended in my classroom this year. Now I have more students problem-solving on their own

and helping each other. I engage them with their data and now they understand the purpose of being on the computers. I don't have to tell them and they know what to do, and this is very hard to accomplish!

At Rocketship, teacher culture is as important as student culture in creating a mindset around blended learning. Caryn Voskuil explains,

> I like to build a culture with my teachers that stresses a co-investigation mindset. If I don't know the answer, I will set aside time to co-plan with the teacher so that we can learn it together. Our blended implementation varies year to year as well, and we are always dreaming up new value hypotheses. Once we have a hypothesis about how to improve, we set out to demonstrate or prove the concept and then create the exemplar to demonstrate how to replicate the idea.

Engaging teachers as partners in learning what works in blended learning classrooms is a recipe for success.

EVERYTHING IS A TRADE-OFF

In my wildest blended learning dreams, here's what I want: K–12 high-quality software products, all Common Core aligned, integrated, and adaptable and assignable—oh, and with game mechanics and embedded formative assessments. I want to build a common school culture around the software and the data, with a common language and metrics. I want to have fiber piped into all of our schools and laptops for all our kids at school and at home, with connectivity, and supporting materials translated into Spanish for the majority of families we serve. I want data dashboards for kids, parents, and teachers, with truly actionable data. I want on-site support from all our vendors, truly flexible seating, amazing support, and all of our products integrated together. You know what? I can't have it all, either because it doesn't (yet) exist, or because I couldn't afford it on current funding levels if it did exist.

Since I can't have it all, it's incredibly important to always communicate the trade-offs. Transparency in decision making will help you manage expectations with all stakeholders and foster a clearer understanding of what's actually possible. Popular imagination about technology often paints a very different picture, and your job is to make sure folks are realists so you're not setting them up for disappointment later.

LOOK FOR OPPORTUNITIES

Most recently, we've begun to ask, "How can we use blended learning to support the instructional shifts we need to make to teach the Common Core State Standards?" With the addition of increased technology in our classrooms, we see opportunities to access electronic resources, allow content creation more rapidly, and [fill in the blank with the latest and greatest innovation]. However, rather than make arbitrary use of technology because it's available, we're thinking strategically about instructional methods like close reading of complex texts that can be better supported with a blended rotation in place, so the teacher can engage in a Socratic seminar using the text with fewer students at one time. At this time, we've only begun to uncover the synergies between blended learning and the Common Core. As we deepen our work each year, the possibilities to consider are exciting!

PHASE IN THE WORK

Not only should you pilot (*and you should*), you should also consider phasing in the work over time. This approach will allow you to work out your technology problems with only a portion of your staff, support the school culture and teacher professional development shifts that will inevitably take place, and learn from your mistakes without affecting the entire staff (ideally). As I've mentioned earlier, at Aspire we phase in the work of converting schools to blended learning over the course of two years. Table 4.1 illustrates the ways in which we articulate the conditions necessary to move forward with rolling out blended across a school.

Table 4.1 Conditions for Multiyear Implementation

Year 1 Conditions	Year 2 Conditions	Year 3 Conditions
Strong principal who is eager to do it. At least 4–8 teachers who are • Interested • High-performing • Strong classroom managers • Already doing solid small-group stations work Bandwidth upgraded by first day of school. IT has sufficient capability to intensively support, given other priorities. Funding allocated.	Successful Year 1, as measured by student achievement data and teacher survey data; school shows fidelity to model. Interest from principal in rolling out to other grades. Majority of teachers are • Interested • Strong classroom managers • Already doing small-group stations work IT has sufficient capability to support, given other priorities. Funding allocated.	Successful Year 2, as measured by student achievement data and teacher survey data; school shows fidelity to model.

GO FOR THE BADGE!

Determined Decision Maker

- Figure out how and where you can focus your blended learning work so you start small and smart, and maintain high quality.
- Build a community of thought partners outside your school, district, or organization to help you do this work.
- Learn from the sector by engaging with outside organizations and resources focused on this work.
- Recognize and articulate the trade-offs when making decisions.
- Build in processes and a culture to ensure that you identify opportunities for improvement and learn from your mistakes.

PART 2

Planning for Implementation: Strategic Decisions and Considerations

Once you've made the fundamental decisions of identifying your focus, determining readiness, and building a strong team, you'll move into a series of strategic decisions to make when going blended. In this section, we'll cover choosing your model, identifying quality software and hardware, navigating student data, choosing furniture, and making sure your network is up to speed. While each of these decisions is operational in nature, how they're made will directly impact the teaching and learning environment. See appendix E for a sample project plan for a full blended learning implementation.

5

Choosing Your Model and Crafting Your Pilots

Running online learning software and piloting a blended learning model are two very distinct activities. Focusing on what model you plan to pilot is imperative, as the model will drive your selection of tools, resources, and supports. When we started out, we explored whether a blended learning model (existing or not) could allow us to have an even greater impact on our students and better utilize our talent, in a way that would contribute to our financial sustainability. We created some clear criteria around which to evaluate models:

Impact on schools and students

- A new model will have a positive impact on schools, students, or both
  - Teachers will be able to use their time with students more effectively
  - Teacher workload will be similar or less, not more
  - Student achievement levels will increase or stay the same

Economics

- A new model will contribute positively to our financial sustainability
  - The model will lower costs and/or
  - Funders (both current and new) will see the benefits of implementing a new model and support it

Organizational fit

- Implementation of a blended learning model will align with our organizational culture and values
  - Student-teacher relationships will remain strong
  - We can maintain a strong school culture

Feasibility

- We have—or, with reasonable expenditures and time, can build—the capacity and capabilities to implement a new model successfully, consisting of
  - Technology needs
  - Training and change management

Originally, we learned about four different blended learning models of implementation: flex, station rotation, enriched virtual, and self-blend. The Clayton Christensen Institute has codified some of the more common blended learning models across the United States. Much continues to change from year to year as more schools explore blended learning. Explore the Christensen database of models, FSG's Blended Learning Case Studies, and the Next Generation Learning Challenge models for ideas and examples of blended learning models in action. If possible, visit blended learning schools so you can see the work first-hand. There's much to learn from each model, and yet, despite the differences among models, the issues in implementing blended learning are strikingly similar.

We landed on the classroom-based, station rotation model: a common implementation of blended learning, especially in the K–5 setting (see figure 5.1).

During a 90-minute instructional block, for example, students in small, differentiated groups rotate across learning stations at 30-minute intervals:

- Group 1 = teacher-led (small-group) instruction
- Group 2 = independent and collaborative practice
- Group 3 = personalized, online instruction

Each of these components plays an important role in helping students apply and contextualize what they learn. This station rotation model affords targeted

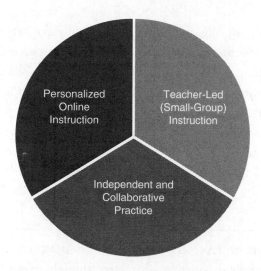

Figure 5.1 Station Rotation Model

teaching and learning opportunities for teachers and students, while simultaneously providing multiple data points to help inform instructional practice. Time frames vary, in order to allow teachers to be responsive and proactive to meet students' needs. Additional, whole-group instruction provides experiences for students to learn and discuss common texts and concepts.

CRAFTING YOUR PILOTS

We bring the same strategy to bear whether we're piloting a model in a few classrooms or converting an entire school or multiple schools to blended learning. If you're going for the badge, you're on the right track!

Why we pilot: We pilot a model to really learn what works and what doesn't; to challenge our assumptions about teaching and learning; to uncover what we don't yet understand about technology infrastructure, hardware, software, and integration; and to learn from our mistakes in a less impactful, less expensive way! We also pilot to show any nay-sayers what's possible and, when needed, to move a culture slowly or begin to build momentum (sometimes you need to go slow to go fast later). Ultimately, I needed to pilot a model to make the case that Aspire should invest in this work, and when the pilot was successful, the results spoke for themselves and made it much easier for me to scale this work.

*How we **don't** pilot*: We don't pilot by throwing spaghetti against a wall and seeing what sticks. So many factors contribute to the success or failure of any technology integration: teacher development, class composition, political environment, school priorities, and so on. Frequently, teachers will ask to pilot blended learning software in nonblended classrooms, but because we focus on getting the model right and try to tightly manage our pilots so we can learn more from them than just teacher opinion and anecdotal evidence, we decline. We'd rather do a few things well than many things possibly not well.

EVALUATE YOUR PILOTS

We looked at student achievement data, IT help-desk tickets, teacher and student survey data, and anecdotal evidence. Ultimately, though, in our teacher surveys, we asked teachers, "What evidence do you have that we should or should not do this again this year?" Overwhelmingly, our teachers cited evidence that we should continue doing blended learning and scale it across the school. Among the most compelling evidence: multiple teachers stated that although going blended was not less work, it was more sustainable work because they were able to see every student grow in achievement levels in the data that teachers held as truth. Teachers no longer spent their Saturdays building workstations for students and instead embarked on a new learning curve to better understand the software programs and ramp up the quality and quantity of small-group instruction. The initial, upfront costs for teachers were large, but the payoff is that they are now getting completely individualized data and analysis of what students are and aren't making sense of and have a model that supports teachers' desire to truly differentiate instruction for all students in a variety of ways. We also found student feedback overwhelmingly positive in each of the surveys we ran, as well as anecdotally.

Key Idea

Keep a disciplined eye on what works and doesn't work in your pilots. Constantly troubleshoot problems by looking at the systems you've put in place (or forgot to put in place).

We ran a few other less successful pilots that ultimately pushed us back to the drawing board when it came to running blended learning in secondary classrooms. In one case, we couldn't figure out how to scale the work once we stabilized it. In another case, the teacher loved the digital tool but couldn't integrate it successfully with her curriculum. In yet another, we found we needed to give students much more support with heavy online coursework. Piloting prevented us from making more costly mistakes, and nobody says you have to roll out a program across the school just because you piloted the program. Sometimes, you learn more about what you shouldn't be doing than about what you should be doing.

A WORD ABOUT NEXT-GENERATION MODELS

Across the country, districts and charters are trying out new blended learning models, many of which have challenged our existing assumptions about the dissemination of content, how technology is used for learning, what instruction can look like, how we utilize time and space in schools, and how teachers can work. Some of these models are radically different from what many of us experienced when we attended K–12 school. Summit Public Schools, Rocketship Education, and the Alliance for College-Ready Public Schools are among many organizations and schools on the bleeding edge of this work. Chris Liang-Vergara explains:

> Starting with a "clean slate" or "reviewing school from the bottom up" helps to encourage people to do more "radical" things. Speaking from a team that settled on a lab rotation model six different times—we reviewed and rebuilt the schedule and student experience from scratch at each school—and it helped (unintentionally) clean up a lot of inefficiencies that otherwise would be hard to remove. So, going through the thought exercises of Next Generation models (or fresh models as I like to call them) has major wins for a school and organization—apart from blended learning.

Learn from others doing this work and have it inform your thinking on what's right for your school.

Ultimately, at Aspire we weren't ready (or even willing) to throw out our instructional model to try out something we weren't even sure was right for us in our existing schools. We appreciate our colleagues at other CMOs and districts who have taken radical steps to go blended. Culturally and practically speaking, with 34 schools at the time, it just wasn't possible or smart for us to do that kind of work.

GO FOR THE BADGE!

Strategic Planner

- Determine your criteria and limits for evaluating blended models first.
- Articulate your model and theory of action.
- Carefully craft pilots to test the key assumptions in your model.
- Study and learn from other models to figure out what might work for your context.
- Evaluate your pilots to use what you learn to make decisions about going blended moving forward.

6

Finding the Right Software and Hardware

If there's one question I'm asked more than all the others, it's this one: "What software programs do your blended learning schools use?" My answer is always, "It's complicated." When we started this work, I believed that I should be looking for the best content, for each grade level, in each subject area, for each student proficiency level. After a few years of trial and error, I've realized that choosing software for student learning is a series of trade-offs to arrive at what's "best right now" for the students we serve. In this chapter, you'll learn a list of challenges to avoid and criteria to use when evaluating software and the considerations for choosing devices.

WHO SHOULD CHOOSE THE SOFTWARE?

We've chosen software in two ways: I've picked it for schools, and I've narrowed down the products for schools and left it up to the school's leadership team to make the final decision on what to run. Because learning the ed tech landscape and attending software demos can be very overwhelming and time-consuming (30–60 minutes a demo alone!), I've attempted to shortcut the process for our schools so they can make informed decisions and still have ownership over the final decision. Some organizations, like EdSurge and Common Sense Media, are beginning to create software websites that allow visitors to search for software by need and read detailed information on features, which can help narrow the field of software offerings for schools to choose. These websites are extremely helpful, but because products change rapidly (as do people's opinions of them), be sure to talk to teachers actually using the products if possible. In addition, these sites may or may not detail the nitty-gritty challenges of implementing the product, so you'll want to get this information however you can.

Caution 1: Be careful about letting early adopters influence your decisions too much. Frequently, teachers who are early adopters want to influence purchasing decisions. While these teachers have great expertise that should be tapped, be mindful of the following questions:

- Does the suggested software directly address the data problem you're trying to solve?
- Is it software that more hesitant teachers could learn to use easily?
- Does this software make sense in your overall budget? For example, if a teacher is hot for a software program solely focused on fractions, consider the cost of that program and weigh that price against the size of your school-wide math program. Can you afford additional software to address your other math problems? If not, maybe you need another product.
- Is the data compatible with the data you consider to be "truth"? That is, does the software provide standards-aligned data that focuses on your standards, and can you export the data so that you can use it in concert with your other student achievement data?

Caution 2: Get good ideas from others implementing blended learning, but be sure to ask lots of questions to ensure you're willing to make similar trade-offs. I'm frequently asked what we use for software, and I'm always wary of answering the question because I'm afraid the questioner won't weigh the trade-offs I've made or will assume that the software can solve an instructional problem totally different from the one I have.

When I call a friend to ask her about her use of a particular product I'm interested in, I ask a bunch of questions:

- What grades or classes are you using it in? With all students or those at certain RtI (Response to Intervention) or proficiency levels or proficiency bands?
- How much time do students spend on the program per week?
- Have you seen data gains outside the program yet? (A no answer to this question isn't a deal-breaker for me, as this metric can be very hard to gauge. However, the answer to this question gives me a much clearer sense of how people at a school are thinking about the program in their instructional context.)
- Why did you choose the program? What do you like about it?
- What do you not like about the program? (With this question, I very much try to probe for all the challenges—both technical and instructional. You'll want to take careful notes as you'll need this information to smooth your implementation should you choose to move forward with this product. A trusted friend I once asked about a product shared that students got bored with the program about six weeks into implementation. This was such helpful information!)
- How responsive is the software company when it comes to solving problems? Do you like working with the company?

Potential tech challenges might include buggy software that freezes often, a frustrating interface for kindergartners to sign into, students' inability to see their own progress in data, support for the program in some web browsers but not others, poor customer service from the software rep, weak or not exportable data dashboards ("exportable" means that a file can be easily shared from one software program to another) or data dashboards that require a crazy number of clicks to get to the data you want, slow loading of software on certain devices, clunky content-provisioning (determining the content students will work on)—the list is endless.

Potential instructional challenges might include these: student engagement is spotty; the training burden on teachers or students is heavy; some students really struggle and need additional adult support (which can really inhibit a teacher's ability to pull small groups); "mastery" seems questionable; some content is better aligned with the Common Core State Standards than other content; the content targets one population well, but not others; and, again, the list goes on.

Depending on your plan, some of these challenges may be worth taking on, while others may not, depending on how you intend to support implementation. And we've taken on quite a few products that we thought were going to be great after we really did our homework on them, but at the end of the day, the products just weren't the right fit for us. Plan to make some mistakes, and *never* enter into a multiyear contract to save money, as you'll end up spending years undoing that mistake!

Highline Public Schools in Washington State took a slightly different approach to choosing software, as district leaders wanted schools to make their own choices across the district based on teacher input. Rachel Klein, director of student advancement at Highline Public Schools, shares, "We narrowed down the content choices to three elementary math software choices, and then had schools choose a maximum of two to use across grade levels. With that, we held a festival together across our 18 schools. Teachers came together and shared their different perspectives with each other, the technology vendors were there to answer questions, and then schools chose what they were going to use for the next year based on each other's input." This method allowed teachers and school leaders to collaborate and spend very little time in a targeted way and yet still be able to make choices about what software to use in their schools.

Don't forget to include input from students and former students. Chris Liang-Vergara at LEAP Innovations takes this approach:

> Take one of the toughest topics you teach, and go into the software and experience how your *students* will experience it. Is it superior to your current lesson? How can it supplement what you're teaching? Is it even worth students' time? Look at one of the topics your students master well each year. Go through the same exercise: have your teachers and curriculum leads experience that same lesson in the program. Games, bells, points, and all that are fun—but at the end of the day they wear off quickly, and you're stuck with either a provider of quality lessons and instructional content or a bunch of flashy-looking, shallow edutainment games.

Lesson Learned

Use student achievement data in the software to better understand where the software is working and not working. Before we were officially doing blended learning, we were running some software programs in many of our schools. The implementation of these programs would vary greatly: in class, after-school, for remediation, as supplementary instruction, to fill skill gaps, with teachers, with substitute teachers, with long-term substitute teachers, with instructional aides, and with ed specialists. We didn't have implementation guidelines or a commonly held theory of action around using this software. In many cases, teachers and principals believed that something was better than nothing, regardless of usage or fidelity of implementation. We ran one particular software program across our schools, and, during one year, 2,000 separate students signed into this program. Yet we didn't have a clear, data-driven answer as to whether or not the software was effective at improving student achievement. After the year, we did a massive data dump to figure out the answer. What we learned was enlightening. After much analysis, we determined that students made significant gains on the State Achievement tests *if*

- They were in grades 4–7, *and*
- They were at proficiency levels of "far below basic" and "below basic," *and*
- Most important, they were on the software for more than 30 hours.

While this was all very encouraging news, we were disheartened by the number of students on the program for fewer than 30 hours or for whom the program had little impact because they were not the target audience. Twenty hours of instructional time wasted could be much better spent in small-group instruction or engaging in really purposeful learning activities. Adhere to recommended times and audiences when implementing software in order to leverage data gains for students.

Caution 3: Don't trust the data from the software or the research from the vendor until you've validated it. "At this point, anyone can say they're aligned to the Common Core State Standards, yet until their product is validated against a reliable assessment, they can say whatever they'd like," reminds Rachel Klein of

Highline. Validating data is incredibly challenging without a robust data system in place, but creating even simple spreadsheets of achievement data from software and trusted assessments can help teachers gain insights into alignment and the efficacy of online activities. Fidelity of implementation can also greatly affect achievement data, so the software provider's research-based results might differ from your results. Find out the amount of time per week students should be spending on the program and, if possible, the number of lessons or percentage of mastery students must achieve each week to make the greatest gains, and then check your own implementation against that metric.

HOW TO CHOOSE THE SOFTWARE

Getting up to speed on knowing what you want and don't want from educational software takes time and energy.

Key Idea

Start the process of choosing your software first by making a list of your nonnegotiables, as doing so will help you greatly narrow the field of software offerings. Take into account your technical limitations, your educational vision, and your blended model. Although this exercise may feel limiting at first, it will help you remain disciplined when it comes to making hard choices among providers.

These are our nonnegotiables:

- The software must be web-based, rather than locally installed, as we don't have the manpower to install and update software programs on all of our computers.
- The content must be standards-aligned to Common Core State Standards.
- Content must be adaptive or assignable, or both.
- Students must be able to work independently in the product without involvement from a teacher (as we want teachers focusing on small-group instruction, not troubleshooting student work on computers).

- The product has data dashboards that track student progress, mastery of standards, and time on task, and that data is exportable to our system.
- The system continues to provide other lessons once a student has completed an assigned lesson or standard.

Our friends at Rocketship Education greatly helped us in learning how to choose the right software by sharing with us their rubric for evaluating software. Although we don't fill out the rubric per se while evaluating new software, we do use the categories on the rubric as a way to screen each product. Our descriptions of each criterion are the ways in which we think about this rubric. Rocketship Education has also generously shared their original rubric for inclusion in this book; you will find this rubric in appendix F.

Alignment and Content Coverage

It's imperative to us that we start with standards-aligned, quality content, and a lot of it (at least 100 hours of content per subject, per grade). We've found many engaging software products on the market without clear standards-alignment and lacking data dashboards to illustrate student proficiency by standard. Without standards-based data, we're unable to test the efficacy of the program clearly against our other measures. And honestly, content that is not aligned to standards communicates a lack of disciplined thinking or awareness of public education on the company's part. Say to software providers, "Show me *how* it's aligned." Additionally, we appreciate when a program can provide the actual percentage and list of Common Core standards covered, so that teachers know what is and is not addressed in any given product.

In addition, we look at how much content a product actually has at a given grade level and in a particular subject area. If the product has fewer than 100 hours of content at each grade level, we're not confident that students won't exhaust the product in less than a year, and we have limited budget and time to add a new product and additional training midyear. We've looked at a few online libraries of books that on the surface have appeared to be great; however, when we've done the math about how many books are available per grade level, we quickly become underwhelmed.

If you plan to use more than one software program at a grade level, consider how the programs will work together, and be deliberate when scheduling how they'll be used. Chris Liang-Vergara at LEAP Innovations explains,

> A cocktail of solutions is an option and also provides necessary variation and unpredictability in the student experience. If the students go to the same math program every day for a year or two or three years, most likely they'll be incredibly bored of it. Have a bench to pull from, but still have your lead-off hitter. Consider diversification of experience as well. Having a "boring" program that is peppered throughout can make another one look amazing (comparatively).

All of this advice assumes that the chosen programs have quality content, of course.

Assessments

When software assigns leveled pre- and post-assessments to measure student growth and readiness for future units and, ideally, provisions content based on the data, the software offers teachers a way of assessing growth or mastery within the product. We take that assessment data and examine it against our internal benchmark data and state assessment data to evaluate the efficacy of our chosen software. Not all software provides diagnostic assessments; some offer embedded formative assessments that push students along independent learning paths. Whether formative or summative or both, the software's assessment engine should provision content for each student based on his or her assessed level. Ultimately, we won't choose software that doesn't have some kind of viable assessment system built into it. Without such a system, the software offers little to teachers in terms of student learning and accountability.

Adaptivity

When the term *adaptive* is used to describe software, the implication is that the software assesses students and adjusts to meet a student where he or she is and to provide instruction at that level. However, the actual employment of this term varies from product to product; the logic in assessment engines varies widely (see

Table 6.1 Pros and Cons of Adaptive Software

Pros	Cons
Allows students to follow individualized learning paths Leverages technology to do what teachers can't do (or can't do easily) Maximizes directed learning on the computers, as students are less able to click around and jump from activity to activity	Can be a "black box" in which teachers are left out of decision making Can be incredibly frustrating for teachers who are accustomed to controlling what content students work on If there's an inherent expectation that the program will inform interventions or other moments of instruction, teachers need to find a way to trust the software and the assessments

table 6.1). Here's an excellent list of questions to ask of the potential software provider:

1. Does the product constantly adapt to where students are in real time (as the student is working in the program)?
2. Does the product use adaptive testing to determine content provisions (what content students will be working on)?
3. Does the software do both—adapt in real time and use adaptive testing to determine content?
4. Does the software merely reassign content if a student gets a problem wrong?
5. Do students repeat lessons they've failed, or are they assigned new lessons?

Lesson Learned

Start early sending teachers the message that they should make their peace with asynchronous learning. Identify examples in your instructional program of students learning content asynchronously (such as independent reading and math projects). You'll need a culture that is comfortable with students learning different things at different times, as that's how you will truly leverage individualized learning in software.

Assignability

Assignable content allows teachers to have some measure of control over content assignment in an automated, efficient way. In this way, teachers can "assign" certain content to some groups or students and other content to different groups or students. While assignability can allow a teacher to sequence content to parallel instruction or differentiate content based on instructional needs, this functionality comes at a price: teacher time. Depending on the software, assigning content uses up teachers' time. If some students complete their folders of digital content in one week, and another student completes her folder in three weeks, and yet another group of students completes their folders over the course of five weeks, teachers need to stay on top of provisioning challenges. Some software products make this task easy. Others do not.

Partly Adaptable, Partly Assignable

You can't really have it both ways (yet), but some software products try. While products will continue to evolve, it's important to manage teachers' expectations about wanting both adaptability and assignability. If teachers try to control everything students do on the computers, the teachers are not allowing the technology to individualize student learning and, in some cases, could be just digitizing the worksheet experience. We've seen some teachers assign students "extra lessons" on computers, to pre-teach or review a concept, and then have students resume their individualized paths. In this way, teachers have been able to take advantage of limited assignability for pre-teaching but also to leverage adaptability so that students can still work on individualized learning paths based on the students' own levels.

Application Programming Interface and Data Integration

When student achievement data is exportable, teachers and school leaders can analyze the efficacy of a blended implementation, identify strengths and weaknesses of the program, and ultimately visualize student data alongside other trusted data. *Application programming interface* (API) is the somewhat daunting term used to describe how two systems communicate. If a vendor has an open API, we can easily connect the vendor's system with ours, and, as a result, we're able to integrate the program's data with our data warehouse pretty seamlessly and to look at the program's data in real time in our system. This kind of connectivity is our ideal as we continue to deepen our use of software data. However, few products we use have open APIs, so vendors willing to work with us to integrate their program's data with our existing data warehouse or other systems also deserve a gold star, as we want and need the ability to triangulate our student data to draw conclusions about the efficacy of our implementation and student achievement. We've begun to build our own data dashboards based on teacher input so that we can identify ways of strengthening our implementations. Although some products have lots of data dashboards for teachers, we find ourselves wanting new and even more detailed ways of slicing the data to make it actionable for teachers.

We appreciate vendors with single user sign-ons, automated account provisioning, and data integration potential. If we can't get our data exported out of the software, we're not interested in even trying the program.

Curriculum

We look for a research-based instructional design and demonstrable student outcomes in field testing and a system that teaches and re-teaches using multiple pedagogical approaches. Granted, many of these products are new, and some of the internal "research" companies use is for their own marketing benefit. However, we still look for research when we can get it. We look for multiple pedagogical approaches, which include audio, written instructions, and multiple visual manipulatives to teach concepts. We don't want students to do digital test-prep "worksheets"; we want students to learn concepts and skills in a variety of modalities, and, when students struggle, we want the software to provide a different pedagogical approach to help students master the material.

Engagement

Although technology may be engaging initially, with any program, over time, student engagement wanes. We look for programs that offer a built-in incentive system (like games or rewards) for students as they demonstrate their learning. We take student engagement seriously. If a program isn't engaging for students, we know that students will veer off task, and learning will not progress.

Cost

Cost is an important factor in making decisions about choosing products. When calculating costs of software programs, be sure to add in the cost of training (if there is a cost associated or required) and divide by the numbers of students served to get apples-to-apples comparisons, as many software providers have different prices for training and support in addition to the software license cost. We create an average per-student budget for software, which allows us to understand important trade-offs when purchasing for entire schools, even though we recognize that this cost will be higher or lower at some grade levels and with some populations.

With a limited budget, we have to ask ourselves, "What is the best allocation of limited resources for the biggest impact on student achievement?" If we budget an average per-student amount of, say, $100/student, we know we may need to make some trade-offs when choosing software. For example, if I find that the most ideal K–5 math program for a school is only $25 per student, I have more wiggle room to find a great program for English language arts and potentially even a digital reading program. But if the math program I love is $75 per student, I know that my choices for ELA software will be limited. Although there are some good software programs for teaching fractions out there, I don't have the option of committing even 20 percent of the budget just to fractions, when I'm looking at both ELA and math achievement and taking into account that fractions might be a challenge only at a few grade levels. Likewise, if one teacher loves a program, but it's not something that makes sense for the whole school to adopt, you'll need to weigh conclusions from student achievement data and the costs of other software programs to evaluate the trade-offs and make a thoughtful purchasing decision.

When getting software quotes, always check and double-check your quotes and invoices. Of all the different types of purchasing orders we place each year for blended learning, we invariably get many more mistakes (rarely in our favor) in our software quotes than in our quotes for other types of purchases. And remember, everything is negotiable!

Training

All software training is not equal. With some software, we prefer a train-the-trainers model, while in other cases, we prefer the software representatives to provide the training. Our decision about training usually depends on the complexity of the software, the strength of the trainer, the cost of the training, and the time commitment involved in the training. Ultimately, we look for minimal, just-in-time training that we can customize to our needs. When reps tell me they need a full day for training, I just laugh: To wrestle a full day of professional development from our principals for software training would be unheard of at Aspire. If a product needs that much training to get off the ground, it's probably too labor-intensive to run in the first place. Once a school is interested in a product, we expect principals to invest in professional development on the product, but the software still needs to be a "self-starter," or nobody will use it in the first place. Schedule follow-up training to dive more deeply into product features and data analysis, once students have generated 6–8 weeks of data in the software. Chris Liang-Vergara at LEAP Innovations suggests, "Structure touch-points of support so there's some prep prior to the start of the year, a 1–2 month milestone, and a 4–6 month milestone at a minimum." We've found that having more than one training frequently creates even greater buy-in for a product, and the follow-up training is even more positively received than the initial training.

Software Management: Less Is More

With each program you add, you take on another layer of complexity around managing the software on devices. This complexity includes whitelisting and imaging documents for each software program, determining which web browser supports each program, figuring out which reps are supportive and helpful when bugs arise, distributing data to teachers, and analyzing data school-wide. The more programs you run in a school, the less the principal is able to build school-wide culture around achievement in the various programs, and the less teachers are able to collaborate with each other and troubleshoot around the software.

Feasibility

Sometimes, the best program is not the easiest program to get off the ground when starting blended learning in a school. Implementation might be harder because of technical requirements to run the program on your devices or the amount of teacher training necessary to ensure the success of the program. We've erred on the side of having easier-to-implement programs in year 1, as programs are much easier to switch in year 2. Keep ease of implementation in mind when choosing your initial software programs to run.

Never Underestimate the Value of a Great Software Representative

Originally, we hadn't thought much about the role the software representative plays in our implementations; to us, they were the folks we faxed purchase orders to and provided student account information to. We quickly realized that a software rep can make or break the success of a product implementation in a variety of ways. Find someone who answers the phone when you call, is helpful and responsive (especially when you encounter bugs or when unexpected updates cause the software to not work), and ideally is open to negotiating for better data and/or lower prices. Avoid software reps who text you at 7 am, or who just float the idea of creating a quote for all the schools in your system when you've asked for a single school quote, or who have to call you back every time you ask them a question. Ask blended learning leaders at other schools about their reps, and really interview your own reps during the bidding process.

Understand the Trade-offs

Honestly, even though the number of software offerings out there is increasing, if you're looking to get blended learning off the ground you may find very little. Start with the data: What student achievement problem are you "hiring" the software to help you solve? Is it a math skills problem? A reading problem? A writing problem? Consider this question in two ways:

- Software that supports student learning (practice, activities, and so on) *and*
- Software that supports teacher instruction (that is, it allows teachers to teach a smaller group of students while one group is on the computers).

Both offer opportunities to increase achievement.

Run Short Software Pilots

Piloting software for 2–6 weeks can be a good way for teachers to try out products and get a better idea of what your needs really are and how the software can work within your piloting structure. Chris Liang-Vergara at LEAP recommends,

> Pilot, pilot, pilot; prototype, prototype, prototype. Talk to experts (other districts, schools, users) to get your short list of software, but then you need to try it with your staff and your students. This helps with the learning curve. You will also find you don't know what you really want until you try things in the real world. For example, our staff initially wanted high assignability in all programs because they were accustomed to that level of control in a paper-based environment. After two days into the pilot, at the team check-in there was a resounding consensus that this wasn't practical and something with pre-set curriculum or adaptability was needed. But we never would have known we wanted this feature if the teachers didn't actually pilot options in their *real,* day-to-day work cycle. Also, make all decisions prior to summer break or earlier so resources are established prior to summer planning.

What works for the setting of a particular school or organization might be quite different from what works in your specific setting. Pilot to make sure the software works in your school. Anirban Bhattacharyya of KIPP Foundation explains, "Start with the academic goal, and make sure all decisions have been made regarding model, schedule, use of physical space, etc. Many programs 'choose themselves' after all of these parameters are put in place."

Involve Other Stakeholders in the Decision-Making

Rachel Klein at Highline Public Schools has a slightly different process. Before school leaders put anything out, they have lots of conversations with vendors and friends whom they trust. Then, Klein and her team run it by their district-level content specialists. Their schools get all their categorical money, but they can buy back services from Highline's pool of content specialists. Their content specialists are very well aligned in terms of philosophies, pedagogical styles, and so on, so they're a great resource for Highline to investigate something before talking to teachers about it, and possibly to use the tool in their coaching with teachers. And generally, the specialists take the tool out to the schools and talk to teachers about it in job-embedded way as needs arise.

Jeanne Chang at E. L. Haynes Public Charter School offers this perspective on helping school leaders make software decisions:

> To make the most efficient use of any school-based staff member's time, I typically try to narrow down the choices to highlight the top two or three options, then outline each one's various pros, cons, and differentiating features. When I was at the District of Columbia Public Schools, Central Office was exploring which math blended learning platforms and resources we should consider supporting at a district level. Prior to making any major purchases, we invited teachers, instructional coaches, and school administrators to listen to a series of vendor presentations over the course of two weeks and asked participants to provide feedback immediately following each session. This opportunity gave educators the chance to see (and often directly explore) each program for themselves, ask tailored questions, and gauge whether or not they would want to use that specific resource in their own classrooms and schools. At the same time, Central Office staff could "check our understanding" of how effectively we thought the programs could meet the targeted needs through the eyes of our school-based staff. At least one person should have the perspective of the field of offerings, and should take input from teachers and principals on what may best meet the needs of students.

Take into Account School Culture

Although we feel school culture is a cornerstone of our work at Aspire, we didn't quite understand how blended learning would fit into our culture. Originally, we defined cultural fit in three ways. Our blended learning implementation had to

- Be aligned with Aspire's Instructional Methods, the best practices that we support in teaching

- Be aligned with our Strategies and Priorities, our big organization-wide goals
- Give us data that was seamless with our other data; for example, our student information system, our student achievement data, and our assessment data

We didn't want to run a program that ran in parallel to other Aspire schools so that we'd have two systems going simultaneously. In short, we wanted blended learning to "scream Aspire," or else we would make the decision that it wasn't for us. Only you and your team will know what it means to "scream [Your School Name]," and I'd encourage you to explore this further and keep it in mind as your gold standard.

In hindsight, culture is more than just the alignment on paper and in data systems. Culture includes how seamlessly (or not) blended learning fits with the day-to-day teaching and learning in our schools. We don't want to trade off fundamentals of our instructional program (our team meetings, data talks, professional development system, instructional methods, "College for Certain" program, and so on) for blended; instead, we want to integrate blended learning so that we can't imagine a time when we didn't have blended in our schools. Chris Liang-Vergara puts it this way: "Blended learning should be integrated into the core school culture. If there's an awards ceremony for academics or athletics, blended learning should be a part of it. Culture systems used in classes should be used for blended learning. It's part of the core DNA of school." We know we've had a successful implementation when a teacher or principal says to us, "I just can't imagine our school now without blended learning."

Lesson Learned

Pay attention to the effects of software choices on your overall school culture.

WHEN WE STARTED

- We chose the best program for best content area at each grade level.
- We assumed that the software was a resource like curriculum that had been adopted.
- We assumed that teachers would "own" the role of software in the classroom.

(continued)

(continued)

THE CHALLENGES

- Teachers couldn't compare student data with one another.
- Teachers couldn't use one another for support in learning the programs.
- The principal couldn't help teachers set goals around so many data systems.
- We couldn't build in any school-wide data incentives.

NOW

As much as possible, we limit our software choices to one ELA program and one math program for grades K–5, and a different pair of ELA and math programs for grades 6–8. We couldn't find anything that could span K–8 effectively, so we're limiting the number of programs we need to manage while still balancing the need for quality content.

Some Thoughts About Beta Products

Software that is still in its testing phase, also referred to as "beta" software, can be an attractive option to those on a limited budget or those who are interested in potentially customizing features of a product still in development. I'm really clear that I will not use beta products to roll out blended learning in our schools. I don't have the capacity in my team, nor the patience to deal with early-stage problems and promises, and I don't want my successes in rolling out blended to hinge on a software product's ability to deliver on the functionality that developers hope to make possible over time.

If you're thinking about using a beta product, ensure that you know what you're getting *now*—and make sure that what you need now isn't on the development path, as frequently software development takes longer than you'd like. Chris Liang-Vergara at LEAP puts a finer point on the issue of beta products and says,

> In fact, it *always* takes longer than you think. Also realize that besides being a beta product, it's also a beta/young company. We've found that in addition to bugs, the company is learning how to scale, provide customer service, etc.—so you'll feel the pain in multiple areas as a customer. Don't

believe anything in a PowerPoint presentation or word of mouth. See it functioning in front of your eyes. I don't think they do it maliciously, but over-promising is everywhere in beta-land! Assume those features they promised will come at least a month to six months late. Or never.

However, some organizations, like our friends at Summit Public Schools, see beta products as huge opportunities to customize or shape a product to meet their needs. At Rocketship, Caryn Voskuil explains,

We are open to using a beta product, especially if the company is open to feedback. Shaping the product to fit our use case can be extremely valuable. We did this with one product we needed to do something very specific: math fact fluency for about seven minutes a day. We helped incubate and build the product, and as a result, our teachers and school leaders are very invested in it.

CHOOSING THE RIGHT HARDWARE

Deciding which devices to purchase can be equally fraught with difficulty. Since you've gotten this far in the book without yet purchasing devices for your blended learning implementation, you're on the right track! Devices should be one of the last considerations and purchasing decisions, as your device should not drive your instructional program—the problem you intend to hire blended learning to solve should drive the program.

Have a Clear Understanding of Device Costs

The purchase of devices, whether tablets, laptops, or something else, costs more than the initial price of the device. Where possible, identify the repair costs and potential replacement time lines to get a clearer understanding of the costs of ownership. Be sure to add in the costs in staff time to image computers (if necessary), manage the devices and accounts, and provision student accounts. Talk to your IT team and finance colleagues for time and cost estimates, and keep good records as you roll out blended learning so you're able to revise these numbers if necessary.

Ask Yourself: What Do I Want Students Doing on This Device?

Ultimately, this question becomes most important, as it will drive your device procurement decision. If your answer includes bandwidth-intensive, flash-based programs (especially ones with plug-ins), it is imperative that you check to see that the technology requirements of the software are actually compatible with the device or devices you're considering. We've rejected devices that wouldn't run the software we had chosen. Also, if you want students typing on tablets, don't forget to add in the cost of keyboards (and take into account that those wireless keyboards can contribute to additional network traffic and even interference).

We have been lured by low-cost devices that we thought would solve many of our problems. However, when we ran tests with some of our software, we found that students using some of our software were being perpetually kicked out of the program and having to log in again. Engaging or low-cost or cutting-edge devices offer seductive solutions when you're looking for devices. And, I must admit, we've almost fallen into the trap of choosing the device and then figuring out what we could run on it. *Don't do this.* A device should not be in charge of solving your instructional problems! At the end of the day, because of the problems we experienced with low-cost devices, we ended up moving toward getting fewer really good devices instead of more low-cost devices.

Test Your Devices

I remember what we did before we knew better: We tested each of our programs on one device, in our Home Office, on our network, by adults. Let me tell you, that is *not* the way to test devices and will not yield the critical feedback you need to make a thoughtful procurement decision.

Lesson Learned

Thoroughly test your devices before making a final decision. We "tested" a laptop before making a large purchase for one of our schools for their blended learning implementation. However, once we put all the devices in place, problems started happening. In our kindergarten and first-grade classes, the

BLTA noticed that by the end of a rotation, many students would have 20 or more browser windows opened. When he investigated further, he identified a curious feature: The laptops had the buttons at the top of the track pad, instead of where they normally are at the bottom. When our youngest students clicked the track pad (rather than the buttons), the students frequently clicked on the right-hand side of the track pad, resulting in a pop-up window appearing. Fearing that they had done something wrong, they just started clicking madly. When they did this, the Chrome browser "learned" that they wanted to open a new window (even though this is not what they wanted to do). And, to make matters worse, we couldn't disable this function or "teach" Chrome not to do this. Luckily we were able to solve this problem in a single day: We bought mice for all the laptops.

We cannot state this enough: Test multiple laptops with students, on the school network, using the actual software you plan to buy. Our school networks are significantly different from our Home Office network—from the speed, to the way traffic is managed, to the filters in place.

Consider How the Device Will Function in the Room

Managing 30 laptops or tablets that potentially will face in all different directions in a classroom is quite different from managing 10 desktops lined up along the wall facing the teacher, not only in a classroom management sense, but also in terms of power source, battery life, and connectivity, not to mention storage and cord control. Think about how you want the flow of the classroom to go, how students will pick up and put away devices, how teachers will know what's happening on the devices, and how teachers plan to use the devices pedagogically. Will students use the devices flexibly throughout the period? Will students need typing time? Will they need to carry the devices back to their desks? (This last item was something we didn't really want kindergartners doing with laptops.)

Budget for the Long Term

I've seen many a principal order a laptop cart and be done with it, hoping that it would last for the next 10 years. And I've seen many a computer lab with painfully old computers and no clear plan or budget to replace them. When we order computers for blended learning schools, we now budget into school budgets to replace one-third of the devices each year, so there is a plan for the long term.

What About BYOD (Bring Your Own Device)?

Do you have the IT support structure to manage a bunch of different devices? We don't, so I don't even consider going down this road. Talk to others who have piloted and modeled a Bring Your Own Device (BYOD) program to learn from them if you're thinking about going this direction. Be sure to consider the impact of BYOD on teachers. The strongest impact may end up being in the classroom, as not everything runs on every computer in quite the same way.

GO FOR THE BADGE!

Strategic Planner

- Start with some clear understandings and parameters around choosing software:
  - What does your student achievement data point to in terms of need?
  - How many programs can you realistically manage at once?
  - Which programs are feasible in terms of initial training and launching?
  - How responsive is your rep?
  - Do you have the capacity to run beta products successfully?
- Articulate the trade-offs you're willing to make when choosing programs.
- Evaluate software products using a disciplined mindset and criteria to weigh the trade-offs.
- Consider how devices will be used before making a device choice.
- Understand the true cost of devices and figure out what you have in your budget to purchase (and replace after a few years).
- Test your devices in the school setting, with students, on the school's network, using the software you intend to buy.

7

Making Use of Student Data

At Aspire Public Schools, we have a robust data-driven culture, thanks to an amazing data and analysis team, Aspire's data solutions team (named Godzilla, which eventually spawned Schoolzilla, a company creating data solutions for districts and charters across the country), Aspire leadership and culture, our data champions (colleagues who help visualize our data for teachers and school leaders), and our data drivers (teachers who support other teachers in learning best practices for using data to drive instruction) at school sites. Aspire teachers are very committed to effective data usage. Our Godzilla data and technology team has received national and international accolades, and Schoolzilla is now making some of these tools available to school districts and charter management organizations (CMOs) more broadly. Our educators access a suite of user-friendly data analysis tools that allow them to view, in one friendly portal, a diverse array of data about student success and educator effectiveness. Teachers meet every week or every other week in teams for data talks in which they do cycles of inquiry to identify trends and inform what the teachers will teach next; administrators look at a variety of data points to make staffing, resource, support, and budgetary decisions on an ongoing basis. Yet, despite a data-rich culture, we still had to figure out the role of blended learning software data in our classrooms. This chapter explores a variety of ways to use blended learning data.

USING BLENDED LEARNING DATA

The learning software programs our students use in blended learning classrooms generate data about student progress. In many software programs, data is available in a variety of forms and dashboards. The following are ways that teachers can use the data generated from the online software.

Setting Class Goals: The teacher may want to create a class growth goal for students based on their performance on the online software. It is crucial that goals are attainable for all students. These goals, in particular, are useful for building a culture of blended learning at the classroom level.

Setting Individual Goals: Certain students might struggle with a specific standard, so setting goals for individual students may motivate them to practice challenging standards.

Informing Instruction: If a majority of the class struggles with a certain standard, the teacher can decide to include additional practice in whole-class spiral review sessions or in targeted small groups.

Observing One-on-One: Sometimes the data will show something that doesn't make sense, either with the student's record or the program itself. The teacher or the blended learning teaching assistant might need to sit down next to a student to observe the student's activity on the computer.

Checking for Fidelity of Implementation: You'll need to look at data to determine how effectively the program is being implemented on the school level. For example, are students maximizing their learning time on the computers, or are some students repeating individual lessons and making considerably less progress than their peers? Or is one classroom of students making less progress per hour than their grade-level peers? Or are all students reaching the minute minimums in their rotations? If not, why not? Look for trends across classrooms, grade levels, and proficiency levels to identify ways to improve the actual running of the programs.

Verifying and Validating Other Data: Data held as "truth" in the school is useful for evaluating new software data to identify potential strengths and weaknesses in products. If you have a benchmark system you trust, or the state data, or some other assessment data (like the Diagnostic Reading

Assessment, or DRA), comparing student achievement in both systems can be helpful and informative. While we have not found a way to norm these practices, we have found new insights in the comparison data.

Lindy Brem, blended learning reading specialist at Aspire Titan Academy, shares:

> Our ELA software program provides a lot of really great data to use when tracking student progress. I am still trying to figure out the best way to use this data in combination with the other reading data that we collect. One thing that I did use was the comparison between the first diagnostic test we administered and the second diagnostic test administered. I took the change between the two and the current grade level and put that on the current data page so that the teacher and I could compare the multiple reading data points and see if we were getting consistent results across the assessments.
>
> Overall, I noticed that most students' diagnostic results were comparable to the reading results from the DRA and from benchmark scores. This tells me that when students are consistently using the software, their work really does reflect the work that they are doing in other areas of reading. By placing this information on the data page, it was really easy to spot a discrepancy. When we did find a discrepancy between DRA and the software levels, the teachers and I were able to have a discussion around possible reasons for this discrepancy and come up with some next steps to support the student.

As a Rapid Screener: If a school needs to identify students for specific interventions or groupings around a specific skill or other focus, software might provide a simple way to accommodate this need.

DATA NEEDS TO BE ACTIONABLE

As the blended learning leader at Aspire, I work with principals, teachers, our Home Office data team, and software developers to identify the most useful and actionable data coming from blended learning software. Our principals and teachers want to sit down together in a data meeting with a variety of student achievement data, and ask these questions: How can we tell if all students are successful on a software program on a weekly basis? How can we tell how much each student is learning, week by week? And if a student is not successful, how do we find out why, and what can we do in response? Tom Willis of Cornerstone advises, "There's too much data, so stay focused on what is most important to your school or you'll get overwhelmed." Despite many software products having countless data dashboards, when it comes to the "levers" to allow teachers to change course in implementation or instruction, surprisingly few data points are truly useful.

The information teachers and principals are seeking is intuitive and reasonable, yet getting answers to these questions is no small task, it turns out. I've reached out to vendors, printed out dashboards, created screen shots of data dashboards I can't export, built ridiculously complicated Excel sheets from data sources in the programs, sat behind groups of students and taken notes on what they're understanding, combed software-training manuals, and called my blended learning friends at other CMOs for advice. Some software is better than others. And as someone operating in a school system that has advanced data analysis tools and capabilities, I shudder to think how school systems that are less proficient with data and technology will access the data they need in ways that make it actionable.

I wish I could tell you which data points are actionable, but unfortunately, the useful data points are different in each software program we use and tend to be a moving target. Some data resonates strongly with our teachers, while other data does not. I'll usually sit down with a team of teachers and look through all the data with them to find what is most actionable to them. More often than not, we decide on the data that is easiest to access (without requiring us to click down into each student's record, which is way too time-consuming to do for each student in a class), the data that helps us best understand what the student knows, and the data that reveals steps we can take toward improvement.

MAKE A PLAN FOR USING DATA WITH TEACHERS

Teachers' usage of data can change over time as they develop as blended learning teachers. Mark Montero, blended learning teacher at Aspire Titan Academy, explains:

Initially, I didn't analyze blended learning data on a continual basis, but then I started to realize kids were losing engagement because I wasn't as invested in their progress in mastering the lessons online. I thought it was a student problem, and then I realized it was a teacher problem. This caused me to figure out what my vision should be for blended learning, and now I'm transparent with the data: I celebrate blended learning successes on a weekly basis. On Mondays, I celebrate the most books read, the most growth, and the highest passing rate, and this allows me to celebrate the strengths of the students working on the computers. Now that I use the data purposefully, my students respect their work on the computers more.

By creating a plan for using data, you'll put teachers on their own learning paths for using increasing amounts of data over time. Consider taking these initial steps:

- Articulate the reasons why it's important to use the data: to check fidelity of implementation, to check for student growth and struggles, to best leverage the software as part of your instruction.
- Dig deeply into the data dashboards and understand them before meeting with teachers. Programs are quirky—what the initial data dashboards show you is not always the most actionable data in terms of identifying what's working about implementation. Identify data that can inform what the teacher is already doing in class and that the teacher can potentially act on.
- Use student data to foster buy-in with teachers who may still have concerns about "giving up instructional time to computers."
- Effectively monitor implementation and troubleshoot from a data standpoint, instead of just an observational or anecdotal standpoint.

Other members of a staff can also take on the role of analyzing and distributing software data with teachers. Chris Liang-Vergara at LEAP offers this advice:

Have an RtI (response to intervention) coordinator or local data/assessment person to help you with the wide range of data you'll experience. They can then be agile and be in the different subject or grade level meetings and help guide the entire staff through the data in the way they need it. There is huge value when there is someone, other than the busy principal, having an overall view of the entire orchestra of data and conducting it. They'll be able to spot effective teaching practices and discrepancies quickly and in ways that are impossible in siloed departments or teams. People need a guide to look to for data goals, benchmarks, and milestones. This is very unique from the principal's role.

Our BLTAs get a lot of traction by meeting with teachers monthly to discuss their blended learning data. In this way, teachers can reflect on what's working and not working with the implementation, analyze trends with the achievement data, and troubleshoot areas of concern. This approach also allows the BLTA to hold teachers' hands through the process of trusting or not trusting the data. Table 7.1 is a template of the nature of one of those talks.

Mark Montero, teacher at Aspire Titan Academy, used what he learned from his BLTA to support his data talks with students. He shares,

My blended learning teaching assistant gives us weekly reports on how our students are doing on the computer programs. The one concern for me was their math report. The report identified five students who had spent *at least one hour* and yet completed *zero lessons.*

Table 7.1 Blended Learning Data Talk Form

Blended Learning Data Talk—October Teacher: Brown Date: 10/11/13	
Success	**Strategy**
ELA software: • 12 students are on or above grade level! • Overall, your students' pass rate is 93%.	ELA software: The students seem very self-motivated once they get on the computers. When I see them looking around or off task, I immediately redirect them. -Proximity to students to address students who are not on task

Table 7.1 (*Continued*)

Blended Learning Data Talk—October	
Teacher: Brown Date: 10/11/13	
Success	**Strategy**
Math software: • Alex, Ivan, Roger, and Stephan are excelling in the math lessons. • 10 students are more than 50% completed with 1st grade curriculum!	Math software: Same as above
Reading software: • There has been a noticeable increase in the number of quizzes that your students have taken in the last two weeks!	Reading software: I've been having only 1 rotation stay on the computer per day, so their time on the computer is for 20 minutes vs. 10 minutes. 10 minutes is not enough time to find books and read them.

Difficulties	**Why**	**Solution**
Brian, Stephan, and Georgia are having trouble passing lessons on ELA software.	-Brian and Sebastian are often talking to their neighbors during BL. -Georgia gets easily distracted while she's working on the laptop.	Could we move them to different computer? -Analyze lessons for Georgia and assess if difficulty is too much for her. We can assign easier lessons.
Alicia is having trouble passing lessons on math software.	I often catch Alicia talking during her lessons.	Move her to a clearer line of vision from U table to monitor computer behavior.
Alex, Brian, and Elisabeth are spending the majority of their time outside of the math software lessons.	Possibly disengaged with the math software lessons?	-Encourage them to avoid redundancies (watching reward videos, repeating completed lessons or just staring at the screen). -Talk to them about the importance of moving forward.

(continued)

Table 7.1 (*Continued*)

Difficulties	Why	Solution
		Presentation of software screenshots to remind students which lessons to select and which to avoid. -Buttons (lesson icons) to display on wall of computers to remind students of what lessons to access.
-Class average for reading software: 51% of students are completing an entire book.	Earlier in the year, the students were only on for 10 minutes vs. 20 minutes	Can you try implementing a weekly category? (Mark implemented this strategy in his class.) This should help students stay on task and complete at least one book before going to another. You can also create a book list. Work on motor skills to control mouse/track pad better.
Roger, Brian, and Stephan have dropped Lexile levels.	Not fully comprehending the questions or stories that they're reading?	Encourage them to focus on books that are within their reading range.

Teacher's Next Steps	BLTA's Next Steps
Switching seating arrangement of Brian, Stephan, Alicia, and Georgia. Remind Alex, Brian, and Elisabeth to focus on lesson instead of accomplishment. Check Mark's class for "weekly category" book search Talk to Roger, Brian, and Stephan to focus on books on level and reading questions correctly. Speak to student helper to better utilize time supervising computers.	Presentation of math software procedures and what to select on the overhead projector after fall break. Create icons for computer wall to reinforce appropriate lessons. Additional support with tabs and improper motor skills with mouse and track pads.

My initial thought was one of anger and frustration. How could I have let this slip off my radar? Was I not monitoring them? Were their peers around them not reminding them to try harder? Rather than wallow in my utter dismay, I conferred with each of the identified students. Fortunately, they all admitted to watching the videos and roaming around the program [rather] than actually doing lessons. So, I problem-solved with them and they knew what they had to do (in its most updated version, however, the software has eliminated the videos—yes!).

We went over the purpose for why they have the software, and we also went over concrete steps on what they had to do to pass more lessons. Whole class, I celebrated those students who did exceedingly well (there was even one student who spent two hours working and completed 27 lessons!).

And so, teachers . . . Data is powerful! I'm glad I was able to catch this early on, thanks to my blended learning teaching assistant giving us weekly data. There needs to be a weekly conversation that you should have with your students about student effort and performance around the blended learning programs. Teaching them how to self-monitor their own progress is a powerful tool that they need for all aspects of life, not just academics. And it begins with the teacher modeling this process him/herself when they receive their class's data.

Don't expect to be fully fluent in data analysis practices from the start. Our teachers state over and over that they keep getting better at using data each year; data usage is a journey, not a destination.

Key Idea

The more time and focus you and the blended learning teaching assistant invest in the software data, the greater your ability to manage the efficacy of the implementation. The more time and focus teachers invest in the software data, the greater their ability to manage blended learning in their classrooms and engage students in their own achievement on the programs.

KEEP YOUR EYE ON THE DATA

While data in software programs will change daily, it's not realistic to expect teachers to check the data daily in most cases. However, not checking the data at all or checking it only infrequently, can also be a problem. Jeanne Chang at E. L. Haynes Charter School in Washington, D.C., offers this advice:

> It's critical for teachers to monitor the data and reports to ensure that students aren't "stuck" on a particularly challenging lesson or concept for too long. It's one thing to attempt a lesson three or four times and struggle with it as part of the learning process. It's extremely demotivating and frustrating to attempt the same lesson 30 times without teacher support or proper intervention. Ensuring that teachers are clear on their roles and expectations (e.g., students should not fail a lesson more than X times before getting explicit support from an instructor) can preempt a lot of issues down the line.

Be sure you understand how the program notifies teachers of problems students may be encountering and what happens to students in the program as a result.

Teach Students to Track Their Own Data

Depending on the grade level, we believe students should own and reflect on their individual achievement data with the software. Student ownership builds the connection students need to make between the effort they put in and the achievement they earn. Software programs that provide students with ways of keeping track of their own data free up teachers from finding ways to make student data accessible to students. Chris Liang-Vergara at LEAP Innovations suggests, "Students should be fully aware of their data, and empowering their own self-awareness is your major goal to drive motivation to be based on an intrinsic desire to improve themselves. Chasing candy and carrots on sticks is not sustaining use of data. Students are not animals, so don't treat them like they are." (See photo 7.1 for one way to make student achievement data accessible.)

What data students access really depends on what programs students use, but many programs offer ways for students to track their own progress. Some of our

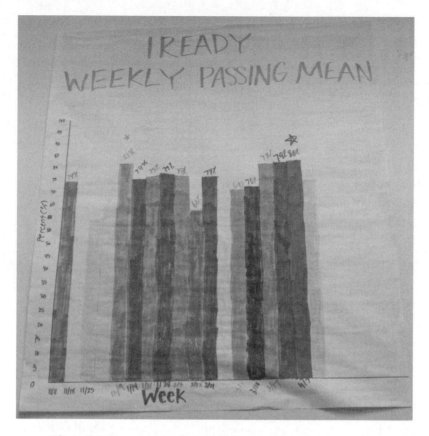

Photo 7.1 Class Average for Weekly Lessons Passed Data Tracker

teachers provide students with paper data-trackers on which they set goals and mark their weekly progress (see exhibit 7.1). With that, Tom Willis of Cornerstone suggests that teachers "keep asking the students what they think" to engage them in the work. Jeanne Chang of E. L. Haynes Charter School explains:

> Having candid, but compassionate conversations with students and help-
> ing them to set and achieve short-term and long-term goals are integral
> ingredients that can make or break the success of the model. Celebrating
> accomplishments of key milestones in a timely manner is important, but
> so is providing regular, positive, specific feedback on a day-to-day basis
> when students put forth the effort to wrestle with a challenging problem,

117

EXHIBIT 7.1 Sample Student Data Tracker

_____'s Tracker

Week_____

Math Software	
Unit Letter: Level: Chapter Test Average:	What did you learn this week?

ELA Software		
Article I Read	**% on Multiple Choice**	**Thought Question Checklist**

Reading Reader		
Book Title	**Quiz Score**	**% of Goal**
Total books read at the beginning of the week: Total books read at the end of the week:		

even if they don't master the concept fully in that particular attempt. Ideally, the program will offer a student dashboard that displays individual achievement over time. At the end of each session, it can be motivating if a student sees measurable gains or mastery to reflect their progress.

Amy Youngman, former middle school humanities teacher at Aspire ERES Academy, shares:

> My biggest blended learning aha around the data was realizing I should be having middle-schoolers track their progress. This meant having weekly trackers on which the kids take ownership of amount and quality of work, and show metacognitive awareness around what they learned and how was it useful. At the middle-school level, the dynamic shifted away from me having to nag and be constantly concerned with what's going on and how well it's going; now, the ownership is on students to complete quality work. And after a few weeks of that, I tailored goals to individual kids. This allowed me to increase the quantity each week (week 1, 50%; week 2, 60% . . . etc.). Having students track their data is also a time-saver for me as well as having the support of a blended learning teaching assistant—we don't have to play with all the reports in these systems. Students fill out the trackers based on what the programs tell them.

Lourdes Meraz, a teacher at Aspire Titan Academy, offers another way of sharing software data with students:

> Since the last [online software] diagnostic assessment, I have had some successes with students in terms of them being more motivated to want to try their best on the computers. Showing students their data from the blended learning binder I created really helped them see that not only was I monitoring their progress and test scores, but also this was available to their parents and fellow classmates.
>
> Seeing their progress on paper and on the graph showed students whether or not they were making gradual progress or if they were see-sawing on their tests. Students who did drop were surprised and very reflective on what they need to concentrate on. As a result, students who saw their data and knew they needed to raise their scores, were motivated. They would rush over to me to let me know they passed that difficult lesson or unlocked new lessons as a result of passing old ones. Granted, I do not let them get off their computer time unless it's an emergency,

seeing how happy and excited they are for passing gives them a pass. Acknowledging their successes gives them that extra external support they need to keep on going.

I want to work on being more on top of checking their progress on my own so that I can have one-on-one conversations with students who are less likely to let me know if they passed a lesson or unlock new lessons. This way I am more aware of what all students are doing and not just the students who are more vocal about it.

DATA INTEGRATION

We maintain our own data warehouse, in which more than 40 of our data systems, including our student information system, our state assessment data, attendance data, and others are brought together, and then we visualize it in a whole host of dashboards through Tableau, a software product that helps users visualize and understand data. When we started getting blended learning data, we became excited about the prospect of bringing blended learning data into the data warehouse and triangulating it against other student achievement data. However, incorporating blended learning data into our data warehouse has proved to be easier said than done with most software providers. We request automated nightly uploads of software data, and only a few providers actually have the willingness and capability to do so. Some of them have worked closely with us and generously built customized data sets for export, which we, in turn, have visualized in our own dashboards. These customized data sets are the ideal, as we've been able to build dashboards for our teachers that allow them to see the data and make it actionable in their classrooms. Most providers, however, are not there yet and we struggle to find software partners who will work with us on this.

ACCOUNT PROVISIONING

One consideration in setting up software accounts is account provisioning. This involves creating student accounts (their user names and passwords) in the software. With each program you add, you'll need to figure out how to provision student accounts.

While account provisioning may seem to be a truly minor part of the process, remember that student account creation can happen throughout the school year if student enrollment is not static. Every time a new student enrolls in the school, an account (or even multiple accounts, depending on how many software licenses each student has) will need to be created. We recommend pushing the software company to have an automated solution so you can do this centrally, rather than having individual teachers do this work. We've gotten to the point where it's completely unsustainable to do this work without automating it, so if a software company can't do at minimum a batch upload of student records, we won't use the product.

We've tried four different ways to provision student accounts, all of which have their own trade-offs. Table 7.2 lists the pros and cons of the different methods of account provisioning.

Lesson Learned

Be sure to use a standard convention when creating student accounts so that you can do widespread analysis of the data someday. Before blended learning started, we ran one particular program in 20 of our schools, and as we started thinking about blended, we thought it would be a good idea to test the efficacy of that program. However, this was no small task, as teachers had used a broad variety of conventions when creating student accounts:

- Student first name, last initial
- Student last name, first initial
- Student full name and grade level
- Student full name
- Student full name and student ID number

Helpful tip: Whenever creating student accounts, *always* use student ID numbers, as they'll enable you to do large-scale data analyses and track longitudinally student progress—as well as spare you a bunch of headaches you haven't yet experienced! We manually matched up all 2,000 student accounts with their student IDs, and trust me, we'll never do that again.

Table 7.2 Account Provisioning Pros and Cons

	Pros	Cons
Manually: We have typed in student information into spreadsheets generated by the software program.	Not many, unless you have only a few students. Free.	Easy to make mistakes. Tempting to shortcut process by not entering information into every field. Slow. Time consuming on the front end, and throughout the year as students come and go.
Half-Manually: This process involves pulling student information from the Student Information System (e.g., PowerSchools) into a spreadsheet and uploading it/sending it digitally to the software company.	Less likely to skip fields or create errors. Free.	Can be done at the beginning of the year, but ongoing accounts must be created manually, which is slow and has a potential for errors.
Via a Blended Learning Service: Companies like Education Elements provide as part of their services automatic account provisioning. This entails connecting your Student Information System to the Ed Elements platform; then the company connects to the software.	Does account creation at the beginning of the year and throughout the year. Accounts created automatically as students transfer in and out.	Entails a cost. Requires significant effort to make the connections to get started. Not all software providers are integrated with these types of systems.

Table 7.2 (*Continued*)

	Pros	Cons
Using a Third-Party Provider: Some companies serve as a connection between the student information system and the software provider (e.g., Clever).	Free. Simple to manage. Little work involved in connecting SIS to system. Automatically creates new accounts throughout the year.	If passwords are not part of your SIS, you'll still need to go in and manually create passwords, which can be time consuming. Not all software providers are integrated with these types of systems.

Overall, we vastly prefer automatic account creation and provisioning, especially with whole-school conversions. However, if automation is not an option for you, figure out ahead of time who will create accounts, and be sure to standardize the types of information captured in the system.

USER NAMES AND PASSWORDS

One of our earliest challenges in this work was figuring out our conventions for user names and passwords. Some advice:

- If possible, create user names that can be used for a student's entire time in the school.
- Use the same user name and password for all providers. This uniformity is especially important if you don't have a single sign-on solution for students logging in.
- Create a convention for student passwords, ideally something that can be automatically generated, like a color and a four-digit number (e.g., purple1234).
- Determine the process for changing a student's password should a student's account get breached.
- Do not use a student's grade level in the user name or password, or you'll have to change all the user names or passwords each year.
- Set policies and routines around password management. Who will provide students with their passwords if students forget the passwords? The teacher? An administrator? We highly recommend keeping passwords secure, or you'll spend an inordinate amount of time changing passwords in your system.

If you decide to have students use their student ID numbers or lunch numbers as their passwords, be mindful that you'll need a Plan B if an account is breached. Depending on the size of your school, organization, or district, you should probably run a test on your student user names to determine how many collisions you might have. We thought our user name convention ([first letter of first name].[last name][graduation year]@aspirestudent.org) would be fine, but when we ran a script to see collisions, we found out that with almost 14,000 students we had more than 1,400 collisions. Yikes!

Single Sign-on

Single sign-on allows students to sign into multiple software programs with a single login and password. This functionality can be enormously helpful, especially in the younger grades when students are still learning basic keyboarding skills and have a more difficult time remembering their user names and passwords, but also in the higher grades, so students don't have to remember different user names and password conventions to sign into multiple programs. Caryn Voskuil, formerly at Rocketship, states, "We have also found single sign-on to be an incredible asset with our school staff. If teachers can log in to each program with a single click they are much more likely to use the program's data as well as modify individual students' pathways for further personalized learning."

WHAT GOOD DATA LOOKS LIKE

How *should* data coming out of programs look so that it supports teachers' efforts to provide differentiated instruction to students and so that the data helps students see and own their progress? Blended learning data has the potential to be *part of* the most meaningful data teachers use, if it has these characteristics:

1. **The data is easily accessible and transparent.** Our teachers have a lot of robust data they trust that is easily accessible at a glance: grades, exit tickets, benchmarks, other formative and summative classroom assessments. This data is transparent, reveals student misconceptions, and most of all, is easily accessible and can be linked to other critical data. Many of our data dashboards at Aspire allow teachers to see a whole class's data on benchmarks, for example, by student,

by standard at a glance. Easily accessible and exportable blended learning data, for teachers and students, will help teachers know where students stand, help students own what they're learning, and why, at a glance.

2. **The data is actionable without being burdensome.** This means, when a teacher sits down with a principal or his or her team, the data informs her thinking around measures of success, groupings, progress, management, interventions, and how to best meet the needs of a particular student and of all students. If a teacher can only look at detailed student achievement data by burrowing down into individual student records, that's a burden. If a teacher has to export Excel docs and spend 30 minutes cutting, pasting, and highlighting data to visualize a classroom at a glance, that's a burden. The last thing teachers have is too much time on their hands. Teachers and principals need blended learning data that helps them draw conclusions about success and leads teachers to feel more effective and efficient in their work with students.

3. **The data is trustworthy.** We're speaking the same language, but meaning different things: Each program has a different definition of "mastery," "red flags," "time on task"(if any), and "standards-aligned," and often that definition is either opaque or found only in conversation with a software rep. Teachers and principals need data presented in a way that answers more questions than it raises.

PROTECT YOUR STUDENTS' DATA

While laws are in place around the protection of student data, in the current climate of public anxieties about schools giving student data to companies or schools letting student data sit on company-owned servers with no way to get it back, you should take every precaution to protect your data. When engaging with software contracts, check provisions around student data privacy, and write your own in the contract if the software company's language is not sufficient. In addition, when creating student accounts, there's no reason you should be sharing student birthdays, addresses, and any other personal student information with software companies, even if the field requires this. Contact the software company and air your concerns, and object to open sharing. When sharing data dashboards openly (in presentations or otherwise), obscure all student names and IDs so that the records are not attributable to individual students.

GO FOR THE BADGE!

Strategic Planner

- Create a plan for using software data with teachers. Involve your blended learning teaching assistant in the process.
- Where possible, use software data with students so that they are partners in the process of their own learning.
- Determine what conventions you will use for user names and passwords.
- Figure out how you will effectively and efficiently provision student accounts and access software data.
- Identify accessible, actionable, and trustworthy data you can use to assess and improve your blended learning implementation.
- Involve students (where possible) in owning and tracking their data.
- Review all contracts carefully for data-protection clauses and make every effort to secure student data.

8

Setting Up the Space

Surprisingly, furniture and the classroom environment overall play an important role in blended learning rollouts, as how students and teachers move in the space is even more important in blended learning classrooms than in other classrooms. How teachers make use of space directly impacts learning, and how you move in to alter a teacher's space can directly impact how the teacher feels about going blended. In addition, how technology is fixed or moves around a room can impact its usage (and durability, in some cases). Space matters!

When we started this work, I learned quickly that choosing the right furniture is not as easy as it might seem, especially in space-constrained schools or schools in which every classroom has slightly different dimensions. Logistically, figuring out a way to use technology productively in a classroom is both a challenge and an opportunity to rethink learning spaces.

Add to this complexity teachers' understanding that blended learning is going to change not only their practice, but also their classrooms, and you've potentially increased the anxiety that may accompany the change.

Chris Liang-Vergara at LEAP Innovations offers, "Everything should be flexible—a young teacher should be able to rearrange the room on his or her own without calling in facilities or another person."

Thinking through the furniture procurement and placement at the beginning of the process is important, not only because of these factors, but also because, in our experience, nothing takes longer than the furniture delivery.

Nothing. Every time, furniture has held up our launch, even though we've tried desperately to order it earlier and earlier each time we roll out blended learning in a new school.

Key Idea

Be sensitive to the fact that many teachers take great pride in how they've organized their classrooms and, up until this point, may have had total autonomy in how they've used space. Listen carefully to their concerns, and offer support and thought-partnership if necessary in helping them reconfigure the space.

To begin the furniture decision-making process, start gathering key information (room dimensions, wall lengths, power locations, existing furniture that can be repurposed), all the while keeping in mind the instructional problem you're hiring blended learning to help you solve.

IDENTIFY THE RATIO OF STUDENTS TO COMPUTERS

If the ratio of students to computers in the room is 1:1 (1 student to 1 computer), where will students store their devices when they're not using them? Where will they power them? Keep in mind that carts are an added expense, as is rewiring classrooms, and you'll want to keep the electrical configuration flexible if possible.

If the ratio is 1:2 or 1:3 (2 or 3 students to each computer), consider how flexible you want your rotations to be. Will you have half or fewer of the students on the computers at one time? Or will you have no more than one-third of the students on the computers at one time? Your ratio impacts the instructional program and teachers' ability to implement blended learning differently. Where will the computers be used? Will students move computers to their desks at rotation time, or will the students move to an area of the room where the computers are stationed?

Consider the trade-offs you'll need to make regarding where students will use the computers (see table 8.1).

Table 8.1 Trade-offs Between Computer Desks and Stations

Device at Desk	Device at Station
• Save on furniture costs • Charging challenges • Potentially hard to see what all students are working on (which could be a classroom management challenge) • Takes time for students to move the device to a desk/station and back to charge	• Need to purchase tables, chairs/stools, which adds to cost • Takes up more room • Can plug into outlets • Easy to see everyone • Saves time for students to sit down and just get to work

And think about how you'll store the computers. Laptop locks are cheaper than carts. If security is less of an issue and laptops are at tables charging, choose locks. If you can't charge laptops in a central place each night, you'll need a cart. Buying one cart per classroom adds up quickly, and carts can take up a lot of space!

FIGURE OUT WHAT YOU HAVE ROOM FOR

When we walk through classrooms, we bring a tape measure to measure all long walls, a notepad to inventory classroom furniture that can be repurposed, and a camera to take pictures of each wall. We also draw a quick sketch of each room to show the current layout of furniture, dry-erase boards, doors, sinks, and so on.

We know we want to create the least obtrusive layout in each room, so we listen carefully to teachers. Some don't want to change the orientation of their space; others are fine with whatever we recommend. (See photo 8.1 for one possible layout.) We try to honor teachers' feelings overall, as they're the ones working in the space each day, and only rarely have we had to reach a compromise because their resources and the new computers wouldn't fit.

Rule of thumb: Allow no less than 20 inches per K–4 student at a long table.

Chair size matters! Choose the smallest chairs you can (or even stools) so you can fit more kids per table if you're space constrained.

Photo 8.1 Classroom Rotation Model

Think about headphone storage. Will headphones be on the tables, in the desks, in a pouch on the chair? Or will students carry them around in their backpacks? We cooked up a great headphone storage solution with some of the packing material from the laptop boxes. (See photo 8.2.)

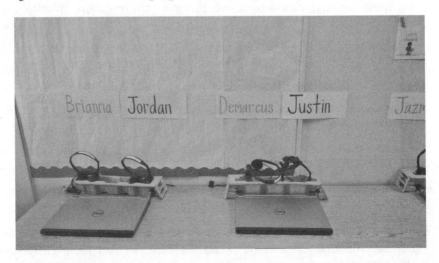

Photo 8.2 Organized Computer Workstations with Seating Labels and Headphone Holders

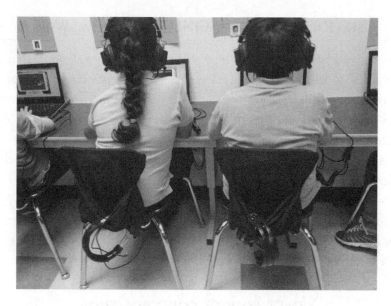

Photo 8.3 Students at Computer Workstations

FIGURE OUT WHAT YOU HAVE BUDGETED FOR

Tables and chairs can add up quickly in blended costs. In general, we try to use existing furniture to save costs. In my opinion, however, don't skip furniture to save costs unless you are confident that students (and the adults who manage them) can manage the technology effectively at their seats. We don't want kindergartners walking around with laptops, so furniture in our kindergarten classrooms is a must. Most of our teachers find it easier and calmer to have a station kids can travel to, so we put computers along the wall in the majority of our blended classrooms (see photo 8.3). If you've got the budget, purchase adjustable height tables that are 17–19 inches deep. These tables take up less classroom space but are fine for laptops.

LOCATE THE POWER SOURCES

Are you using a wireless network? If not, you'll need to find where the wires come into the room so you can power your devices. Figure out where in the room you'll charge your computers and make sure those outlets are nearby. You'll need to know where the wireless access ports are located, too.

HELP TEACHERS IMAGINE THEIR NEW SPACE

We've been asked by many teachers how planned changes are all going to work, and when we've had a clear, reasonable answer about how their room could look, they're much more reassured about the entire process. Be imaginative when considering what the space could look like. If setting up a lab, don't make it look like a call center. Our friends at Milpitas Unified set up an amazing lab space for kids that really pushed our thinking about warm, inviting places for kids to work. These school leaders filled the lab space with risers, giant bean bag chairs, café-style seating booths, and other fun furniture that made the entire lab environment comfortable and inviting. If you have the luxury of having a budget that permits you to imagine new ways to set up the space, you should! Talk to people at other schools who have designed new spaces to get ideas and rethink your options.

DON'T FORGET CORD CONTROL

We've walked into some crazy classrooms with all sorts of power-strip daisy chains at play; we even once saw a room with an extension cord draped over a nonworking sink. Yikes! Be sure to budget for power strips!

AND THEN, BE OPEN TO CHANGE!

Chris Liang-Vergara at LEAP Innovations suggests that "within the first month of school, your staff will want to move the furniture around after seeing how the space works, so make sure they're able to."

Lesson Learned

Streamline devices to save space and IT support. Our principals hoped to use their existing desktops in their classrooms to save on purchasing additional laptops. Ultimately this wasn't feasible: Desktops took up more space, were less flexible in terms of room placement, and required more IT support because they were older. Get those old machines out! They're not worth it!

GO FOR THE BADGE!

Strategic Planner

- Gather key information about your classroom space, including room dimensions, wall lengths, power locations, and an inventory of existing furniture that can be repurposed if necessary.
- Determine the ratio of students to computers in the classroom by considering your instructional problem and your model's design.
- Assess what you have budget and room for and, if necessary, repurpose some existing furniture to save money. If you have the budget, reimagine what the space could look like, and seek out examples from other schools that have built innovative learning spaces.
- Use this opportunity to reimagine what learning spaces could look like in your school.
- Be sensitive to teachers' concerns around reconfiguring their space, and communicate your ideas clearly to teachers to minimize anxiety.
- Identify where the power is and what you'll do about headphones, storage, and cord control.
- Be flexible, as everything (especially your ideas about what works) could change over time.

9

Getting Your Network
Up to Speed

Honestly, as someone who has spent years working in classrooms with students and then with teachers, nothing could bore me more than conversations about network infrastructure—it's the educational equivalent of watching paint dry. Network infrastructure is the least exciting, least romantic topic related to going blended, yet knowing about network infrastructure is a complete necessity. The sooner you accept that network conversations are an important part of your repertoire, the better. Sorry to be the bearer of potentially bad news! Don't expect to become an expert, but do expect to get super-excited when anyone talks to you about dark fiber—even if you can barely understand it now.

If you have a strong network in place, it's the foundation upon which you can build just about anything. Bryant Wong, chief technology officer of Summit Public Schools, explains, "Technology's job is to remove hurdles, so you can increase full adoption across your entire school and organization." You don't want technology to *be* the hurdle; you want technology to allow you to *eliminate* the hurdles, like integrating online content into the curriculum, or adopting 1:1 initiatives in the classroom.

Consider these three layers of decision making and some key terms to help you understand the technology and how it works.

LAYER 1: HOW YOU APPROACH TECHNOLOGY FROM THE START

Ask yourself this question: Do we currently make technology decisions from a tactical perspective or a strategic perspective? Most schools and districts can be successful in the short term by being tactical, but if all decisions are made from a tactical standpoint, technology integration is not scalable, especially when you are scaling blended learning. Strategic decision making is important for technology, because strategy aligns with where you think your model is going and makes your technology department partners, rather than just implementers. *Tactical* and *strategic* can be confusing terms. Tactical decisions allow you to complete an objective without knowing the entire context or goal, like ordering a class set of iPads. Strategic decisions, in contrast, require you to have an overall vision and plan within a larger and broader context or goal (see table 9.1).

A critical part of strategic decision making with technology involves developing the talent of your IT department, something that takes time and energy to understand the skill sets they bring to the table, and to create opportunities to broaden their expertise and understanding of your strategic vision. Bryant Wong, Summit Public Schools' chief technology officer, explains his journey from being a

Table 9.1 Examples of Strategic Versus Tactical Questioning

Strategy (What)	Examples	Tactical (How)
What are the academic outcomes we are going to achieve and what additional tools will be used in the classroom?	1:1 computing	How will we support the increased number of laptops in the classroom?
What resources are available to provide long-term, cost-sustainable, and stable Internet services that allow schools to use online resources in the classroom with little interruption?	High-speed Internet	How much bandwidth do I need?

technology leader to becoming an education technology leader who understands deeply schools' technology needs:

> I came to Summit Public Schools with a strong technology and business background, but without a strong understanding of what schools need in terms of tech. When Dianne Tavenner (Summit's CEO) brought me on board, she invested real time and energy into making me a partner in Summit's work to transform their schools. She created a culture of high trust, autonomy, opportunity, and probably the most impactful thing she did was make me teach Intersession my first year and for two additional years afterwards. I spent 40 full days a year teaching and differentiating technology instruction for a group of students. My final project asked students to develop a personalized website based on virtualization technology and open source software for public display. I worked tirelessly to build a curriculum and reached out to Silicon Valley companies such as Google, Microsoft, and Apple to provide meaningful and life-changing tours that would promote college readiness and technology. I became cognitively aware of the personal impact of technology in the classroom and to students, and teachers saw me differently, which resulted in a different buy-in from them for my work—I was no longer the tech guy who didn't understand their day-to-day lives in the classroom. This has directly impacted my work: I understand the challenges teachers face in a classroom, the impact on instruction when technology does not work and when it works, and most importantly I understand deeply the countless hours of preparation necessary for teachers to differentiate instruction for a diverse group of students using technology. And now, when I bring new tech folks on board, I insist they spend at least a few days in classrooms teaching, so they better understand what we're trying to do and how their work affects teachers and students every single day.

LAYER 2: HOW YOU APPROACH YOUR PHYSICAL INFRASTRUCTURE

The physical infrastructure refers to the power and data cabling in the building and in your classrooms. Both need to be in place, and you'll need experts to help you figure it out. All leaders need to understand student and classroom flow when implementing technology. Simply adding cable or power outlets is a quick fix as it does solve the problem of getting power and connectivity to a classroom. Understanding the flow of teacher and student activity in the classroom (see, for example, photo 9.1) and how technology will be used at a school and in the classroom helps to ensure resources are maximized and not wasted. Becoming familiar with some key terms related to physical infrastructure will help.

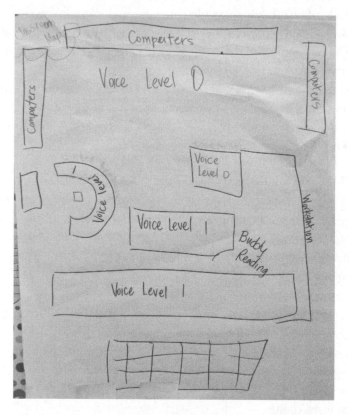

Photo 9.1 Classroom Layout Map Identifying Voice Level at Each Workstation

KEY TERM: POWER

What it is: Electrical power in the school and specifically the classrooms. Additional power allows schools to adequately charge laptops and other technologies properly without overloading or blowing out the main electrical circuit. A lack of power can negatively impact a school's ability to use technology. Adding too much power can be a waste of resources that could have been used in other areas of the organization.

Why you need to know about it: You need to get your power checked to see whether it's set up for the infrastructure you intend to run. For example, if you plug a laptop cart into a regular outlet (as opposed to a dedicated one), you run the risk of overloading the system and bringing down all of your power.

What you need to have: Enough power to safely run the number of devices you plan to run, along with whatever else is being powered in the room. Keep in mind that laptop carts need significant power!

Questions you might ask your IT people: Can the building's outlets support the amount of power that a laptop cart would draw out of it? Are there enough outlets to support the number of power strips we would need? How can we get the power to the right areas of the classrooms and building?

KEY TERM: CABLING (DATA CABLES FROM THE SERVER ROOM TO THE DATA OUTLETS)

What it is: The conduit that connects all the devices throughout the school to a single point of access.

Why you need to know about it: You need to make sure the current cable is compliant with the latest networking technologies.

What you need to have: The minimum in technical terms is Category 5e (CAT5e). This specification is the bare minimum that allows you to use the most current technologies without having a negative impact.

Questions you might ask your IT people: Is the current cabling capable of supporting our technology needs? What are the pros and cons of using the bare minimum versus the newest cable? What are the cable needs for technology-rich classroom instruction?

LAYER 3: HOW YOU APPROACH
YOUR NETWORK INFRASTRUCTURE

The term *network infrastructure* can be scary and daunting to people without technology backgrounds. Your IT department's job is to help demystify your network infrastructure, which is the foundation for all of your technology, just as a school is the foundation for students' college readiness. The network consists of many types of technology and, most significantly, provides teachers and students access to online resources, academic content, e-mail communications, data files, and more.

Whether you want to have a few or many computers in your school, your network will support all of your technology initiatives. We live in a time when almost everything we do at work utilizes some type of technology, and the information we access or create most likely lives in the cloud. Your network helps you access all the resources that you need to achieve your goals.

Despite the critical importance of your network, you do not have to spend lots of money on it; on the contrary, your IT department can design a network that is lean, sustainable, replicable, and scalable and that aligns to the mission and objectives of your organization. If technology is a critical component of classroom instruction and student academic outcomes, then it's important to understand how to design the network to align with those objectives; otherwise, roadblocks to adoption will appear and slow or inhibit your progress.

KEY TERM: NETWORK INFRASTRUCTURE

What it is: The hardware and software resources of an entire network that enable computers to connect, communicate, operate, and be managed in an enterprise network. The network infrastructure connects users, applications, services, and the Internet.

Why you need to know about it: This is the universe that makes or breaks your blended learning implementation. The network infrastructure is what controls your security, your wireless network, your content filtering, and your switches. For example, when your network goes down, students cannot log in to computers and

(continued)

139

(continued)

do work. If your network goes down in the middle of the school day, chaos can result for teachers and students.

What you need to have: Something at an enterprise level that can grow to meet your needs and can be customized.

Questions you might ask your IT people: What equipment do we have? Is our networking equipment up to date? What do we need to put into place to effectively run our software programs? What will an upgrade cost? What are the steps we'll need to take to put an enterprise system into place?

KEY TERM: INTERNET CONNECTION

What it is: Your connection to the World Wide Web. If you need Internet access, then you will need to select a type of Internet connection to get you online.

Why you need to know about it: Three prominent types of Internet connections are widely used by schools, home, and business: DSL, cable, and fiber optic. All three types provide access to the Internet, but each has its pros and cons. Talk to your IT team to find out which one might be right for you.

What you need to have: You must have a really deep understanding of the needs of the school beforehand. This understanding will guide the process of selecting the proper Internet connection.

Questions you might ask your IT people: What type is our current Internet connection? How might our instructional goals for technology in the classroom and online resources be affected by different types of Internet connections? What Internet connection will fulfill current and future needs?

KEY TERM: BANDWIDTH

What it is: The amount of data that can be carried per second from one point to another, measured in bits per second.

Why you need to know about it: Knowing your bandwidth will give you an idea of how many students can work online and how effective the connections will be. If you don't know your bandwidth, you have no data about the speed of your network and no way to determine whether your network can handle the work you're planning to do. One of our amazing tech team members, Brian Sullivan, puts it this way: "If you're trying to get 100 cars from Oakland to San Francisco, would you get them there faster with 5 lanes or 50 lanes?"

Take EducationSuperHighway's SchoolSpeedTest to assess your current bandwidth. Slow bandwidth can also kill a blended learning implementation, as nobody wants to watch students wait more than a minute for a page to load on the screen, least of all the students. Some software programs freeze and need to be refreshed multiple times when the bandwidth is slow. Such problems can greatly affect student engagement and achievement if students need to log back in to programs multiple times during a single session.

How much you need: As much as you can get. Really. Speeds are getting faster and faster, and if you're running bandwidth-intensive programs, you'll need it.

Questions you might ask your IT people: Can our bandwidth support the expected amount of devices in a classroom? Are there other computer programs or websites being used on the campus that would compete with blended learning for bandwidth? Are there ways to optimize the bandwidth for blended learning? Can we run a live test of all the devices running at once on a program?

KEY TERM: WIRELESS DESIGN (WIRELESS ACCESS POINT PLACEMENT)

What it is: The plan and design of wireless access point coverage in a technology-enabled school.

Why you need to know about it: Designing wireless coverage for a school before deploying the technology is really important. Crafting a successful design that meets the needs of a technology-enabled school requires a lot of expertise. Bryant Wong advises,

> At Summit Public Schools, we have developed expertise on wireless design through lots of professional development and working with our wireless hardware vendor to educate us on how to properly design wireless at all of our school locations. I would highly suggest developing someone on the team with this expertise. It has been a godsend to have members of the technology team be well versed in proper design wireless coverage for all of our schools.

What you need to have: Time and a strong partner relationship with your wireless-hardware vendor to help with some of the professional development in deploying their technology properly throughout your school.

Questions you might ask your IT people: What is the purpose of wireless? What is its value, and what contributions can the technology make in the classroom?

(continued)

141

(continued)

What is our current wireless technology, if any? How much coverage do we currently have, and is this adequate to meet our needs?

KEY TERM: WIRELESS ACCESS POINTS (APs OR WAPs)

What they are: Transmitters of wireless radio signals.

Why you need to know about them: You can have great bandwidth, but if it doesn't reach your computers when computers are connecting to the Internet via the wireless (rather than by cables into walls), you'll be bummed—it'll be like you didn't get your fast bandwidth after all, even though you paid for it. This is the most rapidly evolving of all tech components, and the standard for wireless is changing rapidly. Access points can now do many things that switches, firewalls, and other tools did previously. If your student computers are not plugged in to the walls and the wireless goes down, they will not be able to continue working on online software programs unless they're locally installed, which means their learning and engagement will suffer.

What you need to have: There are lots of different camps out there with ideas about ratios of WAPs to devices, and less consistency than you'd think. Ask around, but make sure to ask folks other than vendors, so that you get advice from people who don't have a stake in selling you anything. Purchase enterprise wireless, especially for blended learning environments.

Questions you might ask your IT people: Are the access points adequate to run as many computers as we want to run simultaneously? Do these access points require a security password? If they do, how can someone get access to that? (Just an FYI: The data can be altered if someone has access to it, computers can be hacked, and so on.)

KEY TERM: E-RATE

What it is: A federal program that provides subsidies for data, voice, and network access equipment.

Why you need to know about it: Understanding how E-rate works and how it can help subsidize your data and voice services is really important. E-rate is a beast to fully understand, but with help from a reputable E-rate consultant you can reap huge benefits in subsidized telecom services and even rebates for your network infrastructure. E-rate also requires Children's Internet Protection Act (CIPA) compliance.

What you need to have: Your free and reduced lunch information, a technology plan, and a really good E-rate consultant. A good E-rate consultant can get you funded and doesn't charge you a percentage of the savings. Look for an E-rate consultant with a good reputation who works for a flat rate regardless of the subsidy size.

Questions you might ask your IT people: Do we have an E-rate consultant? What has the consultant obtained funding for, and what were we charged? What is the E-rate funding cycle? Are any of our technology purchases discounted? What is the process for receiving our rebate on purchases that are not initially discounted?

KEY TERM: CONTENT FILTER

What it is: The use of a program to screen and exclude certain websites from access.

Why you need to know about it: CIPA requires that all schools put in place filters to protect children from certain websites. You must understand your obligations under CIPA and ensure that you're keeping students safe based on the requirements of the act. Beyond these legal obligations, however, you'll probably want to control what students can and cannot access on the computers to a certain extent anyway, so you don't have kids checking Facebook when they should be doing quadratic equations.

What you need to have: Ideally, something sophisticated enough to create different levels of filtering for different groups: teachers, students, different grades, and so on. And, you'll need something that can be managed centrally.

Questions you might ask your IT people: Are we able to filter selectively for different stakeholders or at different times? Where should the filters be set? Are filters controlled at the school or district level?

KEY TERM: LONG-TERM SUSTAINABILITY

What it is: The life cycle of technology hardware and systems. Each and every system and hardware component will eventually need to be upgraded and or replaced due to obsolescence.

Why you need to know about it: Technology continues to change at a rapid pace, and the network, software, and computers you're using now will likely need improving (or replacing) in the next one to three years. Computer replacement and the soft costs associated with ongoing maintenance and replacement will impact your budgets, so think strategically about what you need to make work.

(continued)

(continued)

What you need to have: You'll need to understand all the costs and ways of budgeting in the short and long term to pay for those costs.

Questions you might ask your IT people: What are the actual costs for computers, the network, and the support they require? Does the amount of support vary throughout the year? (For example, do the computers require more support with initial setup and less ongoing support?) What is the projected life of the computers and network equipment we plan to choose? If we're using one-time funding for this purchase, what ongoing costs should we plan for down the road?

Obviously, the list of key terms here is far from exhaustive, and by no means is it going to be of any help to your IT team, as they already have this expertise. Rather, you need to know these key terms so you can engage your IT team in conversations and not completely embarrass yourself. You should not outsource all tech talk and not know what's going on with your network infrastructure, as you can't run blended successfully without that knowledge. Really.

EXPECT CHANGE WITH YOUR IT TEAM

Blended learning can change the focus of your IT team. Brian Sullivan suggests, "The nature of IT tech support needed in a blended environment should be more network based than your traditional desktop support based." Help them connect with others doing this work to further build their capacity and strengthen their understanding of how other schools have fared on this journey. Jonathan Tiongco of Alliance College-Ready Public Schools in Los Angeles recommends,

> Build your network, literally and metaphorically. Literally, infrastructure is a huge piece of the blended learning environment puzzle. When the infrastructure and network is strong, students can utilize their technology tools and digital content for their designed purposes. Without it, or having a weak network in general, causes disruptions to learning. Metaphorically, network engineers and IT leaders should reach out to their colleagues in other organizations to build their network of professionals. These can be

thought partners for network design, Internet routing, learning management system development, etc. To do this well, we need to reach out and support one another and share best practices.

Invest in your IT team and help them make the shifts they may need to make as a result of your going blended. Don't just let blended happen to them.

SHOULD YOU HIRE A NETWORK CONSULTANT?

Experts are mixed on the need for network consultants. On the one hand, for some districts with a lean central office, Chris Liang-Vergara suggests, "Bring in a network consultant. Have an IT/network audit. Have them visit another school with a rock-star network to learn about how they do it. Put serious time into the evolution of your facilities and IT team the same way you're going to nurture the transition for your teachers. Blended learning significantly changes the role of the traditional IT department." On the other hand, Bryant Wong suggests, "Network consultants offer expertise on networks, but their area of expertise is commonly not for school networks, and they frequently build their networks for all the wrong reasons, at very high costs, and not necessarily in alignment with your strategic plan on how technology will be used in the classroom by teachers and students for its community." Reach out to colleagues in other neighboring charters or districts to get their opinions.

GO FOR THE BADGE!

Strategic Planner

- Start making technology decisions strategically instead of tactically.
- Develop your IT team by investing time and energy into helping them understand your educational program and vision.
- Approach the building of your physical infrastructure from the perspective of technology's function in daily classroom flow.
- Know your key terms, why they're important, and what questions you should ask your IT team:
  - Power, cabling, network infrastructure, Internet connection, bandwidth, wireless design, wireless access points, E-rate, content filter, and long-term sustainability
- Approach the building of your network infrastructure by focusing on designing a network aligned to meet your objectives.
- Be prepared to manage the change with your IT team, and if necessary, bring in supports.

PART 3

Launching Blended: Helping Teachers and Students Be Successful

You've now made your critical decisions and laid down clear plans. It's about time to launch! Launching doesn't merely mean turning on the computers and sitting students at them to begin working; launching involves a whole series of actions teachers take to prepare their classrooms and students for success with blended learning. With targeted professional development, teachers can confidently and successfully launch blended learning in their classrooms. And, with solid preparation—what we call "readiness"—teachers can maximize student learning from the teacher and on the computers. In the next five chapters, we'll detail what targeted professional development teachers need and the key steps for teachers to take to get their classrooms ready to successfully launch blended learning with their students.

10

Training Teachers and Other Leaders

We made a deliberate choice not to create a blended model that hinged on a large amount of teacher training, as we wanted teachers focusing on their content and the craft of instruction, not on a deep understanding of how to use technology to deliver instruction. We've taken a "marathon" approach to teacher growth with technology, as we believe that once the technology is stabilized in classrooms and teachers feel more comfortable with the tech, they will begin to iterate with the tools. Some teachers will identify all sorts of ways to use the tech in their classrooms in new and innovative ways the moment they get the technology in their classrooms. Others may not initially. But our expectations of teachers in years 1 and 2 of an implementation do not have to be our expectations moving forward. We want teachers to have a sense of ownership of their own learning about the technology; frequently, different teachers develop this sense of ownership at a different pace. Rachel Klein of Highline suggests, "The key is to leverage and develop teachers and school leaders into conscious consumers so they take over the up-front work and have more ownership throughout." Adult readiness for new technologies varies tremendously, and we want to support teacher growth at all stages of the process.

To focus your professional development for teachers, return to the instructional problem you want to use blended learning to help you solve, and take

Table 10.1 Types of Blended Learning Professional Development for Teachers

Instructional Professional Development	**Running Blended Learning**
Small-group lesson planning and instruction based on student achievement data. Systems for flexible grouping. <u>Sample focus</u>: How do I plan for small-group work where each of my students is working with 3–5 other students on a small-group project or independently?	Routines and procedures around getting students on and off computers efficiently. Putting incentives into place. <u>Sample focus</u>: How do I ensure that students maximize learning when they're working independently on the computers?
Software Training	**Technology Training and Tech Resiliency Support**
Running programs in your class, looking at data, maximizing effectiveness. <u>Sample focus</u>: How do I manage the provisioning of content on the computers to ensure every student is meeting the goals set for him or her?	Backup plans, just-in-time lessons, keyboarding, cyber safety, and commonsense media lessons. <u>Sample focus</u>: How can I teach my students to troubleshoot technology problems they may encounter while in the programs?

into account professional development both on the instructional side and the software side. See table 10.1 for a framework to help illustrate the different types of blended learning professional development for teachers.

We provide instructional professional development as part of our summer training for new teachers and our ongoing professional development days. When we took on blended learning, we provided blended learning training and software training at the beginning of the year, and we had our blended learning teaching assistants provide technology and tech resiliency training on an ongoing and as-needed basis. We expect to provide teachers with training and support to make major changes in their classrooms; blended learning training goes hand in hand with the instructional training we provide teachers. Aspire has a robust professional development support system for teachers. We didn't want to create a new system or a different set of expectations for our blended schools. We wanted our professional development for blended learning to dovetail with the instructional professional development teachers were already receiving. We prefer providing our professional development in-house, as we want the messages teachers receive during training to be in complete alignment with our instructional program.

PROVIDE "JUST-IN-TIME" TRAINING WITH A CLEAR OVERVIEW

A clear sense of the purpose and path of your school's conversion to blended learning is important in planning training. Work with your software representative to ensure that software training is focused solely on what teachers need to get blended learning going in their classrooms and is supportive of your instructional program. Sometimes I talk to trainers, and they suggest that teachers need to change their instruction in ways that we totally disagree with. I explain that teachers will tune them out if what the software trainer says contradicts what we're telling teachers and that I want the trainer to be successful. When possible, give teachers software program logins ahead of the training so they can play around in the program and start generating questions they can ask during the training. Teachers will (appropriately) ask a lot of questions, especially when all this technology is new. Help teachers appreciate the value of just-in-time information and training.

Key Idea

Micromanage software reps and trainers. Ask to see training agendas ahead of time, and eliminate or postpone elements that are unnecessary or not timely. For example, teachers do not need to spend time learning how to create accounts if you're automatically provisioning accounts! Nor do teachers need to learn how to read data dashboards if students haven't yet generated any data. Ensure that the training messaging is consistent with your school's messaging.

DON'T SKIP THE TRAINING

I've experienced my fair share of webinars and trainings that have totally wasted my time, and chances are your teachers may have, too. That said, do not skip training. You'll regret missing the opportunity to set a tone and create a baseline of knowledge that you expect all teachers to have before you launch blended learning. Hold teachers accountable for attending and learning the information. Chris Liang-Vergara puts it this way: When training teachers, "do practice lessons and classes. Move from theory to practical/clinical models of mastery as soon as possible. Like students, don't give teachers a 'pass' because they sat in training for 60 minutes. They need to demonstrate understanding and mastery, too."

SCHEDULE FOLLOW-UP TRAINING, IF NECESSARY

Assuming the initial training is valuable, schedule a follow-up training six to eight weeks after the first training, once students have generated data and teachers have begun asking deeper questions about functionality. Again, go over training agendas meticulously. Jeanne Chang of E. L. Haynes explains,

> Most teachers find that a single introductory professional development session without any follow-up is far less effective than experiencing periodic, year-round support. For example, learning how to access and interpret the data through program-specific reports may require additional sessions. Alternatively, some educators find it helpful to have live coaching or modeling by an experienced specialist in their own classrooms in front of their students to better understand what highly effective implementation looks like. If you have in-house expertise and capacity to offer this for your teachers, fantastic! If not, I would recommend looking for vendors with the ability to properly supplement any initial training sessions to meet your teachers' and administrators' needs as they arise throughout the year. Asking for references or connecting with other blended learning teachers or staff at schools in your area that also use a particular program may prove to be especially beneficial as they will most likely give you honest reviews of the level and efficacy of vendor-provided support.

Table 10.2 Time Line for Blended Learning Professional Development

Before Blended Starts (could be done anytime during the year leading up to implementation)	Starting Blended Learning	Once Blended Learning Starts/While It's Running
• Basic "What is Blended Learning?" overview • Instruction based on changes to program • First level of software training • Routines and procedures related to blended	• Basic technology use and care • Teachers teach blended learning routines and procedures lessons to students	• Pedagogy and instruction based on observed needs • Follow-up training on reading and using data reports and deepening understanding of software

If possible, calendar these trainings at the beginning of the year, so you're not angling for teacher time down the road. Consider the time line in table 10.2 for planning your training throughout the year.

INTEGRATE TRAINING WITH OTHER PROFESSIONAL DEVELOPMENT

Don't make blended learning "one more thing." Blended should be part of the school culture. You don't want teachers "blaming blended" for whatever problem may arise. Would they blame their classroom libraries for taking up too much space? Let's hope not. Blended learning is about making systems work together. Rachel Klein of Highline suggests involving people who provide instructional supports in trainings, too: "Include the trusted coaches and specialists who are working with teachers already around instruction. This builds teachers into good leaders, saves money, and helps target our professional development." Blended learning is a team sport, and you want all the players who are focused on student learning in alignment with your goals.

FOCUS ON TEACHERS' NEEDS

Teachers' needs will differ based on experience and readiness. Jonathan Tiongco of Alliance College-Ready Public Schools suggests,

> We need to understand our teachers' proficiency and comfort levels when it comes to going blended. A first-year teacher teaching his or her first classroom ever is going to have a different set of skills and knowledge compared to a veteran teacher who has been teaching for a while. There may be different levels of proficiencies for teachers when it comes to technology use, classroom management, lesson planning, etc., so we need to understand the continuum of teachers and work to support their individual needs.

Every teacher's needs are a little different, and teachers will require varying amounts of support and patience. Sandy Jimenez, teacher at Aspire Gateway Academy, explains that the change and the challenges are worth it:

> As a first-year teacher teaching a first-grade class, I am very familiar with change and challenges. So when I heard that I would be piloting blended learning, it was a change and challenge I was a bit nervous about. I worried about scheduling, procedures, and transitions when launching blended learning. Once scheduling was done and procedures where set, the biggest challenge I faced was running transitions, especially with students who have high behavioral needs. Since learning on the computer was something new and exciting for my students, it was difficult for some to log off from their computer in a timely manner and move on to their next task. This caused valuable instructional time to be lost and delayed my guided-reading instruction. So after countless days of modeling and having students practice, I decided to chart/graph students' transition times and attach an incentive in order to improve transitions. And it worked! Now, transitions have improved tremendously and students are able for the most part to reach their two-minute transition goal. I am now able to efficiently get to my guided-reading groups and work with them effectively.

Aside from having challenges with transitions, blended learning has been an overall great change. I am able to better meet the needs of more students through smaller guided instructions during mini-lessons. I am able to see misconceptions I would have otherwise missed with having a bigger group during lessons. It has been a great experience watching children grow and apply what they have learned on the computer to their learning during mini-lessons. I'm excited to continue blended learning and grow as a teacher as well as watch my students grow academically through blended learning!

DON'T FORGET TO SUPPORT INSTRUCTION

We want instruction to change when classrooms go blended; specifically, we want teachers providing *more* individualized and small-group instruction, which can pose challenges for teachers. While we provide training and ongoing professional development for small-group instruction as part of our regular support for teachers, in a blended learning environment the instructional demands on teachers can increase. They need to shift some of their lesson planning of whole-group lessons to creating multiple small-group lessons each day. Teachers need great systems for keeping clear records of how students are progressing in order to form dynamic groups. Teachers may need to learn new instructional methods to replace some of what they needed to cut out when they went blended. Christian McGrail, teacher at Aspire Titan Academy, shares,

> As a first-year teacher it is difficult to say how my job has changed since implementing blended learning, but I can say that it is vastly different from last year when I was a resident. First of all, [having blended learning] makes me think so much more carefully about how I group my students. Since the class is being split in half, I have to figure out who will push others, who needs help from other specific students, and who can't be grouped together. Within those half-class groups, I then have to split students into pairs and trios for workstations and small groups. In a way, it has helped me get to know my students better, not only because I have more face time with each individual student, but also because of the data

that I am constantly getting back about their academic performance. Blended learning has really pushed me to think about who my students are as people, how they best learn, and how I can maximize my time to make sure that they make as much growth as possible.

Listen carefully to how teachers talk about how their work is changing, and be responsive to creating supports to continue helping them make the transition.

Likewise, scheduling can be a challenge for teachers. We've learned that crafting sample schedules for teachers is an effective support as teachers transition to blended learning. See appendixes L and M for sample K–5 instructional schedules.

SURVEY TEACHERS FREQUENTLY

To figure out how to improve professional development, get teacher feedback after every training and at points throughout the year. Heather Kirkpatrick, our chief people officer at Aspire Public Schools, emphasizes that this input is completely critical to everything we do at Aspire. Feedback in real time and a culture of user-friendliness are huge contributors to the success of our programs. In blended schools, we survey teachers each semester, compile the feedback, share it back with the principals, reflect on it when making our next steps, and continue to invite teachers and principals at every turn to let us know what is working and what isn't. See appendix H for a sample teacher survey. While feedback may be painful at times, it is also very illuminating and ultimately leads us toward being more successful.

GO FOR THE BADGE!

Intrepid Launcher

- Identify the types of professional development your teachers will need: instructional professional development, training in running blended learning, software training, or technology training and technology resiliency support.
- Sequence training to be "just in time," and be sure to schedule follow-up training if necessary.
- Integrate blended learning professional development with existing teacher training so blended learning training is a part of school-wide work around instruction.
- Micromanage training agendas from outside providers to make sure the training is focused, purposeful, "just in time," and in alignment with your instructional program.
- Solicit feedback to inform and improve future professional development.

11

Teacher Readiness and Classroom Readiness

Although teachers and students will be excited to start working on the computers right away, much instruction must happen before students sit in front of the screen. At this point, you'll want to revisit the instructional problem you're hiring blended learning to help you solve, and plan to prepare students for blended learning. Computers can be highly engaging—initially. Once that engagement wanes, students may start to find other (sometimes sneaky and usually not productive) ways to use the computers or students' time while seated at the computers. By spending the time to teach routines and procedures for computer use first, teachers set up students to be more successful and purposeful with their time on the computers and create routines that allow teachers to focus on spending their time on instruction instead of managing behavior on the computers. Don't shortcut this important step! When a classroom is "ready," learning from the teacher and on the computer is maximized. In this chapter, we'll detail the steps teachers need to take to get students and classrooms ready to go blended.

Teacher and classroom readiness are critical for evaluating when it's time to launch blended learning. When we opened our first schools in Memphis, Tennessee, we realized that we'd be opening schools with new teachers and new students and would not be able to roll out blended learning in the same ways we do when we convert schools. Our Memphis colleagues piloted a blended learning readiness program with great success. We've learned three lessons that helped shaped the blended learning readiness program:

1. Not all classrooms are ready *yet* for blended learning.
2. Once the computers are put in place, the classroom can be more difficult to manage if students are not already strong at working independently.
3. Coaches and principals find that it is more difficult to give teachers support in blended learning classrooms if teachers or their students are not ready.

Mindful of these lessons, the team articulated steps to readiness; once teachers and their classrooms were ready, the teachers would get the computers put in their classrooms and would be ready to run blended learning.

WHAT IS READINESS? AND WHY DO YOU NEED IT?

Just as not every school or principal leader is ready to go blended (yet), nor is every teacher ready to make the instructional changes necessary to go blended. Teacher willingness is critically important, but if a teacher's classroom management is not tight, and the teacher's instruction is not solid, putting new technology in a classroom is not going to improve management or instruction—it will make both worse.

> **Key Idea**
>
> Don't put computers in the classroom until teachers and classrooms show readiness. When a classroom is ready, learning from the teacher and on the computer is maximized.

HELP TEACHERS GET THERE OVER TIME

Teachers develop readiness for blended learning at different rates: some have tight systems and procedures that seamlessly allow for them to easily incorporate blended learning into their current work, while others may struggle with the changes in management or instruction necessary to run blended smoothly. This unevenness is part of the process; it's important to recognize that everyone can get there from here.

Our team in Memphis, when readying to open two new blended learning schools, wanted to ensure that every classroom was ready for blended learning before putting students on the computers. The team built blended learning training into summer training as a seamless part of the instructional program. When school started, the team sent teachers the letter presented in exhibit 11.1.

EXHIBIT 11.1 Readiness Letter for Teachers

Hello Teachers,

The academic year is off to an exciting start! It's great to see so many scholars engaged in learning and happy to be at school.

During summer training, we mentioned that we wanted you to have time during the month of August to build relationships and develop routines with your scholars, while promoting independent practice. As we prepare to launch blended learning, we want to make sure that we are actively supporting you and your scholars in the implementation of the model. To ensure that blended learning is off to a great start, we want to make sure you don't feel rushed or unprepared. Rather than a definitive time line for a campuswide implementation, we want to support each of you on an individual basis.

To help with this, please see the **Teacher Self-Assessment: Blended Learning Readiness** document [both on page 161 and in appendix G]. You'll notice that it has three columns: the domain, description, and next steps/goals. Please use this document to self-assess in each domain, and work with your instructional coach to develop a plan for next steps, as needed. Katie and Tommy will work with each of you to review and utilize this document, and Chris will coordinate with you to have blended learning laptops set up in your classroom. Once the laptops are in your classroom, Chris, Sherita, and Vernice will work with you to provide lessons and supplementary resources to support rotations and laptop expectations.

Please see any of us if you have any questions. Thanks for all that you do!

The team devised this reflection/walk-through form to help teachers reflect on their classrooms and to support coaches and principals using the form to identify specific supports for teachers to help them on the journey toward readiness.

TEACHER SELF-ASSESSMENT: BLENDED LEARNING READINESS

For you to successfully launch blended learning in your classroom, instructional, behavioral, and data-driven elements need to be in place. Use this document with your instructional coach to determine your classroom readiness.

Instructional Elements	Description	Next Steps/Goals
• Students know and have extension work that they complete without prompting. *They can complete this with 100% independence (for 25–30 minutes)* **Example:** *When finished with Independent work during math mini-lesson, students have flashcards that they take out and work on independently, without disturbing classmates.*	List or describe what students do for ELA: Math:	• Discuss ideas for building independence with coach. • Focus with class to build independence. • Ask for coach observation of students working independently.

(Continued)

(Continued)

Behavioral Elements	Description	Next Steps/Goals
• Behavior management system is implemented in a way that positively supports student behaviors. **Example:** *Teacher gives consequence to a student that requires him or her to go to the reflection table and the student does so without disruption or question.*	Behavior management system • Is displayed in the classroom • Is used effectively so that instruction or flow of the class is not interrupted by its use • Supports a positive classroom culture	• Discuss ideas to make behavior management system more seamless with coach. • Focus with class to build buy-in. • Ask for coach support.
Use of Data	**Description**	**Next Steps/Goals**
• Teacher has a clear sense of how students will be grouped, based on data (either behavioral or academic).	Articulate your plan for using data to group students	• Discuss ideas for using data with coach. • Make groups with rationale for discussion with coach.

By sharing the form before blended learning even started, the team was able to communicate their expectations for readiness with all teachers, and teachers had a clear idea of what they needed to do to get their classrooms and students ready for blended learning. Coaches and principals also used this form as a planning tool to identify specific supports to provide to teachers if needed.

STUDENTS ALSO EMBARK ON BLENDED LEARNING JOURNEYS

The importance of teaching students to value self-sufficiency cannot be overstated. This skill is important for anyone using technology. (See, for example, a chart that helps teach students how to decide what they need to be doing and in what order, in photo 11.1.)

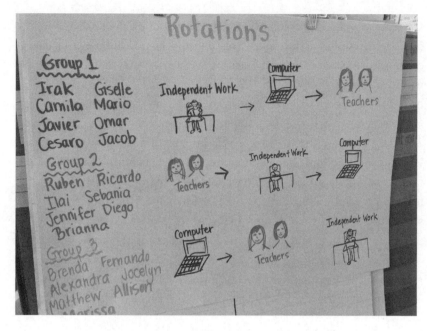

Photo 11.1 Classroom Rotation Chart Showing Groupings

Key Idea

We want students to engage in "productive struggle" on the computers. We don't want students to fail, but we cannot assess their abilities on the computers until we truly let them be on their own. Use the data to determine who is struggling, and encourage teachers to let students struggle first, rather than helping them every step of the way. Stepping back can be hard for teachers who empathize with others who struggle with technology, but students are sometimes surprisingly much more comfortable with technology struggles than we are.

Allyson Milner, teacher at Aspire Titan Academy, sheds light on the challenge some teachers face in letting students struggle while they're on the computers. She explains:

I learned a valuable lesson about my students' problem-solving ability on the computers. Thursday, I was out and a substitute was in charge of monitoring their blended learning. I was nervous that my students would have so many issues. I feel like they have questions or need help problem solving anywhere from 5–10 times a computer session. However, when I was gone, students asked the substitute only about 2–3 questions for the day! I got this information from our blended learning teaching assistant and came to the realization that they were taking advantage of how willing I was to help, or ask our blended learning teaching assistant to come in for help. After that, I told the students to try to solve the problem on their own. Giving them that push resulted in a much more independent computer time. There was only one problem that I helped problem-solve. This was an important realization of when to help and when to push students to become independent critical thinkers and problem solvers!

STUDENT READINESS TAKES TIME AND DELIBERATE PRACTICE

Time and time again, teachers tell us that they will end up paying the price later if they give in to student excitement and put their students on the computers too early. Taleen Dersaroian, teacher at Aspire Gateway Academy, recognized that blended learning routines are not unlike other instructional routines she teaches. She shares,

> Now that I've been running blended learning in my classroom for about 2.5 months, looking back there is one thing I wish I had done differently: build student muscle memory. When we were given the lesson plans to roll out blended learning, I just taught them; however, I recently realized I should have spent more time on building computer/sitting stamina and endurance, and actually wondered why this wasn't in the plan. When we rollout Daily 5 [a literacy program] in class, it's usually a 4–5 week process because we practice correct and incorrect models to build muscle memory so students know what it feels and looks like when Daily 5 is done right. We also practice with a timer, building up to 20 minutes of student independent work time;

Photo 11.2 Student Stamina Tracker

as soon as one student is off task, we reflect individually upon what went wrong and what went well. I have found that muscle memory practice really helped keep my students on task and productive for Daily 5. Most importantly, with muscle memory students self-regulate! I look at my students now at blended learning and I can see behaviors that should have been nixed had we done a longer roll out + stamina plan. Muscle memory is huge for students. So next year when I roll out blended learning again, I plan to have stamina graphs and have students practice correct and incorrect model (muscle memory) for at least a few weeks so correct blended learning behavior is ingrained into them.

(See photo 11.2 for one way to track student readiness.)

CELEBRATE THE PROCESS OF CONSTANT IMPROVEMENT

Our colleagues in Memphis also created "The BLEND Award" to acknowledge and celebrate teacher perseverance in getting blended learning off the ground in their classrooms (see figure 11.1). Each week at the faculty meeting, one teacher is awarded the BLEND Award (an old trophy with a blender glued on top) for having the knowledge and determination to keep working toward an excellent blended implementation. The school plays "Eye of the Tiger" for the announcement (as the school's mascot is the tiger), gives the teacher space to make a speech, and interviews the teacher about what the teacher has been doing in the classroom. In this way, the school takes the sting out for teachers who are trying hard and

The "BLEND" Award

This award recognizes teachers for their dedication, perseverance, and collegiality in the launch & ongoing support of Blended Learning.

As the recipient…
Be a thought partner for at least one other teacher:
Provide support, strategies, and encouragement.

Each Friday, I will present the trophy to a teacher at the team meeting.

Blended Learning Exemplar – ✖Nowledge & Determination

ASPIRE
PUBLIC SCHOOLS

Figure 11.1 The "BLEND" Award

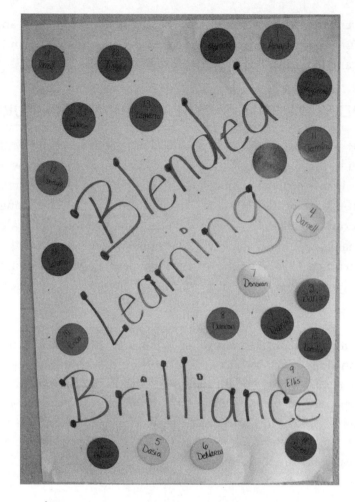

Photo 11.3 Computer Groups and Workstation Numbers

celebrates the process of constant improvement. (Finding creative ways to illustrate student information, as in photo 11.3, may also help.)

BUILD COMMUNITY WITH A NEWSLETTER

Because going blended is a work in progress, you'll want to continuously engage teachers in their own learning and development. A weekly blended learning newsletter is a great vehicle for communicating useful information about the

167

software over time, celebrating achievement, sharing best practices, and building school culture around blended learning. Please see appendixes I and J for two different examples of blended newsletters in our schools.

UNDERSTAND THAT BLENDED LEARNING IS A JOURNEY

Much of the work in going blended is focused on managing change with teachers, which includes managing both their expectations and your own while making major shifts in instructional practices. Going blended is not flipping a switch; it's a process that takes time, flexibility, and openness to learning and changing. What your classrooms look like in year one will be different from how they look in year two, and chances are, classrooms will continue to evolve after that.

Keep teachers focused on the instructional problem you're hiring technology to help you solve. Tom Willis of Cornerstone Charter Schools offers a similar perspective:

> When teachers show they have an open mind and are focused on trying most anything to help kids learn in better ways, to me this is a more fundamental question than the question "How do you know when a teacher is ready to do something different?" which is really an age-old question around getting humans to change. And to try to get folks to change, you can either force them or they can want the change themselves and clearly, the latter is the better way to go.

GO FOR THE BADGE!

Intrepid Launcher

- Identify what "readiness" looks like for teachers and classrooms, and communicate measurable steps to take toward readiness before launching blended learning.
- Emphasize that building up to readiness takes time and deliberate practice.
- Celebrate the culture of constant improvement with rituals like the BLEND Award.
- Create newsletters and other ways of communicating the work and engaging teachers in the process of going blended.
- Recognize that going blended is a journey for teachers and students that will change over time. Manage expectations and celebrate achievements.

12

Teaching Lessons to Support Blended Learning

We learned quickly that the classrooms with smooth blended learning implementations were the ones where teachers spent a lot of time teaching students strong routines and procedures for being on the computers. Sometimes, teachers tried to shortcut this process and get students on the computers more quickly, but ended up having to re-teach their routines and procedures to get blended off the ground and be able to leverage blended to allow small-group instruction. We strongly recommend not having students get on the computers in the first two to three weeks of school, and taking the time to really teach the lesson plans we've included.

The resources in this chapter are based on our station-rotation model in K–8 classrooms, but many of these lessons can be adapted for other models and contexts and students, as they involve the movement of students to and from technology.

We've heard teachers say, "Once we go blended, I can teach in small groups. That will make everything better." However, in reality, teaching in small groups will mean that teachers will be planning, teaching, troubleshooting, and solving problems in an exponentially more challenging environment. Teachers who haven't really managed a class of 24–30 students separated into diverse, flexible groups will need additional professional development that is beyond the scope of the lessons detailed in this chapter.

Paying attention to student voices is equally important as you launch blended learning. Students will let you know what's working and what needs more support. My blended learning teammate in Memphis, Chris Florez, says:

> I've heard some great things from students about how much they value spending quality time with their teachers in small groups. They recognize—now that they're in a blended environment—that they haven't really had such quality instructional time with their teachers in the past. They recognize that there's value in what they're learning on the computers, reinforced in teaching and learning moments with their teachers that can be more conversational and personalized than in whole group settings.

TEACHING ROUTINES AND PROCEDURES TO FOSTER STUDENT INDEPENDENCE

Ideally, if teachers launch blended learning at the beginning of the school year, they're able to incorporate routine and procedure instruction for blended with the other classroom routines and procedures they plan to teach, so that blended learning isn't set apart from the regular instruction of the classroom. Our teachers suggest erring on the side of more practice with routines, rather than less. Contessa Cannaday, teacher at Aspire Slauson Academy, explains:

> The advice that I would like to give new blended learning teachers is to practice a lot of procedures before you let students on the computers. We practiced a lot of transitions and we even used a song at first. I told the students what the expectation was with lining up, standing in line, the order of going to their computer and how and when to log in. This practice really allowed the students to do the best job possible when it came time to transition into blended learning.

Student independence is key to the blended learning model and must be explicitly taught. In our classrooms, student independence means that students can locate and complete extension work without prompting and can work

Photo 12.1 Daily Focus for Students to Search for Books

independently for 25–30 minutes (the length of one rotation), whether doing independent work, reading, or some other learning activity. (For example, in photo 12.1, a teacher chooses a daily focus for students to search for books, minimizing searching around by students and giving the teacher an opportunity to make connections with other content being learned in class.) If students can't work independently for sustained periods during regular instruction, students will likely struggle to stay engaged on the computers, which will in turn compromise the teacher's ability to focus on differentiated instruction, requiring the teacher instead to spend valuable instructional time managing student behavior on computers. In order for small-group instruction to be meaningful and uninterrupted, students will have to be experts in remaining on task during their independent work. These routines should be taught and practiced before students work independently. (For example, see photo 12.2, showing students how computer transitions should occur, and photo 12.3, showing students' daily schedule.)

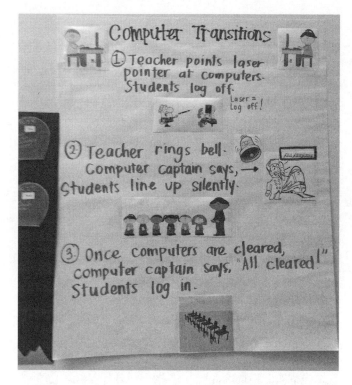

Photo 12.2 Chart Illustrating Classroom Rotation Procedure for Students

Routine instruction not only involves student independence and movement through the classroom, but also should focus on how students should use the computers. Nithi Thomas of Mastery Charter Schools reminds us, "Do not over-assume tech savviness of students—like in a regular class we need to intentionally teach our students routines and procedures and what success looks like. Create structures that promote independence from the beginning—encourage your students to make mistakes and not get frustrated."

In appendix N, you'll find a sequence of recommended mini-lessons to teach routines and procedures in a blended learning classroom during the first three to four weeks of the school year, or whenever you launch blended. Blended learning works best if the teacher takes ownership of the lessons and incorporates the gradual release of responsibility, based on students' needs.

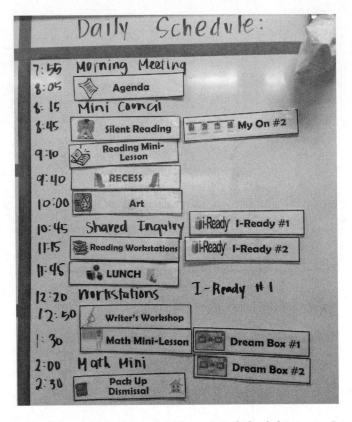

Photo 12.3 Daily Schedule Illustrating Placement of Blended Learning Rotations

THE FIRST FEW WEEKS OF GOING BLENDED

Blended learning lessons begin with a discussion of what students already know about computers (see table 12.1). Students are likely quite knowledgeable already and will be excited to tell all they know!

Table 12.1 Blended Learning Classroom Rollout

Week 1	Week 2	Week 3
The first three days of lessons about computers are spent discussing students' prior knowledge about computers, how computers can help us, and class-generated computer rules. The teacher creates daily class posters (or possibly, a daily page in a class big book) to document the discussions about computers. The teacher continues to build anticipation and excitement about computers as the lessons progress. In the days following the initial discussions, the teacher models how to log in and out of the computers and how to use the specific programs. The programs are projected, so that all students can clearly see them. Rather than telling students what to do in each program, the teacher can ask students what they think they are supposed to do. Each day, the class will revisit the posters, and	Lessons focused on routines and procedures related to blended learning continue.	By Day 12, or when students are demonstrating responsible behavior with the computers, it is time to invite students to interact with the programs. At this time, the blended learning teaching assistant begins to work with the teacher to take a co-leadership role. One group will use the computers, and the other will work on an independent activity that has been pre-taught in the previous weeks. After time at the stations, invite students back to the rug to discuss the progress of each group. The purpose of the check-in is to continually remind students of the importance of their independent work time. The class is divided into small groups of 6–8 students for practice two times per day—reading and math. For each successful practice session, 1 more minute is added to the following day's practice. The goal is for

(*continued*)

Table 12.1 (*Continued*)

Week 1	Week 2	Week 3
students are reminded of the purpose and usefulness of the programs. At this early stage, students will not use the computer programs independently. Instead, they will practice going from the rug or station to the computers safely and responsibly. After each practice, the class will discuss how they did, and the teacher will help students chart their progress on a class graph. Each practice session will be only a few minutes long.		students to be able to work independently for 15–20 minutes, while building up to at least 30 minutes. Student practice should be stopped early any time that 100% of the class is not working independently. At the end of the first month, students will be ready to rotate between activities.

WHEN STUDENTS AREN'T WORKING ON THE COMPUTERS

Teachers will need to make many other instructional decisions around what non-computer activities students are doing, whether independent, in collaboration with other students, or with the teacher receiving one-on-one instruction or small-group instruction. The more explicit and clear these activities are for students, the more orderly the learning environment, and the less management the teacher will have to do during rotations, allowing the teacher to really focus on providing the most targeted, focused small-group instruction.

When students work directly with the teacher, it's usually at a teacher table. Giving students an independent activity to work on right away at the teacher table can be helpful. At reading time, students can sit down and read quietly. At word work, students can practice reading the words from their word sorts. At math time, students can skip count, sort coins, create patterns, and so on. For the teacher, having the freedom to walk around the class at the beginning of the rotation is incredibly useful to ensure that students get right to work. Photo 12.4 shows a traffic light chart that helps students self-reflect on their own focus at computer stations after each rotation.

Photo 12.4 Traffic Light Chart

Key Idea: A Few Teacher Tips for Getting Blended Off the Ground

Some teachers graph the progress of the class each day. The teacher or students can color in boxes on a graph for the total number of minutes students were able to work independently each day.

The teacher should not remind students to stay on task during the practice time. If students are off task, end the practice session and bring the group back to discuss what happened. The teacher does not want students to be in the habit of staying on task only when reminded.

See photo 12.5 for an example of a transition time tracker that allows teachers and students to gauge how quickly students can transition among blended learning stations and then incentivize efficient transitions.

See exhibit 12.1 for a list of lesson plans on classroom procedures with technology. These lesson plans are detailed in appendix N.

Stay positive! Congratulate students on their progress, and remind them that each day that they practice their independent activities with consistency, they are improving.

TRANSITION TIMES TO COMPUTERS

Date	Group 2 IREADY	Group 1 IREADY	Group 2 DREAMBOX	Group 1 DREAMBOX
4/17/14	1:24.4			
4-21-2014	1:31.7		1:33.7	2:08.0
4-22-14	1:59.8	1:59.8		
4-22-14	2:01.0	2:01.2	2:00.9	1:32.2
4-22-14	1:57.4		1:31.6	
4-23-14	1:49.7	2:23.7	2:23.9	
4-28-2014		1:26.4	1:35.3	1:06.4
4-29-14			1:38.7	2:05.9
4-29-14				1:32.3
4/30/14	1:40.4		2:08.2	1:20
5/1/14	1:43.6			
5/2/14	1:38.3	1:35		
5/6/14	1:36	1:34.1	2:10	2:03.5
5/6/14	1:52.7		1:40	1:35.0
5-7-14	1:10.6	2:39.7	1:40.6	
5/8/14			1:13.7	1:07.3
5/19/14	1:37.4	1:28.5		1:45
5/20/14	1:41:2			
5-21-14	5:27			

Photo 12.5 Transition Time Tracker

WHAT ABOUT STUDENT TECH LITERACY?

Organizations like Common Sense Media have created a host of user-friendly lesson plans for teachers to tackle the challenges of teaching technology literacy and cyber-safety to students. Students need instruction on cyber-safety when using

---

EXHIBIT 12.1 Lesson Plans on Classroom Procedures with Technology

1. Location of workstations
2. Noise level at workstations
3. Correct behavior at computers
4. Correct behavior at workstations
5. Necessary materials at workstations
6. Quiet and efficient rotations
7. Computer workstation etiquette
8. Preparing to rotate
9. Staying comfortable at the computers
10. Caring for the computers, part 1
11. Caring for the computers, part 2
12. Correct keyboarding position
13. Using the track pad or mouse
14. Logging in
15. Logging out
16. When the computer is loading
17. Troubleshooting problems during login
18. Closing the program and logging in again
19. What to do when there's a computer problem
20. Adjusting the volume
21. Handling headphones

---

computers and on tech literacy throughout the school year as the need arises during instruction. We frequently charge our blended learning teaching assistants with initially rolling out these lessons with teachers as appropriate.

As with any instructional program, teachers must balance positive classroom culture with effective instruction, procedures, and management.

Jonathan Tiongco of Alliance College-Ready Public Schools in Los Angeles offers this perspective:

> The first thing to understand is that students don't really think of their learning as being "blended" or "technology-integrated." For our digital natives, this is how they live, work, and communicate. When I think about learning 20–50 years ago, no one ever talked about it being chalkboard integrated or pencil-and-paper integrated, so why do we do this with technology? Students are so accustomed to using technology in their personal lives. When I talk to students, they say that technology makes their work and their social life faster, more engaging, and more efficient. It's up to us, as the adult educators, to prepare them to use the technology for academic purposes.

DON'T FORGET KEYBOARDING INSTRUCTION

We've found that the keyboarding demands in many software products rise dramatically in the switch from fifth to sixth grade, yet prior to going blended we hadn't thought much about keyboarding instruction as part of the curriculum. The Common Core State Standards state that students will need to be able to type a page of text at one sitting by the end of third grade. As a result, teachers have started creating small keyboarding rotations with free typing software. Some of our kindergarten teachers put students on an early keyboarding program for a week, just to familiarize them with the location of letter keys before starting blended learning.

GO FOR THE BADGE!

Intrepid Launcher

- Build in enough time prior to launching blended learning (at least two to three weeks) in which you'll teach the routines and procedures necessary to run blended learning in your classroom.
- Create back-up plans for when the technology doesn't work.
- Maintain high standards for accountability when teaching students lessons on using the technology; the better they understand how to use technology correctly, the more you'll be able to focus on small-group instruction.
- Identify where and when tech literacy, cyber-safety, and keyboarding instruction should take place.

13

Setting Up Your Classroom and Students for Success

In addition to teaching the necessary routines and procedures to get blended learning started, you'll need to take other steps to get your classroom ready and maintain student engagement throughout the school year. This chapter begins with an explanation of considerations for teaching the programs themselves, followed by a detailed look at how to think about and teach ways of rotating on and off the computers and methods for dealing with headphones. We'll then discuss creating incentive systems, troubleshooting problems that arise, and finally soliciting support from others.

TEACH THE PROGRAMS THEMSELVES

Teachers need to spend time navigating through the software programs in order to anticipate potential issues that may come up for students during independent work time. Sometimes, the ways in which programs ask students to sign in and out might be unfamiliar to students or challenging for nonreaders; explicitly teaching students how to sign in and out of programs will save time in the long run (see photo 13.1). Many teachers use the bulletin board above the workstation to organize students onto specific computers, highlight the reading focus for the week, and give directions for logging in to and navigating some software programs (see photo 13.2).

Photo 13.1 Student Signing into Computer Program

Photo 13.2 A Bulletin Board Above a Workstation

Most programs are intuitive, and chances are, many students will have amazing preexisting knowledge about how to use computers and how to solve problems that arise. Invariably, error messages will come up, and students will need to learn the process for dealing with errors and bugs. Teachers can use screenshots, short digital videos, PowerPoint presentations, and whole-class lessons to demonstrate these skills. To promote efficient rotations, some of our teachers ask students to time how long it takes to sign out after the signal has been given to rotate.

Some programs have diagnostic assessments that set content levels for students, while other programs allow students to move at their own pace through similar content. Our students had no prior experience with online adaptive testing before we introduced blended learning in our schools. Teachers had to familiarize themselves with how adaptive testing works, teach students ways of taking adaptive tests (to prevent frustrated clicking through and "throwing" the test), understand the results, and explain how the results set the learning paths for students. In short, the software wasn't just "plug and play"; teachers had to pre-teach the software or they would get very mixed results and potentially waste valuable instructional time having students work on content that was not at their level if they threw the test.

See appendix N for lessons on teaching the programs (Lessons 14, 15).

ROTATING OR MOVING ON AND OFF THE COMPUTERS

Invariably, moving to computers (or taking them out) or moving away from computers takes time for students. Teaching students how to rotate—what rotations look, feel, and sound like—pays huge dividends once blended learning starts in the classroom. Ensuring that rotations are effective and efficient is a step no teacher should miss teaching. The tighter the rotation, the less time is lost! To reinforce and support this lesson, a teacher could use a poster like the one shown on page 184.

After creating the poster, have students practice rotating. Just as students need multiple opportunities to practice independent computer behaviors, they should also practice rotating. The teacher will need a timer and a nonverbal signal to communicate to students when to end an activity and rotate. At the signal, students will sign out of computers or clean up their activity, stand behind their chairs, and

What will it look like when we rotate?

- Students quickly signing out of computers
- Students cleaning up independent activities
- Students standing behind chairs
- Students looking at the teacher
- Students walking to next rotation
- Students starting work right away

What will it sound like when we rotate?

- Quiet voices
- Quiet feet walking
- Fingers typing
- Pencils writing
- Students reading

What will it feel like when we rotate?

- Calm
- Focused
- Safe
- Responsible

then walk to the area of their next activity. (See photos 13.3 and 13.4 for examples of pocket charts showing reading and computer rotation groups.)

The class should review the rotation chart daily before the rotation practice begins. On the day of the first rotation lesson, students should practice just moving from rotation to rotation. On the following days, after students have practiced moving from rotation to rotation, they should practice the actual activities for 15–20 minutes. When the rotation has been completed, students should return to the rug, or starting position, and rate their rotations with a thumbs-up or thumbs-down.

A clearly labeled chart needs to be posted so that students know where to go for each rotation. The chart should be large and easy to see. Figure 13.1 is an

Photo 13.3 Pocket Chart

example that visually depicts online instruction, independent or collaborative practice, and teacher-led instruction. (See also photo 13.5.)

Many of our teachers create digital rotation charts that they project onto the board. Doing so allows them to make changes easily as groupings change.

Other teachers create signals students can use to help notify students that it's time to move. Raul Gonzalez, teacher at Aspire Titan Academy, shares:

185

I remember the first time I had my students rotate, and I didn't anticipate the rush of students for the computers while the others were still putting away headphones and logging off. I was quick to suggest the following procedure that has been working like a charm . . . sort of.

When students are rotating:

- Students at the computer log off and prep headphones to be stored.
- As they finish they walk over to the other person assigned to that computer.
- A pat on the back lets the other student know that the computer is ready for use.

This procedure keeps students from going over to a computer that is still in use by the student packing up. The reason why I said it "sort of" works for all is because I've noticed some students still forget to pat their partner on the back, and if the student is not very assertive they'll sit there instead of realizing that their partner is already off the computer. I guess it goes to show that at least they follow the procedures and wait to be patted on the back.

Rotations

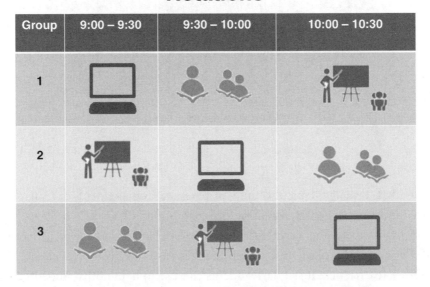

Group	9:00 – 9:30	9:30 – 10:00	10:00 – 10:30
1	💻	👥	🧑‍🏫
2	🧑‍🏫	💻	👥
3	👥	🧑‍🏫	💻

Figure 13.1 Rotation Chart Illustrating Where Students Should Be

186

Photo 13.4 Pocket Chart

CREATE INCENTIVE SYSTEMS TO KEEP STUDENTS ENGAGED

As highly engaging to students as computers can be initially, we know that engagement will wax and wane throughout the school year. Teachers need to

187

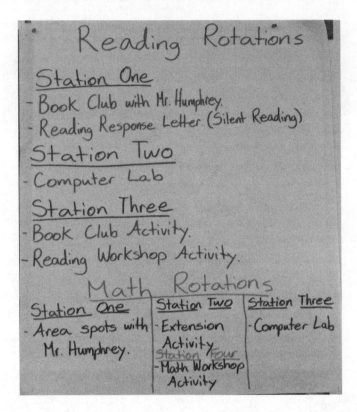

Photo 13.5 Rotation Chart Illustrating Student Options at Each Station

put classroom incentives and school-wide incentives into place to foster increased engagement and build momentum for learning in the programs. Student engagement will wane, so teachers need to figure out how to counter that tendency. Allyson Milner, teacher at Aspire Titan Academy, explains:

> We have been using computers now in the classroom for a couple of months. Before the computers arrived, my students could not wait to get on them. Once they got here, my students asked daily if they could use them already. Two months later, not all students are as excited as they once were. Now, when I look back at the computer area, I notice a couple of students looking around the room, seemingly unengaged. When looking at the data and comparing the estimated time to complete a lesson and the amount of time it took some of my students, there is a big gap.

The challenge for blended learning teachers is to identify the most operable and actionable data from each program on which to base incentives and to craft an incentive that truly engages students in the process. Programs vary widely in what might constitute actionable data: unique lessons completed, standards-mastered, syllabus completion percentage, books read, quizzes passed, and so on. Table 13.1 details some sample incentive ideas; see also photo 13.6.

Table 13.1 A Few Incentive Ideas

Grades K–5	Grades 6–12
Wear the golden headphones for a week.	Earn 15 minutes of free-choice activity or gaming activity on software.
Earn points for a class reward.	Become the tech assistant for the class.
Keep an animal (the class or software mascot) on your desk.	Earn tickets toward free time.
Get a fun worksheet.	Receive a positive phone message or e-mail home.
Student with the highest progress gets to fill in the progress chart.	You're the DJ: Choose the music played during blended rotation transition.
Have lunch with the teacher.	

Photo 13.6 Classroom Incentive Sticker Chart for Blended Learning

Be sure to make your incentives transparent and public by posting the goals and metrics on bulletin boards, and celebrate achievement with class and even school-wide goals. Most teachers we've spoken with use student data from the software to track their incentives weekly; frequently, the blended learning teaching assistant takes care of this task for teachers.

Allyson Milner, teacher at Aspire Titan Academy, keeps her students motivated and invested in their learning on the computers by publicly setting goals and tracking the data each week with her students. She shares,

> To help track our progress, we keep our weekly big goals posted. On Monday, we review the data from the previous week and determine if we met our goals. I set these goals for our class after looking at an initial few weeks of data. This helped me write goals that are challenging, but attainable for my students. Each time we meet our goal, I put a star on our calendar for the week. They can earn up to 12 stars a month! If we earn at least 10, we earn a small reward for our hard work, like an extra 10 minutes of recess time. This encourages teamwork! We can only make our goal if we are all here and doing our best!

Nithi Thomas of Mastery Charter Schools recommends,

> Get your students excited from the beginning; when you have student buy-in, you will be able to accomplish a lot more. Get your culture team involved in creating rewards/incentives that are recognized throughout the school—not just in the classroom. We have students who are recognized during morning meetings, and we have a blended learning bulletin board by the entrance of the school where we post student pictures.

SEATING, LOCATION OF WORKSTATIONS, AND STUDENT BEHAVIOR

Teachers handle seating with computers in a variety of ways, depending on the configuration of the room, the sources of power and connectivity, and the teacher's management of students. In our schools, I do my best to encourage teachers and principals to create a computer workstation area along a wall, so that the computers have a set place to be and students aren't spending time checking out computers from a cart and moving them to a specific place in the room. Such a setup also allows the teacher (and the blended learning teaching assistant) to more easily monitor what students are doing on the computers at any given time without interrupting small-group instruction. However, some teachers prefer having students take computers to their desks. This routine may create additional challenges for teachers in monitoring student behavior on computers and assessing how long it takes for students to log in and out. (Be sure to think about power needs and battery charging if you do choose this option!)

Figuring out who gets what computer is also a key decision teachers need to make. Our teachers assign students to a particular workstation and computer for the year. This option allows teachers to hold students accountable for any damage that might happen to computers and also helps the blended learning teaching assistant troubleshoot problems that may arise with a particular device or software program. However, at certain times of the year, grouping may become so flexible that assigning students to particular computers isn't really feasible. In these circumstances, teachers should teach students about making "wise choices" and finding seats next to friends who can help them do the most learning, or face a consequence of not having that kind of flexibility in the future.

See appendix N for lessons on seating and location of workstations (Lessons 1, 5).

Consider student stamina and the need to take breaks from time to time, and create systems for helping students take breaks productively. Christian McGrail, teacher at Aspire Titan Academy, explains,

> It's gotten to the point in the year [February] when students no longer have the same love and fascination for the computers they showed in August. It's totally natural, but is sometimes hard for me to keep students motivated. I've noticed that my kids love to get up to get a tissue. One idea that I plan on trying is helping students take structured breaks so they can relax their muscles and brains without loitering around the tissue box. My blended learning teaching assistant suggested the idea of having a Velcro sticky above each laptop where students can put a clock stating that they are taking a 30-second break and are free to stand and

have a look around the room. As long as it is used in moderation, I think it will really help students stay on task for the full 30 minutes. The honeymoon phase with the computers will be back again next August, but of course it's all cyclical.

MANAGE HEADPHONES OR THEY'LL MANAGE YOU

We spent a ton of money on headphones, and although they can be inexpensive, they take a lot of time to manage, and costs can add up quickly. Just Google "Kids Chewing Headphone Cords" to see what I mean. Photos 13.7 and 13.8 show two ways to organize headphones.

We've shifted the burden of headphone costs to students and their families by providing each student with a set of headphones at the beginning of the year and then having families pay to replace them should their student break them. We've seen a marked increase in the care given to headphones and a decrease in headphones needing replacement.

See appendix N for a lesson on headphones (Lesson 21).

Think through your procedures and routines around headphone use. A teacher at Aspire Titan Academy explains,

Photo 13.7 Headphone Organizers for Different Student Groups

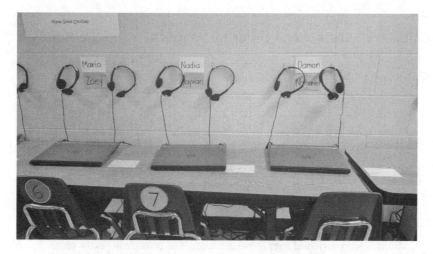

Photo 13.8 Organized Computer Workstations

So, headphones are a headache. Where to put them is the beginning. They are big, the plastic bags that hold them don't hold up, and the students spend too much time trying to close the bag. It adds to the transition time. The students have trouble putting them on. They often pull them and break them as they put them on their head. I know using headphones for K–2 is a better option than the ear buds, but research or trial headphones would be a good idea in the future. Students pull at the wires and insist that the wires pulled on their own. This is an ongoing problem with students. I wish I would have spent *a lot of time* going over how to put them on, how to take them off, and how to use them.

Key Idea

Purchase a set of headphones for each student. If you don't, your chances of a lice outbreak are pretty high!

Included in exhibit 13.1 is the letter we send home to families about headphones.

EXHIBIT 13.1 Headphone Letter for Families

Dear Parents,

We gladly inform you that Aspire Public Schools has officially initiated the blended learning program. It is exciting to introduce new learning innovations to our classrooms. To do so, we have provided each student with headphones to be used during blended learning time. It is important for students to take care of their sets as they will be required to use them as they progress through each academic year here at school. We ask that you talk with your child regarding the importance of taking care of their headphones. Should the headphones become damaged, we will ask that you replace your child's set as we are unable to provide an extra pair.

_____ Student Name

_____ Parent Signature

Estimados Padres,

Es nuestro placer informales que Aspire Public Schools oficialmente ha empezado el programa de blended learning. Nos satisfice introducir nuevos métodos de aprendizaje en nuestros salones. Para alcanzar nuestra meta, cada estudiante ha sido otorgado un par de audífonos que deberán ser usados durante el tiempo de blended learning. Es muy importante que los estudiantes cuiden sus audífonos ya que deberán usarlos en los años consecutivos mientras estén en la escuela. Se les pide a los padres que hablen con su hijo/a sobre la importancia de cuidar sus audífonos. En caso de algún daño, los padres serán responsables de remplazar el par de audífonos ya que no tenemos la capacidad de otorgarles un par extra.

_____ Nombre del Estudiante

_____Firma del Padre

TROUBLESHOOTING PROBLEMS THAT ARISE

Inevitably, technical issues and behavioral problems will arise. Maybe the Internet will be down. Perhaps the power will go out. A former teacher at Aspire ERES Academy recounts one such occurrence shortly after she started piloting blended learning in her classroom:

So after today's power outage (and the subsequent loss of Internet connectivity), I realized that I need to have a solid back-up plan of what to do when our technology fails in the middle of rotations; this resulted in less than magical behavior and a distracted teacher during guided reading groups.

It's a great idea to be prepared for these situations when they come up, because they always do! At times, the problem occurs midway through a rotation. It's important that students know how to navigate technical difficulties, so that small-group instruction doesn't have to stop.

See appendix N for lessons on dealing with problems (Lessons 16, 17, 18, and 19).

No matter how strong your network is, chances are the Internet will go down. When this happens, you'll want to have a plan in place (see table 13.2).

Allyson Milner of Aspire Titan Academy shares:

Last week we were coming in from recess and the first group of students was getting ready to go on the ELA program. The second group knows to get their workstation folder and supplies and start their work. The only problem, the Internet was down. Students were unable to access their blended learning programs. My decision at this point was to have all students go to stations. After all, who knew if or when the Internet would be back up. I was not about to sacrifice guided reading for the day.

Table 13.2 What to Do When the Internet Goes Down

Problem	Solution
The power goes out!	You have pre-copied packets of seat work to work on, or books to read, in lieu of computers.
The Internet goes down mid-rotation.	You have prepared students for the situation! They know to get their book boxes and to sit at their computer spot and read.
A message box pops up on the student's computer.	You have taught students to look for the X and click it, or to click OK if they can.

What ensued was a huge mistake. My students were no longer used to the procedures for working with such a large group. Additionally, the stations currently in place are not designed to be used by the whole class at one time. There are many parts that require student discourse. This made the volume of the room much louder than I like, especially if I am trying to read with a small group.

I learned my lesson. Upon reflection, I decided that there are better alternatives next time the Internet goes down. (1) I can wait an hour or two (depending on the day/schedule) and switch which teaching practices I do and when. (2) I can have half the students remain in stations, while the other half does silent reading or other independent work. This will keep part of the class silent and not overload the stations. As you are thinking about blended learning, remember to keep in mind what you will do when the Internet goes down. I can guarantee that it will!

Include Systems for When Students Are Stuck

Inevitably, programs will have glitches or experience difficulty loading, and computers will not work from time to time, the bandwidth or power will go out, or the network will go down. The list of things that can go wrong with technology are pretty endless. During these times, you'll want a plan for what students should do instead, and you'll need to teach students how to do what you expect them to do. Some ideas:

- Have students carry a book on their rotations, so they can read.
- Place work packets (extra math practice, homework, enrichment problems) in folders near the computers so if the computer goes down, students can just grab a worksheet and keep working without getting up and disrupting others.
- Load a few non-web-based programs onto the computers (typing programs, math practice, downloaded books) that students could access when the wireless goes down, because it will.

Rachel Klein of Highline exclaims, "There's nothing more heartbreaking to a blended learning leader than watching a table of eight-year-olds be sad and frustrated watching the spinning wheel (of page loading) go on and on because the kids want to play their game (even though it's educational)."

We find that our kindergartners and first-graders need considerably more support in blended learning than students at higher grades. Imagine this situation: A teacher has 6 students at the U-table; 6 are working independently; and 6 of 12 on laptops have their hands raised because they get an error trying to log in to the ELA program and don't know what's wrong—you can easily find yourself having serious management issues. Plan on having the blended learning teaching assistant support those classes as students learn how to log into programs, use track pads, and sign out of programs.

Some small actions by students can actually lead to larger problems. While nobody can plan to prevent every mishap, it's worth taking the time to think through potential challenges when putting students on computers. See table 13.3 on page 198 for one example of possible causes and solutions for the problem of the youngest students not being able to log in.

Addressing Student Behavior on Computers

As in any activity, student misbehavior with computers should be met with predictable and logical consequences. This section looks at misbehaviors we observed during a pilot year and ways to handle this conduct. Of course, each classroom may have different rules and consequences (see photo 13.9 for an example). The teacher should do whatever makes the most sense in that particular classroom.

Sometimes, despite all of the practicing students are doing as a class, a student might continue to struggle with on-task behavior. A brief one-on-one conversation and practice at recess time can help to solve this problem. However, if the student continues to veer off task, take a closer look at the activity the student is struggling with. Is it too hard? Too easy? Too long? Make whatever modifications you need to for your students to be successful at independent work.

If students are roughhousing around computers, remove students from computers and give them seat work to do (even if this interrupts a small-group meeting; safety is always the first priority). Follow up with a longer conversation about classroom safety. Students then can write letters to the class about computer safety or create a classroom poster about computer safety.

Table 13.3 Small Things Can Be Big Things

What If a K–1 Student Can't (Consistently) Log In?	• Think about using stickers on the period or comma key.
	• For some programs, passwords are shown on the screen as an "*". This can be really hard for a student to troubleshoot what she/he might have mistyped. Create a plan around this.
	• Consider how to teach/foster digital literacy skills, in addition to procedures and routines.
	• CTRL+ALT+Delete can be a big deal for K–1 students. Do the power settings on the devices require younger students to remember or struggle with an additional username and password convention— just to log into the device? Create a plan for this.
	• Create a plan for how a K–1 student can find/ retrieve his/her username(s) and password(s) if he/she forgets.
	• If a student's username or password has an "l"— lowercase "el" in it—make sure he knows it's not an uppercase "I" (eye), as it looks on the keyboard.
	• Have younger students practice typing their user names and passwords in Word so the teacher can see whether and where students consistently make mistakes.

Children are curious, and at some point during the year a student is likely to figure out how to sign on to a computer as someone else—either another classmate or a sibling in another grade. Explain to the class that teachers use the information from the computers to plan their teaching. Any false information could cause the teacher to teach the wrong thing. Making a big deal out of this situation is worthwhile, as computer ethics will continue to play a part throughout our students' educations.

Any repeat offenses in the types of misbehaviors just addressed should result in losing the privilege of using computers.

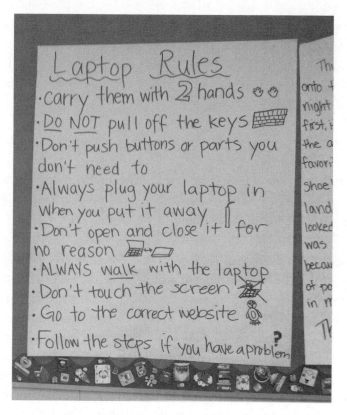

Photo 13.9 Computer Use Rules for Students

Not all misbehavior is wrong. Nancy Pacheco Sanchez, teacher at Aspire Titan Academy shares,

My class is a very chatty group and not even computers stop them. They have gotten better at this, but it is still not 100 percent as I would like. I always correct this behavior, but since I'm always working with students at the guided-reading table it is difficult to hear what students are talking about. Today I had a bit more mobility as one of my students was testing, I let her read the book silently as I walked around to monitor students on the computers. I found that those students who are constantly talking were talking about what they were learning on the computer. I also had one student trying to help another student with *context clues.* He told him

"I learned that last week." I then realized that a lot of students are actually trying to help one another and not talking about other things as I assumed. I think I need to allow some time every day to give them an opportunity to share what they are learning about. Finding the time will be the difficult task.

See appendix N for lessons on student behavior on computers (Lessons 2, 3, 4, and 7).

Help students manage their emotions by teaching them skills for being flexible when working on the computers. Amy Youngman, former teacher at Aspire ERES Academy, explains the struggle of doing this with her students:

> The hardest thing about middle school—like everything else in middle school—is that the range of student achievement is huge. I've got third-grade through eighth-grade readers, and kids who can't text and kids who are super tech-savvy. It's really hard to get everyone in line. I had to teach huge, time-consuming lessons: "How do I put a computer on standby? How do I go from standby to off? How do I restart?" With that, middle-schoolers are moodier—their emotions are really strong when something doesn't work or when they lose something on computers. Trying to teach kids to be flexible on computers is really really hard, but important and a skill they need for college. In sixth grade it's a hard lesson to learn.

INVOLVE PARENTS BY SHARING KEY INFORMATION AND EXPECTATIONS

A year into our blended learning implementation, teachers began to identify useful ways to involve parents in the process of building and keeping students engaged on the computers. Mark Montero at Aspire Titan Academy explains, "With the students who are less motivated or do not always use their computer time wisely, I get the parent on board and share the expectation that the work on the computer has to be as rigorous as the rest of the work in my class." His colleague Raul Gonzalez continues, "We've had a big win with parent buy-in to blended learning because we've given students access to the programs at home.

Now, students have purposeful reading at home in the software, and we've built credibility for the program with parents." Montero continues, "Blended learning gives you something else to talk about with parents. It's one more way to connect home life to school life."

Consider how much information parents need to support their student's learning at home. Lindy Brem, literacy specialist at Aspire Titan Academy, explains,

> I recently had a conversation with a parent about using the software programs over the summer, and he asked me: "Why is the reading software beneficial to my daughter? What are the skills that she is learning on the English language arts program?" At first, I was taken aback and wanted to reply, "Because they're important, that's why!" But obviously this wasn't going to be the right approach. So as I was explaining both programs to this parent, it made me wonder, how many other parents don't know why their students are on the computer for over an hour a day. It also made me wonder, do they need to have a deeper understanding?

Such insights have demonstrated to us the importance of sharing more information with parents about what students are doing on the computers.

Report cards offer yet another opportunity to communicate blended learning achievement to parents. Raul Gonzalez shares,

> With report-card season around the corner, it helps to have an additional piece of information to give to parents. Student reports vary from program to program, but the information their usage provides helps parents get multiple perspectives about their child. At times I think that parents might think that what we give them on report cards is subjective, so to have data from software allows us to affirm our grade decisions supported by the data from their learning on the computers. Many times, those scores are comparable to their classroom performance. I am happy to be able to provide parents with as much information about their child's successes in the classroom as well as with areas for improvement. It's like having another teacher to support your decisions and comments to parents.

GET SUPPORT FROM BLENDED LEARNING TEACHING ASSISTANTS

At the beginning of the year, solicit support from your blended learning assistant to support your efforts. Some helpful activities might include the following:

1. Offer to teach some of the blended learning routines.
2. Label headphones with student names.
3. Create index cards with student user names and passwords.
4. Create posters for procedures on the computers (logging in, what to do when you're stuck, and so on).
5. Teach students what to expect when signing in to the software. Consider making a PowerPoint presentation with screenshots.
6. Create incentive systems for student behavior and progress and post the systems on classroom walls.
7. Establish a plan for when the Internet goes down.

APPOINT TECH HELPERS IN THE CLASSROOM

One way of involving students in tech support is by creating the classroom job "tech helper" to allow a student to address problems that arise on the computers. Create a set of signals students can use to get help to minimize disruptions. At Rocketship Education, they call these students "Junior Techs" and provide them with a manual.

PLAN FOR SUBSTITUTE TEACHERS

We've learned our lesson: It makes little sense to put blended learning in classrooms where the teacher's management is not strong enough to make blended learning successful (with one potential result being damage to the technology). So what happens when the teacher is out and a substitute covers the class? We wondered about that situation and watched our classrooms carefully to find out what would happen. As might be expected, teachers whose routines and class culture were strong enough to sustain a few days of the teacher's absence, by and large, had students who continued with their blended learning work at the same level with a substitute teacher. A former teacher at Aspire ERES Academy shares,

Last week, we had our very first substitute since blended learning has started. Initially, I was very hesitant to run our rotations as usual with a sub. I was worried about kids not taking care of the equipment and not using the technology properly if I wasn't there. (I think this was especially a fear for my class and the upstairs classrooms because kids physically move the computers several times over the course of the day.) However, this situation will obviously come up from time to time, so I gave it a try. I wrote very detailed sub plans, scripting exactly what I say during computer transitions, and thanks to the lovely Julie, everything went great. In fact, she said that the rotation schedule made subbing especially easy. As usual, our blended learning teaching assistant also helped everything run smoothly by being present during all computer transitions (when possible!). So my lesson learned is this: Blended + (competent) Substitute = Magic.

Sometimes, however, a long-term substitute cannot sustain over time the routines and procedures set by the original teacher. In these cases, we pull the computers out of the classroom until the teacher and the classroom show readiness again, as we want to maximize student learning from the teacher and from the computers.

GO FOR THE BADGE!

> ### Intrepid Launcher

- Ensure that teachers are committed to teaching routines and procedures before students get on the computers. Provide guidance around the amount of time teachers should take to teach the lessons.
- Plan for when students get stuck or the technology doesn't work.
- Use support from blended learning teaching assistants strategically.
- Create school-wide and classroom-based incentives to promote student engagement.
- Find multiple ways to engage students.
- Address behavior concerns immediately.
- Make a headphone plan.
- Involve parents.

14

Making Mistakes and Iterating to Improve the Work

We've learned, and continue to learn, many lessons from our blended learning work and that of others. While some lessons are unique to our organization and instructional program, the major ones can apply to nearly everyone doing this work and are worth keeping in mind. Because blended learning is still in many ways in its infancy, you're going to make mistakes along the journey. Mistakes are a good thing; learning from what doesn't work is much easier than learning from ambiguous situations or lukewarm progress.

Key Idea

Embrace a culture of making and learning from your own mistakes!

Looking back on this work, I remember saying to pilot teachers over and over, "We are not sure blended learning is right for us, and we're hoping to learn from you what works and what doesn't." This approach allowed them to make mistakes and took a lot of the pressure off getting things right the first time. Our blended learning implementations in the first year looked quite different from now, and I'm confident that two years from now, these implementations will look even more different. In this chapter, we'll detail some of the bigger mistakes we've made so far and offer alternatives so you don't have to face the same problems. We will also share some mistakes that we haven't made (and that you shouldn't make either).

10 BIG MISTAKES WE MADE (AND HOW WE CORRECTED THEM)

The following are 10 major mistakes we made when we first started this work.

1. **Deciding to pilot blended learning, rather than deciding to solve an instructional problem using blended learning.** The semantics and focus mattered here. Initially, we all focused on "piloting blended" and trying to understand what that felt like. Once we began shifting our focus to the ways in which our instruction could change and student achievement could grow, we realized that our work wasn't all about blended learning; our work was about using blended learning to support good instruction. Stay focused on the instructional problem you're hiring blended to help you solve.

2. **Not managing teacher expectations about what the software could do.** We believed in the power of technology but didn't quite understand initially that the software market is fairly young and therefore products are not quite "there" yet. We assumed that the standards-aligned software taught all the standards. We assumed that the software would be able to adapt in real time to whatever the student might need. We assumed that we would be able to easily get from the software whatever student-achievement data we wanted and needed. Our assumptions were not confirmed by reality. Armed with a much better sense of what we want and need out of software, we now grill providers to find out what we can get, and then we manage teachers' expectations so teachers don't get their hopes up before students start working on the computers. When a software provider tells us that a particular feature is coming, we tend to not inform teachers until the promised feature actually arrives—frequently, it doesn't.

3. **Paying quoted software prices.** We didn't understand that very few products have list prices and that all contracts are negotiable, which meant that initially we paid higher prices than we should have. Now, we build relationships and partnerships with companies we respect, we talk to our blended learning friends to ask them what they're paying for software, and we negotiate like crazy. We're now having all software contracts come through our Home Office, so that individual principals are not negotiating on their own and so we're able to leverage district pricing whenever possible.

4. **Not creating pilot agreements and paying stipends to teachers during the first year of implementation for each teacher.** We were really structured when it came to rolling out our pilots the first year, but at the beginning of our second year of implementation at the first school where we piloted, we just assumed that everyone would remember and uphold the parameters from the first year. We didn't consider enough the impact on the teachers who hadn't piloted the year before, nor the messages we wanted the new pilot teachers to hear. As a result, we spent a fair amount of time recalibrating teachers' performance according to our expectations, and we became frustrated when things didn't look the way we had assumed they would. Now, we share pilot agreements with all teachers at our initial rollout and in blended learning training, whether they pilot the first year or the second year, and we stipend all of them, as going blended does create additional work for teachers in their first year of this work.

5. **Not building strong relationships with our IT team.** Initially, we left it to our IT team to figure out how to solve problems getting schools ready to go blended and how to troubleshoot difficulties that arose during implementation. This approach created many inefficiencies. Communication loops were frequently broken because teachers shared problems with IT but not with the blended learning team, or shared problems with the blended learning team that we then would have to share secondhand with IT, which frustrated all of us. Once we began engaging our IT team in the work as a whole team, the IT team built our capacity on the blended learning side, and we were able to build their capacity on understanding the instructional side. Now, we have bimonthly check-in meetings between the blended learning and IT teams to ensure that we all know the status of each rollout and what we need to be thinking about in the months ahead.

6. **Assuming we could get blended learning off the ground in just a few months.** Everything takes much more time than we ever imagined: getting funding, getting principals and teachers on board, getting IT to agree to supporting and purchasing particular devices, negotiating software contracts, upgrading infrastructure, having furniture shipped, setting up furniture—everything! As a result, we created undue stress for ourselves and everyone else in the process by not managing everyone's expectations. For example, teachers were ready to and wanted to start teaching routines and procedures, but computers to put students on hadn't yet arrived. In one school, teachers had to move furniture after school (instead of us doing it for them during a school break), because the furniture didn't arrive on time. Getting this work off the ground requires a lot of teamwork, and many decisions directly impact other decisions on the time line. Now, we allow 8–10 months to get blended learning off the ground—and if we have more time, we take it! See our sample project plan in appendix E.

7. **Believing we'd be able to clearly see the student-achievement impact of blended learning software.** I used to joke with colleagues during our first year of going blended that if the data showed that student achievement went down, everyone would blame blended learning, but if the data showed that student achievement went up, everyone would say, "It's inconclusive." Our data on student achievement did show increases in the first year of implementation; alas, however, as much as we analyzed a million points of data, we could not separate the impact of the software from the impact of increased small-group instruction. What we do know is that if students get additional small-group targeted instruction from teachers, the data will show that student achievement goes up, and the way to allow teachers to do more small-group instruction is to put blended learning in their classrooms to support their instruction. We continue to pull data from the various programs for analysis, and we have celebrated small wins where the data points to increased reading proficiency, or where the software has clearly taught something well the teacher has not at all covered, but clarifying impacts continues to be a work in progress.

8. **Assuming (or maybe just hoping) that blended learning could make up for a teacher's mediocre classroom management.** Blended learning amplifies everything in the classroom; if a teacher's management is not strong, it gets worse with students on the computers. While students may initially be engaged

in using the technology, blended learning cannot serve as a student babysitter or manager. We need teachers to create tight routines and procedures and to assign consequences when students violate them, and we need students to maximize their learning on the computers by being focused and purposeful in their work.

9. **Not engaging other education leaders, like our education specialists and instructional coaches, from the very beginning.** Our education specialists (special-education teachers), instructional coaches, and other instructional specialists have a great deal of impact and influence on the instructional program in our schools and on student achievement. Initially, we didn't engage these specialists, because we didn't have a clear idea of how to engage them in this work and were concerned that we'd be wasting their time. Now, we engage these specialists as partners in this work so that they can learn about blended learning from their respective positions and improve the program even more by adding their expertise.

10. **Not upgrading our entire school infrastructure before starting blended learning.** We didn't have the money or the expertise to do a full upgrade when we started our first pilots. We believed we could make it work, and to an extent we did make it work. However, deciding not to upgrade the entire infrastructure resulted in our sacrificing teacher goodwill when the network was slow and created much frustration for our IT team, who spent an inordinate amount of time at the school attempting to troubleshoot problems. Now, we know that a partial upgrade is actually more costly in staff time and materials than upgrading the entire infrastructure all at once.

10 MISTAKES WE *DIDN'T* MAKE (AND YOU SHOULDN'T EITHER)

We avoided making the following mistakes and, once you've read about them, you should, too.

1. **Not being disciplined with budgets.** If you're not disciplined, you might have to make trade-offs later that will compromise your plans. Consider one-time and ongoing costs, track personnel costs carefully, figure out your plan for building technology replacement into future budgets now, analyze where you

can save costs every step of the way, read your invoices closely, and by all means stay disciplined and focused on ensuring all your expenses are focused on solving the instructional problem you selected.

2. **Starting blended pilots without really clear parameters laid out for teachers and principals.** If you don't set out clear parameters, you'll waste time trying to understand what's working and what's scalable, and you may not get the learning you really want from the pilots. Create pilot agreements and clearly lay out the parameters of what is and is not negotiable (time, schedule, focus, support, or other aspects). Clearly articulate what you want to learn from the pilots and communicate it with all stakeholders before you even begin to pilot. Make space for teachers and principals to ask lots of questions. Leave room for teacher creativity, innovation, and autonomy, but be aware that sometimes being creative can cost teachers time and energy.

3. **Assuming we could run blended on our own as a little blended learning team.** Blended learning requires the involvement of and support from many departments (advancement, tech ops, data and analysis, finance, special ed, and coaching). Involve others whose work may change as a result of your decision to go blended, so they are partners in the work and don't think blended is something that is being done to them. You need someone to lead blended learning on your team, but the leader shouldn't have to maintain the effort alone.

4. **Not scrutinizing every single invoice for software or services to identify potential mistakes or discrepancies.** If you don't, you will probably pay more, and that money could be better spent on students. We have to be incredibly disciplined with every penny we spend, so we have no problem reading invoices closely. And when mistakes are made or deadlines aren't met, we go back to providers to get refunds or discounts.

5. **"Letting a thousand flowers bloom," or running little pilots all over the place.** We knew we wanted to learn from our pilots, and we knew we had to put parameters around piloting that would allow us to closely monitor a few things at one time. Running many things to see what works can definitely be beneficial, but running tight pilots with fidelity of implementation is a lot of work. We knew we could only closely monitor and support so many classrooms and teachers at one time successfully.

6. **Neglecting to document our process so we wouldn't have to reinvent the wheel with each subsequent rollout.** Some of this work, like crafting tight rollout timelines and teaching blended learning lessons, is the same, year after year. Although many things do change from year to year, we recognized that, with such a small team, we wanted to find every possible efficiency we could. We have a running list in the form of a project plan (see appendix E for a sample) that we revisit and revise with each new implementation. Our blended learning teaching assistants write and archive newsletters to share "just-in-time" training ideas with teachers; our teachers blog their own lessons learned for themselves and one another (and us); and we've begun creating materials to share our practices more widely (like our blended learning implementation guide, which grew into this book).

7. **Keeping our successes to ourselves.** If you do this work in isolation, you'll never learn from others, and you'll miss the opportunity to get critical outside feedback on your work. We've run countless tours to show other educators what blended learning looks like at Aspire Public Schools. The questions our visitors sometimes ask push our thinking around choices we've made and frequently affirm for us that we're on the right track. Education Elements made a beautiful video of our blended learning work at Aspire ERES Academy (www.aspirepublicschools.org).

8. **Underestimating the power and impact of blended learning teaching assistants on the culture of blended learning across the school.** If we hadn't put someone in place to support the technology and deal with problems in each of our schools, I'm confident the tech problems would have gotten the best of us. (I shudder to think of what I would have been doing each day at the school to keep everything going that first year!) Teachers would have quickly lost confidence in our investment in the technology if we hadn't provided the support necessary to keep it running. And, over time, we have realized that blended learning teaching assistants play a central role in how teachers view the use of technology over time. We make sure we hire folks who bring a positive problem-solving mindset to work each day (instead of empathetically complaining when things go wrong).

9. **Letting those who are the most eager about blended learning be the pilot teachers.** Many teachers are enthusiastic about technology and the powerful

role it can play in classrooms. I caution you to avoid letting what I call the "Moodle Teacher" to be among the pilot teachers. The Moodle Teacher is the biggest champion of technology in a school, but although this teacher may run a lot of technology in his or her classroom, those practices have not spread to other teachers at all. While the Moodle Teacher is not afraid of the change that technology can bring to the classroom, this person might be less aware of or sympathetic to teachers whose technology use or developmental stage is not near his or her own. The Moodle Teacher could compromise your ability to scale your pilot by being less patient with others or going off on his or her own to iterate further on something that may not be part of your plan. Not all tech champions are the Moodle Teacher, but you should be aware that the role this person plays in your pilots could be both helpful and hurtful.

10. **Believing that software providers have your teachers' best interests at heart.** Being seduced by bright, shiny objects in the form of flashy devices, super-fun software programs that may not be the best instructionally, or software reps who overpromise and underdeliver will only break your heart little by little. Be a realist and stay focused on your instructional problem, your teachers, and your students.

ITERATING AS A PROCESS AND WAY OF LIFE

Tom Willis of Cornerstone Charter Schools suggests:

> Because we have so much to learn, there's very little that's nonnegotiable. I suppose for us it would be staying focused on three things: (1) better learning for the students we serve . . . if it doesn't improve student learning, then it doesn't matter how fancy the technology is; (2) faster learning (growth each year is crucial to close the achievement gap); and (3) less expensive (we want our model to be more efficient so we can improve the rest of our model and ultimately pay our teachers better if possible).

Chris Liang-Vergara at LEAP Innovations puts it this way: "Everything is open to change, assuming the initial effort/implementation was executed well according to agreed-upon metrics. Being agile and letting staff own and iterate is key to accelerating the adaptation process."

GO FOR THE BADGE!

Intrepid Launcher

- Embrace a culture of making mistakes and learning from them.
- Be mindful of the mistakes others have made (and learned from) so you don't make the same mistakes yourself.
- Instill a culture of iteration in your teachers, but keep your parameters around the work firm.

Conclusion

When I was asked to lead this work at Aspire, I was taken aback. I didn't consider myself a technologist, nor a champion of technology, nor even someone who is particularly tech-savvy. I didn't even know what I didn't know. (And in my first year of doing this work, I definitely learned that there was a whole lot I really didn't know!) Norman Atkins of Relay Graduate School of Education once said to me, "I just don't get it, Liz. Your experience is all in 6–12 content and instruction. You didn't know much about technology. You had no experience or background in any of this. Either your supervisors were very smart or very lucky when they asked you to do this work!" I'm here to say, if you care about students, student achievement, and teacher sustainability, and you are willing to learn and make mistakes, you can do this work.

Our students deserve adults who are brave and willing to take on the unknown when it comes to finding the best ways to use technology in support of student learning. The fact that our students may (or may not) be much more tech-savvy than we are is no excuse for failing to learn about technology. Teachers are best positioned to evaluate the quality of content and to watch and learn from the ways students interact with technology in school. Technology-purposeful classrooms should be part of every student's experience, not just of those students lucky enough to have teachers who are interested in technology or who find it particularly easy to use.

Software companies and others are incredibly interested and invested in this work, and much money can certainly be made in the educational technology sector. But school leaders and teachers know how students learn and what makes most sense instructionally, and we are the ones who should own and lead this work. I hope you agree and are willing to take on this daunting but very important work.

THE BLENDED LEARNING JOURNEY

Teachers can see the benefit of this work once the change begins to happen. Taleen Dersaroian, a third-grade teacher at Aspire Gateway Academy, explains,

> We've now been at blended learning for over a month and I can truly say that I love it. I love seeing all the different skills and concepts all the kids are working on independently on the computers. And now that I'm teaching smaller math lessons, I'm better able to reach more students . . . especially those whom normally I wouldn't be able to provide individual feedback to during a lesson. Interestingly enough, because I'm working with a smaller group, I'm noticing things about my students that I hadn't before noticed in a whole-group setting . . . so I'm making sure to work with these observations to improve my students' learning. Additionally, I can reach more kids during mini-lessons now because I can easily see who needs help or who needs more of a challenge and I can address them instantaneously and individually. I'm actually able to work with a small group during each guided practice to help my struggling students. In essence, I really enjoy blended learning and am fortunate that my class got to pilot it this year! So, am I a believer and convert? You betcha. Would I recommend it to others? 100 percent guaranteed.

Even teachers who initially resist this change can begin to see the value in making it. Carolina Orozco, also a third-grade teacher at Aspire Gateway Academy, explains,

> I was a little weary about incorporating blended learning in my classroom. I had yet to see blended learning work in a classroom much like mine, which made me feel very nervous. After visiting Aspire Titan Academy's blended learning classrooms, the anxiety I felt about going blended quickly dissipated. That anxiety soon turned into excitement and anticipation for a really cool program I knew would be a perfect fit for my students.
>
> Now, a month or so into our fully implemented blended learning schedule, it feels as if we've had blended learning in the classroom all year long. It's been amazing how well the students have reacted towards the

schedule change, the new routines, logging in and out, and those pesky headphones.

We've looked at data very minimally so far, but what I've seen is really astonishing. I have a few kids who are working on sixth-grade math standards and other students who are receiving fifth-grade reading comprehension work. I love that my students have a chance to work on differentiated work at their level. This is a really valuable time for those students who may not have constant success with their own grade-level work. I do have some students who are working on first- or second-grade reading comprehension work, but they come away from their blended learning time feeling successful. I can't wait to delve more into data analysis!

The experience of working with only 12 students during a math lesson (while the rest of the class is on computers) is phenomenal. It's my favorite time of the day as I get to sit with my students to hear and watch them learn. I'm really appreciative of the time I get to spend with those students who need more one-on-one time with me because they're having trouble following along with the lesson. It's a time where I feel most like a truly successful teacher!

This chapter closes with one more teacher journey to underscore that this work is a journey for all of us. I hope your journey will be a rich learning opportunity for you and the students you bring with you.

WHAT'S NEXT?

I'm frequently asked, "What do you think blended learning will look like in 5–10 years?" That's a tough question, as technology and how we use it are constantly changing. I tend to answer, "I don't actually think that we will still call what we're doing *blended learning*. I think it will just be part and parcel of what we do." Think about it: We don't talk about having classroom libraries—they're just a seamless part of classrooms and teachers' reading programs. To me, blended learning isn't an end in itself; rather, it's a way to get to the classrooms of the future.

My Blended Learning Journey

Amy, Sixth-Grade Self-Contained, Aspire ERES Academy

PRE-LAUNCH OF PILOTS, EARLY NOVEMBER

This is where my story of blended learning truly begins. The first few months of the school year I had really struggled with finding ways to truly differentiate the learning in my classroom. I was pulling small groups of students during reading, writing, and math instruction, but it felt forced. I felt as if the time was profoundly benefiting students while they were meeting with me. However, I continually felt as if I were giving other students meaningless seatwork simply to keep them occupied. I was constantly trying to find ways to meet with more groups of students without creating busy work for the rest of the class.

Then, Liz presented me with the concept of introducing students to interactive computer programs that promise to be not only highly engaging, but also differentiated in their content. These programs, she promised, would assess student learning regularly and adjust learning activities accordingly. It seemed too good to be true.

Over the next couple of weeks I tested out a number of different computer programs myself. I was able to pre-pilot these programs on my own and give Liz feedback on how effective I felt they'd be for my students. While working to identify the right programs for my class, I was also grappling with the idea of scheduling. Blended learning opened up doors for differentiation that I didn't think were possible, but they required a huge shift in our schedule and planning models. In this area, I was pretty much on my own. I played with many, many different scheduling options and finally landed on a model that seemed to work for my class. I had to plan for many more small-group lessons and had to tailor each of these lessons to the learners themselves. This was as exciting as it was challenging.

THE LAUNCH, LATE NOVEMBER

Late November and early December were trial-and-error weeks for me. I would try a schedule and find out it didn't work. I would try a lesson-planning format and realize it was unsustainable. I would try a method of tracking and realize it complicated life more than I could handle. These weeks I tried to be as transparent with my scholars as humanly possible. I explained to them that this is a system that is unique to our class, that computers will be a major teaching tool for us, and that we need to be flexible as we experience "innovation pains." We had our fair share of frustrating moments, but learned a ton in the process.

My sixth graders fell into two camps. There were the students who were "technology fluent." These were the students who easily navigated through each of the programs presented to them. They were able to problem-solve effectively and were very self-managed. Then, there was camp number two. These were our "beginning technology learners." These were students who needed far more instruction and required lots of visual and audio reminders throughout their exposure to the programs. I learned to err on the side of providing more resources for students as opposed to less. I provided all students with a "Computer Toolkit," which thoroughly explained common misconceptions (how to put the computer to sleep as opposed to shutting it down, the steps for logging in to each program, etc.).

We also had to work hard on procedures associated with using our computers to ensure learning wasn't lost in transition time. We practiced routines and procedures over and over again until they were perfect. We evaluated ourselves on the effectiveness of each one and wrote personal reflections.

I also learned early on that there had to be a backup plan for when technology totally failed us. I learned this the hard way when the power went out and students had no alternative activity. The next day, I provided each student with a packet of review worksheets titled "My Computer Is Not Working." The expectation was that students would begin working on this packet as soon as they couldn't solve a technology problem. This would signal the problem to me and to Ms. Furukawa (our blended learning teaching assistant) that the student had a problem they couldn't resolve alone. This strategy also prevented students from interrupting me or any other students when a problem occurred. Eventually, we identified tech experts within our class who could support solving more minor technology problems when "less fluent" students struggled.

THE PILOTS, NOVEMBER TO MAY

Throughout the rest of the school year, I continued to tweak and reevaluate structures to make blended learning as effective as possible.

(continued)

(*continued*)

Using data strategically was one area that I learned to better utilize as the year went on. I learned how to better read and interpret the data from the various programs. This understanding helped me blend my instruction more closely with student misunderstandings as well as hold students more accountable for the learning they were doing on the programs. I began introducing student trackers that allowed students to track their own progress throughout the course of each week. There were weekly expectations for not only how much time was spent on each program, but also for how much learning was being accomplished in the allotted time.

As routines and procedures became second nature to my students, I was able to play around with individual student schedules. By the end of the year, I had 26 different student schedules in my class. I could ensure that each student received instruction that they needed, on their level. This kind of differentiation meant that I spent a lot of time looking at small-group data and adjusting my instruction each day according to student understanding. This meant that students were receiving differentiated instruction from me during small groups and from their computer programs. Students received small-group writing instruction, guided reading instruction, and small-group math instruction. Students were also on computers for silent reading accountability, nonfiction reading program, and differentiated math re-teach program. The programs and small groups worked together to meet students where they were at *and* push them forward to where they needed to be.

As magical as this sounds, it also presented its challenges for me. I was charged with doing more strategic planning than I was used to, using data more regularly than I was used to, and relying more heavily on different styles of instruction. I was assessing student learning regularly and found students progressing far more rapidly than I had in the past. Reading levels, math content knowledge, and writing skills were growing dramatically. Furthermore, I was able immediately to specifically target students who were falling behind, instead of waiting for a posttest to signal a red flag. I found myself pre-teaching and re-teaching regularly as student self-confidence rose class-wide. I can't say that it is less work than before, but I *can* say that it is more targeted and efficient in terms of student growth.

CONCLUSION

Blended learning definitely pushed me as an educator and challenged me to target instruction directly to student learning needs. Students were excited about their growth and enjoyed learning in a more independent, focused manner. I can say that there was a visible difference in the behavior of my middle-schoolers when most of the instruction was in small groups. There was less pressure to perform, to be concerned with reputation, or to act out. I am excited to more closely collaborate with other Aspire teachers around the blended learning model. As with any teaching tool, I know that the blended learning model will continue to be perfected each year as we place more technology into the hands of our young learners!

Appendixes

A. Blended Learning Analyst Job Description
B. Blended Learning Teaching Assistant Job Description
C. Director of Innovative Learning Job Description
D. Sample Blended Learning Pilot Agreement
E. Sample Project Plan
F. Rocketship Curriculum Evaluation Rubric
G. Teacher Self-Assessment: Blended Learning Readiness
H. End-of-Year Teacher Survey Questions
 I. Sample Blended Newsletter 1
 J. Sample Blended Newsletter 2
K. Sample Blended Learning Classroom Floor Plans
 L. Sample Common Core Weekly Schedule for Grades K–2 Blended
    Learning Classrooms
M. Sample Common Core Weekly Schedule for Grades 3–5 Blended
    Learning Classrooms
N. Twenty-One Lesson Plans for Implementing Blended Learning

Appendix A

BLENDED LEARNING ANALYST JOB DESCRIPTION

General Summary

The Blended Learning Analyst will be responsible for executing a plan to enable all aspects of our blended learning work, capturing lessons learned and incorporating them into a plan for the 2013–14 school year in Memphis and California schools. The ideal candidate will have K–12 experience and effective project management skills. This is an opportunity for an entrepreneurial-minded, detail-oriented person who is passionate about blended learning and is champing at the bit to do the work it takes to convert and open schools as blended learning models. This is currently a full-time grant-funded position for nine months, with the possibility of extending work based on potential new opportunities.

Essential Duties and Responsibilities

Develop systems to codify all aspects of blended learning implementations to scale future deployments

- Build Aspire's resource database of products, contacts, contracts, and evaluations related to blended learning.
- Identify and source other technology tools, resources, and contacts that can be used in Aspire's blended learning classrooms.
- Capture lessons learned and identify opportunities to share knowledge across the sector.
- Create a blended learning workflow plan in concert with other Aspire teams.

Help Aspire schools plan and execute successful blended learning deployments

- Conduct needs assessments to understand the technology needs of our blended learning schools, including bandwidth, equipment, devices, configuration, monitoring, data visualization, training, and support.
- Collaborate with Aspire's technology team to support effective rollout of new tools and technology.
- Manage procurement of all devices, software, and accessories; track budgets; and manage accounting systems.
- Provide on-site technology support for blended learning schools as needed, working with outside vendors as appropriate.
- Evaluate programmatic outcomes and identify opportunities for ongoing improvement.
- Serve as a champion for students' and educators' needs.
- Become an authority on blended learning systems, and use that expertise to support Aspire teammates.

Help Aspire communicate blended learning work internally and externally

- Build out digital learning space on MyAspire to share updates, resources, and lessons learned.

- Collaborate with teachers to capture learning from blended learning classrooms and create ways to communicate our blended learning work within and beyond Aspire.
- Collaborate with Aspire's development team on grant proposals and reporting as needed.

Organization Relationships

Success in this position requires an entrepreneurial approach to problem-solving, a strong quantitative and qualitative analytical skill set that includes budget tracking, and the empathy to understand the challenges faced by educators at Aspire. This person works closely with staff at all levels within our home office and schools, and with outside consultants and software vendors.

Qualifications

1. Required knowledge, skills, and abilities:
   - Comfort with technology; demonstrated ability to learn new tools, systems, and processes quickly
   - Track record of establishing effective relationships with people in business, educational, and technical roles
   - Excellent organization, time management, and follow-up skills; high sense of urgency; demonstrated ability to successfully handle multiple projects concurrently; ability to work independently
   - Ability to research complex problems and develop cost effective solutions; strong analytical skills, even in the face of ambiguity
   - Exceptional writing skills
   - Skilled in providing technical support empathetically to frustrated users of all skill levels
   - Love of data! Driven to discover data anomalies and understand their implications. Ability to see the forest and a second later zoom in to point out the bug on a tree
   - Tendency to document and ability to do so effectively
2. Minimum education level: bachelor's degree

3. Experience required:
   - Experience working as an educator or on site at a K–12 school environment or 2+ years' work experience doing business analysis, solution support, technical consulting, or product management
   - Familiarity with blended learning a plus
   - Experience working in dynamic, high-performing work environments

Appendix B

BLENDED LEARNING TEACHING ASSISTANT JOB DESCRIPTION

General Summary

Aspire Public Schools is running a series of blended learning pilots in our schools and is looking for someone to serve both as a teaching assistant and a person who can provide tech support and troubleshooting in the classrooms where our pilots are taking place. This is an exciting opportunity for individuals interested in education technology and teaching who are willing to learn and eager to provide support to teachers to ensure the success of the pilots. The Blended Learning Teaching Assistant will provide support to at least six different teachers on a five-day/week schedule. We hope to take what we learn from these pilots and apply these understandings to other Aspire schools.

Essential Duties and Responsibilities

Supports classroom systems/procedures and helps manage student behavior to ensure all students are fully engaged in learning.

Supports teacher's use of technology in the classroom by monitoring student behavior while on computers and performing basic technology functions (e.g., rebooting computers) as needed.

Supports Aspire IT with basic computer setup and maintenance.

Supports software-based assessments, collects and disseminates data, and provides recommendations for program improvement where necessary.

Collaborates with Aspire team members to improve own and others' instructional practices; shares best practices.

Helps classroom teacher(s) provide students and their families with regular and timely information on classroom activities and student progress.

Supports a school-wide culture of high expectations that includes college preparation for all students; works with College and Academic Counselor to support students with academic progress.

Actively participates in professional-development activities related to the pilots.

Demonstrates knowledge of and support Aspire Public Schools mission, vision, value statements, standards, policies and procedures, operating instructions, confidentiality standards, and the code of ethical behavior.

Performs other related duties as required and assigned.

Organization Relationships

Reports to Site Principal. Works closely with other site and Aspire staff. May work with outside consultants and vendors.

Qualifications

1. Required knowledge, skills, and abilities:
   - Strong facility with technology software and hardware
   - Ability to troubleshoot computer issues; inquisitive working style and desire to get to the root of technology issues
   - Ability and willingness to implement Aspire Instructional Guidelines and Best Practices

- Ability and willingness to reflect and improve
- Knowledge of child cognitive development and different learning styles
- Strong written and verbal communication skills; ability to collaborate with colleagues, parents and community
2. Minimum educational level: bachelor's degree
3. Experience required: 1+ year working with students as a teacher, teacher intern, or teaching assistant preferred

Appendix C

DIRECTOR OF INNOVATIVE LEARNING JOB DESCRIPTION

General Summary

The Director of Innovative Learning leads research, design, and implementation of new blended learning instructional model for the Aspire school system. The Director spearheads the blended learning pilot to test and inform model for wide-scale implementation to provide a high-quality, personalized education program for students.

Essential Duties and Responsibilities

- Synthesize research around the effectiveness of blended learning models, internal best practices, and challenges to design and pilot a blended learning model that aligns with Aspire's instructional practices, beliefs, and values, and delivers strong student achievement results.
- Plan and launch blended learning pilot for 20xx/20xx school year; select sites and teachers, and determine performance metrics.

- Research, select, and approve content for blended learning pilots and make recommendations for wide-scale launch.
- Evaluate economic implications of blended learning model for feasibility and short- and long-term cost-effectiveness.
- Partner with cross-functional partners to help determine technology requirements for pilot program.
- Develop and deliver training program for teachers and principals to execute blended learning model pilot.
- Manage daily delivery of blended learning model, addressing issues and problems that arise during execution.
- Evaluate effectiveness of blended learning pilot and distill pilot learnings into planning for wide-scale implementation of blended learning model as appropriate.
- Work in collaboration with principals, Home Office, and external consultants to achieve strategic goals.
- Demonstrate knowledge of and support Aspire Public Schools' mission, vision, value statements, standards, policies and procedures, operating instructions, confidentiality standards, and the code of ethical behavior.

Qualifications

1. Required knowledge, skills, and abilities:
   - Demonstrated knowledge of curriculum development and program design
   - Strong experience in performance assessment
   - Demonstrated commitment to students and learning
   - Excellent communication, presentation, and interpersonal skills with demonstrated ability to write clearly and persuasively
   - Excellent organization, project management, and community-building skills
   - Ability to meet tight deadlines, high sense of urgency; demonstrated ability to successfully handle multiple projects concurrently
   - Ability to lead cross-functional team and to work as a team
   - Entrepreneurial passion

- Demonstrate knowledge of and support Aspire Public Schools' mission, vision, value statements, standards, policies and procedures, operating instructions, confidentiality standards, and the code of ethical behavior
- Perform other related duties as required and assigned

2. Minimum educational level:
- Experience with secondary level education
- Experience developing teachers

3. Experience required:
- Bachelor's degree required; master's or Ph.D. in education preferred
- Administrative credential preferred
- No Child Left Behind Highly Qualified Teacher preferred
- 3+ years working with urban students as a full-time teacher preferred
- 7+ years teaching and administrative experience

4. Physical requirements: The physical demands described here are representative of those that must be reasonably met by a Director of Innovative Learning to successfully perform the essential functions of this job.
- Stand, walk or bend over, kneel, crouch, reach overhead, grasp, push, and pull. Move, lift, and/or carry up to 30 pounds to shoulder height.
- Repetitive use of hands (i.e., fine manipulation, simple grasping, and power grasping).
- Demonstrate normal depth perception.
- Sitting, walking, or standing for extended periods of time.
- Dexterity of hands and fingers to operate a computer keyboard, operate standard office equipment, and use a telephone.
- See and read a computer screen and printed matter with or without vision aids.
- Distinguish colors.
- Read and understand rules and policies, labels, and instructions.
- Hear and understand speech at normal levels and on the telephone.
- Verbal communications, including the ability to speak and hear at normal room levels and on the telephone.

5. Work environment: The work environment characteristics are representative of those in a normal office/classroom/school setting that one might encounter while

performing the essential functions of this job. Reasonable accommodations may be made to enable individuals with disabilities to perform the essential functions.

- Work indoors in a standard office environment, computer lab, and/or classroom environment.
- Work is performed in indoor and outdoor environments.
- Exposure to dust, oils, and cleaning chemicals.
- Some exposure to childhood and other diseases in a school environment.
- May be required to work outside of normal workdays and office hours to meet operational deadlines.

Appendix D

We're excited to study what it means to incorporate blended learning practices in our classroom. In order to get the maximum benefit out of the pilot and to clearly delineate responsibilities, we've drafted this agreement about our responsibilities within this pilot to make it a great success and meet the requirements we've laid out to funders. We're actively pursuing funding for the hardware and infrastructure upgrades for this pilot and if/when that happens, we'll amend this document to reflect the additional responsibilities in possessing the technology. Here are the specific questions we've set out to answer with the pilot:

- Does the classroom rotation model help our teachers better meet the *differentiation* needs of students?
- How can a multiage group create greater efficiencies and opportunities around reading instruction?
- What's the right balance between screen time and teacher instructional time in our elementary model?
- What is the potential for increasing class sizes with classroom rotation? How many additional students feel sustainable?
- What training, structures, and processes need to be put in place for classroom rotation so teachers are well supported in this work?
- How do we integrate data effectively for teachers, whether from computer-based instruction or teacher-facing instruction?

What We'll Do	What You'll Do
Purchase online learning software program licenses for all of your students and 11 computers for each of your classrooms (with the exception of 6th grade, which is already 1:1). Create a single sign-on for students to easily access and enter programs from the desktop. Purchase computer storage and furniture for K–3 classrooms.	K–1 will try a multiage approach in which you'll test what an "early reader" and "late reader" program might look like if you combine and share students in different ways. Grades 2–3 and 6 will replace independent work time and most whole-group instruction with centers-based instruction and small-group differentiated instruction. Students will be on the computers in structured rotations for a minimum of 60 minutes per day on programs TBD in ELA and math.
Work to extract the "back-end" data out of the software programs into existing Aspire data systems. Work with Godzilla and outside vendors to identify ways of incorporating your data into Aspire visualizations to better help you drive your instruction.	Create, codify, and share routines and procedures for managing student use of the technology in your classroom.
Analyze your online learning data to identify trends, patterns, opportunities.	Use the data from the work done online to inform your instruction.
Increase school-wide bandwidth, conduct facility technology upgrades (including WAPs, routers, etc.). Prioritize your classroom for IT support and installation of new computers.	Take care of the technology and communicate with blended learning team about any issues that might arise.
Showcase your classroom as an innovative practice in Aspire.	Provide feedback to blended learning team members on an ongoing basis and to help meet grant-reporting milestones.

Support your efforts to innovate and help troubleshoot any instructional or procedural concerns.	Be open to feedback and revisions of pilot scope to best maximize outcomes. Participate in necessary professional development or training.
Maintain relationship with funders and complete all reporting to funders on the given time lines.	Allow visitors to observe and ask questions about the pilot and your current learnings.
Provide your school with an instructional aide shared across 5 classrooms.	Be willing to take risks and innovate to figure out the best way to support individualized instruction and feel supported.
Provide you with a $2,000 stipend.	Run the pilot for the whole school year with fidelity.

Appendix E

SAMPLE PROJECT PLAN

Task	Who Is Responsible	Due Date	Notes
Send out information to principals	Chief Academic Officer, Blended Learning Team	15-Dec	Send questions for principals to address with leadership team about potentially going blended
Interviews with principals	CAO, Blended Learning Team	9-Jan	Determine interest and readiness for blended
Create final list of piloting schools for school year 2013–14	CAO, Blended Learning Team	10-Jan	
Create rollout calendar for schools	Blended Learning Team	11-Jan	
Meet with each principal to communicate blended learning plan, pilot parameters, and readiness program/checklist	Blended Learning Team	11-Jan	

Share narrowed-down software choices (with demo logins) with schools	Blended Learning Team	16-Jan	
Meet with instructional coaches to communicate blended learning plan and get them on board	Blended Learning Team	16-Jan	
Start thinking about software choices	Principal, School Leadership Team	16-Jan	
Finalize pilot classroom list of teachers	Principal	16-Feb	Only strongest teachers for Year 1 implementation
Meet with teachers (including learning specialists) to share rollout time line, blended handbook, pilot agreement, potential schedules, instructional focus	Blended Learning Team	21-Feb	
Principal rolls out readiness checklist and plan with teachers	Principal	21-Feb	Important for principal to own this part
Finalize Year 1 budgets	Blended Learning Team and Finance	21-Feb	
Identify technology storage needs and electrical requirements	IT and Facilities Teams	23-Feb	

Confirm networks are sufficient	IT Team	28-Feb	Confirm procurement and installation plan is in place to meet launch date
Complete inventory of existing machines	IT Team	28-Feb	Can any of these be used for blended learning?
Identify number of classroom computers needed to be ordered	Blended Learning Team	5-Mar	
Post blended learning teaching assistant (BLTA) job description	Blended Learning Team	5-May	
Screen applicants for blended learning teaching assistant position	Blended Learning Team	10-May	
Make decision on computer device of choice	Blended Learning Team	10-May	
Interview blended learning teaching assistant candidates	Principal, Blended Learning Team	15-May	
Conduct needs assessment/inventory of furniture that can be used for blended learning; identify number of tables and chairs needed	Blended Learning Team	15-May	
Order furniture for blended learning classrooms	Blended Learning Team	15-May	Allow 6–8 weeks for delivery, plus time for assembly and installation

Order computers and additional networking equipment, if necessary	IT Team	15-May	Ensure computers arrive in time for unpacking, imaging, installation
Confirm software decisions for next school year	Blended Learning Team	1-Jun	
Hire blended learning teaching assistant	Principal	5-Jun	Set start date for week before school starts
Negotiate new software contracts	Blended Learning Team	10-Jun	
Book software training dates for end of summer	Blended Learning Team	15-Jun	
Image computers (if needed)	IT Team	1-Jul	
Create draft teaching schedules that include blended rotations	Instructional Coaches	1-Jul	
Order headphones	Blended Learning Team	1-Jul	One pair per student, plus cache of extras
Schedule Saturday schools	Principals	15-Jul	
Set up furniture in classrooms	Office Managers, School Facilities People	20-Jul	Make sure teachers have cleaned rooms and open spaces for tables are marked
Upgrade infrastructure	IT Team	1-Aug	
Provision accounts for all software (after PowerSchools rollover)	Blended Learning Team	1-Aug	

Onboard blended learning teaching assistant	Blended Learning Team	4-Aug	
Conduct software training (2 half days)	Blended Learning Team and Software Providers	6-Aug	
Conduct Blended Learning Handbook training for teachers and ed specialists	Blended Learning Team (Internal Trainer)	6-Aug	
Collect software-training feedback	Blended Learning Team	6-Aug	
Send blog information to blended learning teachers so they can start blogging	Blended Learning Team	6-Aug	Remind teachers that the expectation is that they blog a minimum of once per month
Share classroom incentives with blended learning teaching assistant	Blended Learning Team	6-Aug	
First day of school	Teachers	12-Aug	
Start teaching blended learning lessons	Teachers	18-Aug	
Teachers start teaching routines for getting on and off the computers	Teachers	18-Aug	
Review Year 1 budgets	Blended Learning Team and Finance	1-Sep	

Blended Learning Teaching Assistants set up stools and headphones in all classrooms	Blended Learning Teaching Assistant	6-Sep	
Computers are turned on (first possible date)	Teachers (Who Have Shown Readiness)	9-Sep	
Determine readiness of classrooms starting blended learning	Coaches and Principal	9-Sep	
Set up computers (according to readiness)	IT Team and/ or Blended Learning Teaching Assistant	9-Sep	
Administer diagnostics (first possible date) once computers are in classroom	Teachers	9-Sep	
Blended Learning Teaching Assistant meets with teachers around data; set biweekly routine for sharing software data	Blended Learning Teaching Assistant	15-Sep	
Blended Learning Team meets with principal around blended learning progress; set biweekly check-in for sharing blended learning progress and building principal ownership of blended	Blended Learning Team	25-Sep	

Pull data to check how things are going	Blended Learning Team	25-Sep	
Continue to monitor data and make adjustments to program	Blended Learning Team and BLTA	25-Oct	
Participate in follow-up training (if needed)	Teachers	9-Nov	
Continue to monitor data and make adjustments to program	Blended Learning Team and BLTA	25-Nov	
Administer second diagnostic to have content re-provisioned	Teachers	15-Dec	
Continue to monitor data and make adjustments to program	Blended Learning Team and BLTA	20-Dec	
Analyze data of second diagnostic	Principal, Blended Learning Team	5-Jan	
Review Year 1 and confirm Year 2 budgets	Blended Learning Team and Finance	1-Feb	
Continue to monitor data and make adjustments to program	Blended Learning Team and BLTA	25-Feb	
Start planning for summer training: set date, tentatively schedule vendors	Blended Learning Team	1-Mar	

Continue to monitor data and make adjustments to program	Blended Learning Team and BLTA	25-Mar	
Create evaluation survey for teachers on pilot year	Blended Learning Team	25-May	
Administer final diagnostic to calculate growth	Teachers	25-May	
Complete evaluation survey on pilot year	Teachers	1-Jun	
Analyze data from pilot survey and share out	Blended Learning Team and Principal	22-Jun	
Analyze data from final diagnostic	Blended Learning Team and Principal	1-Jun	
Make changes to software choices if survey data and achievement data reveal a need	Blended Learning Team	15-Jun	
Pay teacher stipends (principal budget)	Principal	10-Jun	
Schedule next year's new training and follow-up training for returning teachers (if needed)	Blended Learning Team	15-Jun	

Appendix F

ROCKETSHIP CURRICULUM EVALUATION RUBRIC

Dealbreakers
Must be either adaptive or assignable content (ideally both; see rubric below)
• Browser-based and no local server
• Able to serve 120 simultaneous users over standard 1 Mbps connection
• Students can work independently without the oversight of a credentialed teacher
• No additional materials/manipulatives required
• System tracks individual student progress by:
○ Lessons complete
○ Percent mastery of individual micro-standards
○ Accuracy
○ Time on task
• System continues to provide other lessons once student has completed an assigned lesson/standard
• Chrome-compatible

Necessary Future Enhancements				
• Alignment: reporting by Common Core Standards at the micro-standard level				
• API: ability to fully adopt Rocketship Teacher Dashboard APIs:				
○ Single user sign-on				
○ Automated account provisioning				
○ Data integration with Teacher Dashboard				
○ Assignability of content via Teacher Dashboard through web services API (requires ability for admin to target Common Core Standards at the micro-objective level)				
		Does Not Meet	**Partially Meets**	**Meets/ Exceeds**
Weighted Decision Criteria Items	**Weighting**	**0**	**(1–2)**	**(3–4)**
• Alignment and Content Coverage—at least 100 hours of content/subject/ grade (exceptions for fact fluency/other targeted skill programs). Content aligned to Common Core grade-level standards at the micro-standard level.				
• Assessments—program assigns leveled pre-/post-assessments to measure student growth and readiness for next units. Independent assessments verify content mastery.				
• Adaptivity—system determines student's				

current instructional level within addressed content micro-standard and adapts instruction to current level.				
• Assignability—ability for admin to influence/control content assignment in an automated, efficient way.				
• API and Data Integration—full adoption of Rocketship Teacher Dashboard APIs for account management and academic data.				
• Curriculum—research-based instructional design and demonstrable student outcomes in field-testing.				
• Curriculum—system teaches and re-teaches concepts through multiple pedagogical approaches.				
• Engagement—built-in incentive system (game, rewards) for students as they demonstrate their learning.				
• Cost—all-in cost proportional to $100/ student total online curricula budget (roughly $15–30 for core program, $10–15 for addressable				

		Does Not Meet	Partially Meets	Meets/ Exceeds

practice, $5–10 for fluency individual skill, i.e., typing).

- Train-the-trainers mode— one time training that we can deliver to ILS personnel.

Total Pre-Screen Score (Max 140)

Verify During Trial	**Weighting**	**0**	**(1-2)**	**(3-4)**
• Assessment and Results— student makes significant gains which can be measured by Rocketship's micro-objective assessments.				
• Confirmation of Adaptivity—system modifies lessons in real time based on student error and alters content to adapt to student's individual level.				
• Confirmation of Assignability—system allows user to assign content and alter scope and sequence at micro-standard level.				

• Student Usability—ease of student navigation and comprehension of instructions.				
• Admin Oversight— simplicity for coordinators to administer program and assist students.				
• Engagement/Breadth— curriculum could be used continuously without burn-out or disengagement.				
• Support—phone/e-mail access to responsive, respectful, effective support team.				
Total Trial Verification Score (Max 112)				

Appendix G

TEACHER SELF-ASSESSMENT: BLENDED LEARNING READINESS

In order for there to be a successful launch of blended learning in your classroom, instructional, behavioral, and data-driven elements need to be in place. Use this document with your instructional coach to determine your classroom readiness.

Instructional Elements	Description	Next Steps/Goals
• Students know and have extension work that they complete without prompting. *They can complete this with 100% independence (for 25–30 minutes).* **Example:** *When finished with independent work during math mini-lesson, students have flashcards that they take out and work on independently, without disturbing classmates.*	List or describe what students do for: ELA: Math:	• Discuss ideas for building independence with coach. • Focus with class to build independence. • Ask for coach observation of students working independently.

Behavioral Elements	Description	Next Steps/Goals
• Behavior management system is implemented in a way that positively supports student behaviors. • Procedures around use of computers have been taught and student behavior demonstrates they have learned them. **Example:** *Teacher gives consequence to a student that requires him or her to go to the reflection table and the student does so without disruption or question.*	Behavior management system • Is displayed in the classroom • Is used effectively so that instruction or flow of the class is not interrupted by its use • Supports a positive classroom culture	• Discuss ideas to make behavior management system more seamless with coach. • Focus with class to build buy-in. • Ask for coach support.
Use of Data	**Description**	**Next Steps/Goals**
• Teacher has a clear sense of how students will be grouped, based on data (either behavioral or academic).	Articulate your plan for using data to group students	• Discuss ideas for using data with coach. • Make groups with rationale for discussion with coach.

Appendix H

END-OF-YEAR TEACHER SURVEY QUESTIONS

General Questions About Blended Learning

1. I am glad my school is a blended learning school.
   a. Strongly Disagree
   b. Disagree
   c. Not Sure
   d. Agree
   e. Strongly Agree

2. Blended learning has allowed my students to make greater achievement gains than before I ran blended learning.
   a. Strongly Disagree
   b. Disagree
   c. Not Sure
   d. Agree
   e. Strongly Agree

3. Blended learning is an effective support as we implement Common Core.
   a. Strongly Disagree
   b. Disagree
   c. Not Sure
   d. Agree
   e. Strongly Agree

4. Running blended learning in my classroom has made this job more sustainable.
   a. Strongly Disagree
   b. Disagree
   c. Not Sure
   d. Agree
   e. Strongly Agree

5. The data I receive from software programs helps me make more informed instructional decisions.
   a. Strongly Disagree
   b. Disagree
   c. Not Sure
   d. Agree
   e. Strongly Agree

6. My students are highly engaged in their computer work.
   a. Strongly Disagree
   b. Disagree
   c. Not Sure
   d. Agree
   e. Strongly Agree

7. I would like to run blended learning in my classroom next year.
   a. Strongly Disagree
   b. Disagree
   c. Not Sure
   d. Agree
   e. Strongly Agree

8. I feel confident in my ability to run blended learning (and the software programs) in my classroom.
   a. Strongly Disagree
   b. Disagree
   c. Not Sure
   d. Agree
   e. Strongly Agree

9. I feel I've received adequate support for implementing blended learning in my classroom from my blended learning teaching assistant.
   a. Strongly Disagree
   b. Disagree
   c. Not Sure
   d. Agree
   e. Strongly Agree

10. Are there other ways you'd like your blended learning teaching assistant, principal, or Home Office team to support you? (*Open Response*)

11. I've increased the number of small groups I pull, as compared to before I ran blended learning in my classroom.
    a. Strongly Disagree
    b. Disagree
    c. Not Sure
    d. Agree
    e. Strongly Agree

12. I find it really challenging to have my students on the computers for 30 minutes for English language arts and 30 minutes for math.
    a. Strongly Disagree
    b. Disagree
    c. Not Sure
    d. Agree
    e. Strongly Agree

13. Comments? Questions? Victories? Challenges? More feedback? (*Open Response*)

Software-Specific Questions

14. What software do you use in your classroom for math? (*Pull-Down Menu*)

15. Please rank the software you selected above on the following criteria:
    Student engagement (1–10)
    Quality of content (1–10)

16. What software do you use in your classroom for English language arts? (*Pull-Down Menu*)

17. Please rank the software you selected above on the following criteria:
    Student engagement (1–10)
    Quality of content (1–10)

18. What software do you use in your classroom for reading? (*Pull-Down Menu*)

19. Please rank the software you selected above on the following criteria:
    Student engagement (1–10)
    Quality of content (1–10)

20. Anything else you'd like us to know? (*Open Response*)

Appendix I

SAMPLE BLENDED NEWSLETTER 1

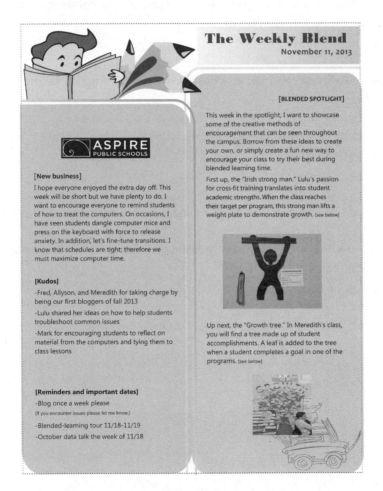

Figure AI.1

Appendix J

SAMPLE BLENDED NEWSLETTER 2

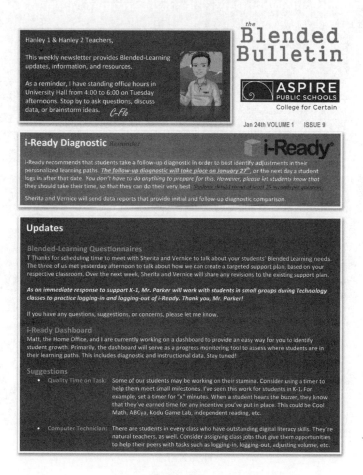

Figure AJ.1

Hanley 1 Update
Mrs. Jones

I want to send a special shout out to Ms. Cornwell & Ms. Caviness for being so supportive of Blended Learning. I appreciate your continuous in-person/e-mail communication and feedback regarding all aspects of Blended Learning.

THANK YOU SO MUCH FOR ALL THAT YOU DO!

Hanley 2 Update
Mrs. Turner

Hello, Hanley 2 teachers!

Shout out to Thaddeus from Ms. H. Jackson's class. He demonstrated fantastic problem-solving skills: the laptop wasn't working, and he immediately checked cords and power to resolve the issue. Shout out to Mrs. Foxx & Ms. Johnson for having 100% of scholars complete unique lessons in DreamBox.

Student Spotlight: What Does "Blended Learning" Mean to You?

Grade: 3   Teacher: Ms. Chestnutt   Student: Gabrielle (Gabby)

Sometimes, in i-Ready, I get mixed up on some of the bigger words. I really, really like how it helps me with my reading, even though it's hard. I've learned how to describe nouns and verbs, like action verbs – "Jump!"

With DreamBox, I've learned multiplication and addition. I really like the mental math. Math helps me in my life...going to the store, counting money, how much change I get back. It's really useful.

I like learning in small groups. I feel supported, and it's not as confusing as when the whole class is with the teacher.

Resource Update

Our Blended Learning Dropbox folder includes a variety of photos, videos, and materials to help you get and share ideas.

Weekly Updates:

- Mrs. Foxx meets with students to walk through the DreamBox interface. This is a great way to help students learn and explain expectations. They worked on sample problems, too. *(see "Foxx_DreamBox.jpg" within the "photos" folder.)*

- Mrs. Quraishi's reading rotation slides. Great visuals to support rotations. Thanks, Shea! *(see "Reading_Slideshows" within the "resources" folder.)*

BLEND Award Winner

Words of Wisdom from Mrs. Quraishi

"Students are the key! On the best days, it's as though I'm not needed. When students have ownership over their learning, they know what to do and how to do it.

It's great to see them get excited about their names on the wall for all of their hard work. They deserve it!"

Figure AJ.1

258

Appendix K

SAMPLE BLENDED LEARNING CLASSROOM FLOOR PLANS

Option 1

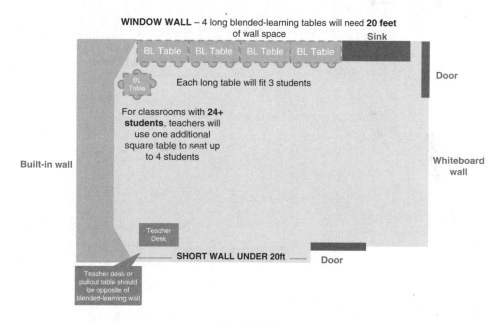

Figure AK.1

Option 2

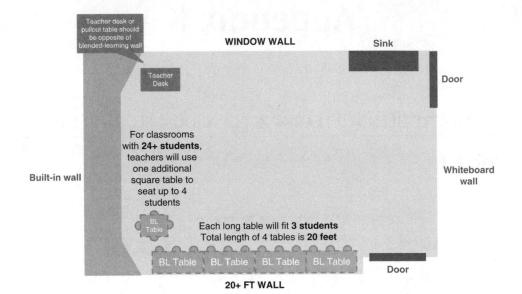

Figure AK.2

Appendix L

**SAMPLE COMMON CORE WEEKLY SCHEDULE FOR
GRADES K–2 BLENDED LEARNING CLASSROOMS**

Blended Learning with Science Teacher (K-2)

MONDAY		TUESDAY		WEDNESDAY		THURSDAY		FRIDAY	
8:00–8:20	Independent Reading/HW Check (20 min)	8:00–8:20	Independent Reading/HW Check (20 min)	8:00	PREP	8:00–8:20	Independent Reading/HW Check (20 min)	8:00–8:20	Independent Reading/HW Check (20 min)
8:20–8:35	Morning Meeting (15 min)	8:20–8:35	Morning Meeting (15 min)	8:45–9:00	Independent Reading/HW Check (15 min)	8:20–8:35	Morning Meeting (15 min)	8:20–8:35	Morning Meeting (15 min)
8:35–9:05	Calendar Math Fact Fluency Number Strings (30 min)	8:35–9:05	Calendar Math Fact Fluency Number Strings (30 min)	9:00–9:10	Morning Meeting (10 min)	8:35–9:05	Calendar Math Fact Fluency Number Strings (30 min)	8:35–9:15	Math Problem Solving (40 min)
9:05–9:35	Math Lesson→ Group 1 (30 min)	9:05–9:35	Math Lesson→ Group 1 (30 min)			9:05–9:35	Math Lesson→ Group 1 (30 min)		
9:40–10:10	Math Lesson→ Group 2 (30 min)	9:40–10:10	Math Lesson→ Group 2 (30 min)			9:40–10:10	Math Lesson→ Group 2 (30 min)		

	MONDAY		TUESDAY		WEDNESDAY		THURSDAY		FRIDAY	
	10:10–10:20	Math Closing/Independent Practice (10 min)	10:10–10:25	Math Closing/Independent Practice (15 min)	9:10–9:40	Calendar Math Fact Fluency Number Strings (30 min)	10:10–10:15	Math Closing/Independent Practice (10 min)	9:15–10:00	Writer's Workshop (45 min)
	10:20–11:00	Phonics (40 min)			9:40–10:10	Math Lesson→ Group 1 (30 min)	10:15–11:00	Phonics (45 min)		
			10:30	PREP/ SCIENCE	10:15–10:45	Math Lesson→ Group 2 (30 min)			10:00–10:50	Content Extensions (50 min)
	11:00–11:15	Content Instruction (15 min)			10:45–10:55	Math Closing/Independent Practice (10 min)	11:00–11:15	Writer's Workshop (15 min)		
					10:55–11:15	Phonics (20 min)			10:50–11:00	Pack Up
	11:15	Lunch/Recess	11:15	Lunch	11:15	Lunch	11:15	Lunch	11:00	Lunch
									11:15	PREP/ SCIENCE
	12:00–12:15	Content Instruction (15 min)	12:00–12:45	Phonics (45 min)	12:00–12:25	Phonics (25 min)	12:00–12:30	Writer's Workshop (30 min)	12:00	Dismissal

	MONDAY	TUESDAY	WEDNESDAY	THURSDAY	FRIDAY
	12:15–12:45 Content Extensions→ Group I (30 min)	12:45–1:15 Content Instruction (30 min)	12:25–1:05 Writer's Workshop (40 min)	12:30–1:00 Content Instruction (30 min)	
	12:45–1:15 Content Extensions→ Group 2 (30 min)	1:15–1:45 Content Extensions→ Group I (30 min)	1:05–1:45 Content Lesson (40 min)	1:00 PREP	
	1:15–1:45 Writer's Workshop (30 min)				
	1:45 Recess	1:45 Recess	1:45 Recess	1:45 Recess	
	2:00 Writer's Workshop (15 min)	2:00–2:30 Content Extensions–> Group 2 (30 min)	2:00–2:30 Content Extensions→ Group I (30 min)	2:00 Content Extensions→ Group I (30 min)	
	2:15 Pack Up				
	2:30 PREP	2:30 Writer's Workshop (30 min)	2:30–3:00 Content Extensions→ Group 2 (30 min)	2:30 Content Extensions→ Group 2 (30 min)	
		3:00 Pack Up	3:00 Pack Up	3:00 Pack Up	
	3:10 Dismissal	3:10 Dismissal	3:10 Dismissal	3:10 Dismissal	

Appendix M

SAMPLE COMMON CORE WEEKLY SCHEDULE FOR
GRADES 3–5 BLENDED LEARNING CLASSROOMS

Blended Learning with Science Teacher (Grades 3–5)

Monday	Tuesday	Wednesday	Thursday	Friday
7:55–8:05 (15 min) Morning Meeting/Social Skills	7:55–8:05 (10 min) Unpack/Check HW/Agenda	7:55–8:20 (15 min) Morning Meeting/Social Skills	7:55–8:05 (10 min) Unpack/Check HW/Agenda	7:55–8:55 (60 min) Unpack/Council
8:05–8:15 (10 min) Check HW/Agenda	8:05–8:30 (25 min) Fact Fluency (5 min) Number Talks (10 min) Daily Review (10 min)	8:05–8:15 (10 min) Check HW/Agenda	8:05–8:30 Fact Fluency (5 min) Number Talks (10 min) Daily Review (10 min)	8:55–9:10 (15 min) Check HW/Agenda
9:50–10:00 (10 min) Fact Fluency		9:50–10:00 (10 min) Fact Fluency		
8:30–9:15 (45 min) Prep	8:30–9:15 (45 min) Science	8:30–9:15 (45 min) PE	8:30–9:15 (45 min) Science	
9:15–10:00 (45 min) Writer's Workshop	9:15–9:45 (30 min) Independent Reading/Digital Reading	9:15–10:00 (45 min) Writer's Workshop	9:15–9:45 (30 min) Independent Reading/Digital Reading	9:10–9:20 Recess
				9:20–10:20 (60 min) ELA
	9:45–10:00 (15 min) Grammar/Conventions		9:45–10:00 (15 min) Grammar/Conventions	10:20–11:00 (40 min) Math Performance Task

Monday	Tuesday	Wednesday	Thursday	Friday
10:00–10:20 Recess	10:00–10:20 Recess	10:00–10:20 Recess	10:00–10:20 Recess	11:00–11:30 Lunch
10:25–10:55 (30 min) Math Mini Lesson-group1	10:25–10:55 (30 min) Math Lesson→Group 1	10:25–10:55 (30 min) Math Mini Lesson-Group1	10:25–10:55 (30 min) Math Lesson→Group 1	11:30–11:50 (20 min) Math Performance Task
11:00–11:30 (30 min) Math Mini Lesson-Group 2	11:00–11:30 (30 min) Math Lesson→Group 2	11:00–11:30 (30 min) Math Mini Lesson-Group 2	11:00–11:30 (30 min) Math Lesson→Group 2	
11:30–11:45 (15 min) Math Independent Practice/Closing	11:30–11:45 (15 min) Math Independent Practice/Closing	11:30–11:45 (15 min) Math Independent Practice/Closing	11:30–11:45 (15 min) Math Independent Practice/Closing	
11:45–12:10 (30 min) Independent Reading	11:45–12:05 (20 min) Writer's Workshop	11:45–12:10 (30 min) Independent Reading	11:45–12:05 (20 min) Content Workshop	
12:10–12:45 Lunch	12:10–12:45 Lunch	12:10–12:45 Lunch	12:10–12:45 Lunch	
12:45–1:15 (30 min) Content Lesson	12:45–1:15 (25 min) Writer's Workshop	12:45–1:15 (30 min) Content Lesson	12:45–1:15 (25 min) Writer's Workshop	11:50–12:50 (60 min) Cycle of Inquiry/Assessment
1:15–1:45 (30 min) Content Workshop→Group 1	1:15–1:35 (20 min) Content Lesson	1:15–1:45 (30 min) Content Workshop→Group 1	1:15–1:35 (20 min) Content Lesson	

Monday	Tuesday	Wednesday	Thursday	Friday
1:45–2:15 (30 min) Content Workshop→Group 2	1:35–2:05 (30 min) Content Workshop→Group 1	1:45–2:15 (30 min) Content Workshop→Group 2	1:35–2:05 (30 min) Content Workshop→Group 1	
2:15–2:35 (20 min) Number Strings & Daily Review	2:05–2:35 (30 min) Content Workshop→Group 2	2:15–2:35 (20 min) Number Strings & Daily Review	2:05–2:35 (30 min) Content Workshop→Group 2	
2:40 Dismissal	2:40 Dismissal	2:40 Dismissal	2:40 Dismissal	1:00 Dismissal

Appendix N

LESSON 1	Locating Each Workstation in the Classroom
Objective	Students will be able to locate designated workstation areas in the classroom by walking to correct location when asked.
Materials	Chart paper (with desks/tables/computers pre-drawn), green marker, red marker
Time	7–10 minutes
Procedures Teacher Models	"I have drawn a map of our classroom, so we can see where we should be in the room depending on the workstation we are working on. Over here (point to the computer wall in your classroom and then the computer wall on the chart paper) will be the computer workstation. I am going to label it in red (red is for voice level 0). Only be in the computer workstation area if that is your assigned workstation." *"Who is allowed to be in the computer workstation area?"* *"Where is the computer workstation area?"* "The next workstation is the read-to-self area. (Point to the read-to-self area in your classroom, and point to it on the classroom map.) I'm going to label this area in red, as well (voice level 0). The only friends who are allowed to be in the read-to-self workstation area are the ones who have been assigned to that workstation." *"Who is allowed to be in the read-to-self workstation area?"* *"Where is the read-to-self workstation area?"* "The next workstation area is buddy reading. (Point to the buddy reading area in your classroom and then point to it on the classroom map.) I am going to label this area in green (voice level 1). You should only be in the buddy reading workstation if you have been assigned to that workstation." *"Who is allowed to be in the buddy reading workstation area?"* *"Where is the buddy reading workstation area?"* "The last workstation area is work on words/work on writing. (Point to the work on words/work on writing area in your classroom and then point to it on the classroom map.) I am going to label this area in green (level 1 voice). The only people who are allowed to be in the work on

LESSON 1	Locating Each Workstation in the Classroom
	words/work on writing area are the ones who have been assigned to that workstation." *"Who is allowed to be in the work on words/work on writing workstation area?"*
Students Model	Call on one student to model walking to the computer workstation, one student to model walking to the read-to-self workstation, one student to model walking to the buddy reading workstation, and one student to model walking to the work on words/work on writing workstation. After you have had single student models, ask one whole row to model walking to a specific workstation area. Practice all rotations.
Number of Lessons	2 or until mastered

LESSON 2	Noise Level at Workstations
Objective	Students will be able to use appropriate voice level at designated stations.
Materials	Computer voice-level poster, PowerPoint
Time	5–7 minutes
Procedures Teacher Models	*"What voice level do we use during workstations?"* *"What does a voice level 1 sound like?"* *"Why is it important to be at a voice level 1 during stations?"* Have students model how to talk in a level 1 voice as they do during workstations. *"What do you think our voice level should be at the computers?* The volume at the computers needs to be at a level 0. (Show PowerPoint slide with Illustration.) It needs to be at volume 0, so that you don't distract your friends at the other stations. You are not going to be working with a buddy, and you will all be doing different things, so there is no talking." "Let me show what my voice level at the computer station sounds like." Model going to the back and sitting down using a level 0 voice.

(continued)

LESSON 2	Noise Level at Workstations
	"What voice level did I use when I was sitting down at the computer?" (0) Place the volume poster on the wall by "computer stations."
Students Model	Call on a few students to model what level 0 sounds like at the computer station. *"What voice level did our friends use?"* *"What voice level do we need to have at the computers? Workstations?"* Remind students to keep a level 1 voice during other workstations.
Number of Lessons	1 or until mastered

LESSON 3	Correct Behavior on Computers
Objective	Students will be able to demonstrate correct behavior (bottom flat on seat, eyes and hands on own computer, headphones on, voice level 0) when sitting at the computer workstation.
Materials	PowerPoint or poster with expectations, headphones
Time	7–10 minutes
Procedures Teacher Models	*"What did we learn about our voice level at the computers? Why does it need to be at a level 0?"* (It needs to be at a level 0 so everyone can focus.) *"Yesterday, we learned that our voice level needs to be at a 0. Today, we are going to learn how to properly sit at the computer station. When you're at the computer station you need to sit on your bottom. Your bottom needs to touch the chair, and your feet need to touch the floor (or close)."* Model doing this. *"Your eyes and hands also need to be on your own computer. You cannot touch your friend's computer, or look to see what your friend is doing."* *"Where should your eyes and hands be?"* (on own computer) Model doing this using your own laptop. *"Why is it important to keep your eyes and hands to yourself?"*

LESSON 3	Correct Behavior on Computers
	"The next thing that you need to remember is to always have your headphones on." Model putting your headphones on. Focus on the string that attaches to the headphones. "The headphones will be in individual bags with the students' names on them." *"What did you notice about my noise level?"* (level 0) Go over the 3 rules one more time. Model sitting incorrectly and have students correct you referring back to yesterday's poster or PowerPoint listing expectations.
Students Model	Have students model the correct behavior for the class using the classroom computers. *"Did they show us the correct computer workstation behavior? Why not?"*
Number of Lessons	1 or until mastered

LESSON 4	Correct Behavior at Workstations
Objective	Students will be able to demonstrate correct behavior (eyes on work, ignoring those using the computer) when working in designated workstation areas.
Materials	Chart paper
Time	10 minutes
Procedures Teacher Models	(Create I-chart with class.) "During workstations, some friends in our class will be at the computers, while others are with the teacher. Others may be working independently or in pairs." "It's important that we're all respectful of where we are—what we're working on—and what's expected at the station. This helps us avoid distractions or being distracting."

(continued)

LESSON 4	Correct Behavior at Workstations
	"What should students who are working at workstations be doing?" (Record responses on I-chart.) *"Why is it important to not distract other students?"* "You only have a short amount of time, so you need to make sure you are able to complete all tasks." "If you look at—or distract—others, you won't be able to complete work." "During workstations, (insert your name) will be reading with students at this station (reading area)." *"What will (insert your name) be doing during workstation time?"* (Record responses on I-chart.)
Students Model	Have a group of students at each workstation model what stations should look and sound like in practice. *"What do you see the groups doing during workstations?"* *"Are they following the expectations of the I-chart?"*
Number of Lessons	Review I-chart each day prior to starting workstations.

LESSON 5	Necessary Materials at Workstations
Objective	Students will be able to prepare workstation materials and place these items on desks before transitioning to designated workstation area.
Materials	Student workstation materials—progress-monitoring form, reading, or math packet for computers
Time	5–8 minutes
Procedures Teacher Models	*"What materials do we use during workstations?"* *"When we begin our transitions, we will need to practice moving quietly and quickly into our ready positions, so we can begin our stations."* Using transition I-chart (from earlier lesson), add workstation materials to transitioning. *"Pencils will cause marks and damage the tables and computers. So, you need to make sure that any writing materials are put away."*

LESSON 5	Necessary Materials at Workstations
Students Model	Have a correct and incorrect model. Have two students model having a hard time transitioning using I-chart. Debrief and review where they made a mistake. Keep same students and repeat with correct model and debrief. *"What did we learn today, and how is this going to help us during our station time?"*
Number of Lessons	At least 5→ going over I-chart each time, adding new ideas as needed for improved transitions/leaving materials on desk and getting started. Time students (4 min, then 3, then 2 . . .).

LESSON 6	Quiet and Effective Transitions
Objective	Students will be able to transition to designation workstation areas with a level 0 voice, walking feet, and with or without necessary materials.
Materials	PowerPoint or chart paper When the timer sounds . . . at computer workstations When the timer sounds . . . at read-to-self workstations When the timer sounds . . . at buddy reading workstations When the timer sounds . . . at work on words/work on writing workstations How to transition
Time	5–10 minutes depending on classroom
Procedures Teacher Models	*"Why is it important to be at a volume 0 and walk with purpose to our workstations?"* (Because it saves time, keeps everyone safe) *"What does a volume 0 sound like?"* "Today, we are going to practice transitioning to our computer station and back to our workstation with a volume 0 voice. This includes walking with purpose. That means that we are not talking to our friends and not touching other students' desks." *"What does walking with purpose mean?"* Model doing this incorrectly.

(continued)

LESSON 6	Quiet and Effective Transitions
	"What was wrong with the way (fill in the name) did this transition?" "That's right! We need to be at a volume 0 and walk with purpose." Model walking to the computers with purpose and with a volume 0 voice. *"What was correct about the way (fill in the name) did this transition?"*
Students Model	Have a student that you know can't do this correctly model it for the class. Ask the class what can be changed so that this transition is perfect. Have the same student model again with the changes—high-five opportunity! Put students in the direction of the path to computers, so students can model going around them. Have a group of students scattered in the path and have 5 students show how to walk around them—not stepping over them—and being safe.
Number of Lessons	Until mastered (it will be different for each classroom)

LESSON 7	Computer Workstation Etiquette
Objective	Students will be able to visualize what their computer stations should look like before and after work time.
Materials	Pictures of clean computer station
Time	5–7 minutes
Procedures Teacher Models	*"Today, we are going to learn what our computer stations should look like when we get to them and when we leave them."* "Before I go to the computer and touch it, I must use hand sanitizer (demonstrate), I need to make sure that my hands are completely dry. This is so I don't get any dirt on the keyboard." "When I get to my computer this is how my computer should look (show picture). The headphones should be placed like this, and the laptop should be open. If you get to your computer workstation and it does not

LESSON 7	Computer Workstation Etiquette
	look like this, the person who used it last did not clean it and leave it correctly." "Even if your friend did not leave the workstation as it should be, you can still use the computer. You just have to do a little extra work to set up. Remember if I don't clean up, the person behind me has to, and that is not being fair or showing respect." *"What should my computer workstation look like when I get there?"* *"What if my computer workstation does not look ready? What should I do?"* "After you are done using the computer, you need to leave it the same way you found it."
Students Model	"Now, let's have someone model how we get ready to go to the computer station." *"What do you need to do before you go to your computer station?"* I need to get hand sanitizer and make sure my hands are dry before I touch my computer. (Have the students model.) *"What should my computer look like when I get to it?"* It should be open. I will get my headphones from the plastic bag in the bin. *"How should my computer look after I am done using it?"* The same as when I got there. (Have students model what it should look like before they leave). *"What should I never bring to the computer station?"* Food and drinks, even water, are *not* allowed.
Number of Lessons	2, review questions on Day 2

LESSON 8	Preparing to Rotate
Objective	Students will be able to pack up workstation materials in 2 minutes and follow classroom map for rotation to new workstation.
Materials	Classroom map created in first lesson

(continued)

LESSON 8	Preparing to Rotate
Time	7–10 minutes
Procedures Teacher Models	"Previously, we learned how to transition into our first workstation group. *Who can tell me how we move into our first workstation group?*" "Yesterday, we learned how to leave our computer workstation for the next friend who will use that computer. *Who can tell me how we leave our computer workstation?*" "We also learned where we keep our materials for our workstation groups. *Where do we keep our materials for our workstation groups?*" (on our desks) "Today, we are going to learn how to transition from our first workstation group to our second workstation group. But first, let's review our classroom map so we remember where we go." (Teacher reviews each station depending on classroom.)
Students Model	Use PowerPoint to teach directions for transitions to next rotation. For each station, have students model the correct behavior. Finally, have students model transitioning from one station to the next. *"What did our friends do well? What do we still need to work on?"*
Number of Lessons	Since the goal is 2 minutes, you will need to build stamina with your class. Start now by timing students during their current workstation rotations.

LESSON 9	Staying Comfortable at the Computers
Objective	Students will be able to model appropriate small stretching and breathing while still sitting silently at the computer.
Materials	Chair, model stretch up, neck stretch, back stretch, breathing techniques
Time	10 minutes
Procedures Teacher Models	"Sometimes, while you are working at the computer your eyes or body might feel tired. If you feel tired, there are some stretches that you can do from your chair while sitting in front of the computer."

LESSON 9	Staying Comfortable at the Computers
	"What can you do if you get tired while sitting at the computers during workstations?" "Let's take a look at some stretches you can do while sitting in front of the computer. An important thing to remember while doing stretches is to not touch our neighbors or the computer." (Model arm stretching up, side-to-side neck stretch, back stretch, and deep breathing.)
Students Model	Have a group of 3 students model doing stretch while working at the computer during workstations.
Number of Lessons	2–3 consecutive days

LESSON 10	Caring for the Computers, Part One
Objective	Students will be able to know what *not* to touch when using computer equipment.
Materials	Artifact poster on what to touch and *not* to touch, and PowerPoint or video of proper care and maintenance of computers
Time	10 minutes
Procedures Teacher Models	Show video or PowerPoint of proper care. *"How should we take care of our computers?"* Have students think-pair-share. "To keep a computer in good working order, it is important to keep it clean and away from snack foods and liquids that can damage its parts or make it sticky dirty. We also take good care of the monitor, trackpad, keyboard, and wires." "There are certain parts of the computer that we are meant to touch." *"Which of these parts are we meant to touch?"* Have students think-pair-share, cold call, etc. (The keyboard, the trackpad)

(*continued*)

LESSON 10	Caring for the Computers, Part One
	"Good, I heard that we are supposed to touch the keyboard and the trackpad or mouse. But, I also heard that we shouldn't touch a few parts of the computer. What are those parts?" Have students think-pair-share, cold call, etc. *"Why should we never touch the computer monitor?"* *"Why should we never press the power button?"* "The screen is *not* an iPad or touch screen, so we don't touch it. We don't press the power button, because this turns off the computer. Only an adult should do this for you."
Students Model	Have student go to a computer/laptop. Have the student point to the things s/he *can* touch (keyboard, trackpad). Then, have the student put an X (with 2 fingers criss-crossed) on the things s/he should *never* touch (computer monitor, power button). Closing of lesson: *"So what are the things we can touch and what are the parts of the laptop that we can* never *touch?"*
Number of Lessons	1

LESSON 11	Caring for the Computers, Part Two
Objective	Students will be able to know what *not* to touch when using computer equipment.
Materials	Artifacts poster on what to touch and *not* to touch Video on playing it safe around electricity and cords
Time	10 minutes
Procedures Teacher Model	Show videos on playing it safe. *"What messages do these 2 videos have?"* Have students think-pair-share. "Yes, as I was walking around, I heard many students say that the message is that we should play it safe when it comes to electronics and electricity."

LESSON 11	Caring for the Computers, Part Two
	"What will happen if we pull or yank the power cord?" *"What will happen if we put our fingers into the outlet?"* "We will never pull on the electric cord, have water near or around the computer, or place our fingers in the electric outlet or in the cord of the laptop because we want to be safe and not electrocuted."
Students Model	As a review from yesterday with addition from today . . . Have a student go a to computer/laptop. Have the student point to the things s/he *can* touch (keyboard, trackpad). Then, have the student put an X (with 2 fingers criss-crossed) on the things s/he should *never* touch (computer monitor, cord, power button). Closing of lesson: *"What are the things we can touch and what are the parts of the laptop that we can* never *touch?"*
Number of Lessons	1

LESSON 12	Correct Keyboarding Position
Objective	Students will be able to demonstrate the right way to type on a keyboard by typing their name.
Materials	Keyboard printout, video on how to type
Time	10 minutes
Procedures Teacher Models	"Yesterday, we learned what we should not touch at the computer workstation. Today, you will learn the right way to touch a computer keyboard, and you will get a chance to practice typing your name." "Now, I will show you the right way and wrong way to type on a keyboard." Teacher models banging on keys and hitting the keys hard and then models the correct way of pressing down lightly on the keys. *"Is this the correct way or the wrong way? Why?"* *"Why is it important to learn the right way to type on the keyboard?"* *"What could happen if we typed the wrong way?"*

(continued)

LESSON 12	Correct Keyboarding Position
	Ask all students to raise both hands in the air like they are about to type on a keyboard or play the piano. Have students demonstrate the wrong way and the right way of typing on a keyboard in the air. "Now, before I show you how I can type my name on a keyboard, here's a short (2-minute) video that shows where the letters are and where I should place my hand on a keyboard to type faster." Pause at 0:26 and have students read some letters on the keyboard (point out the general position of numbers on top and letters in the middle, and the delete/backspace key, space bar, and enter button). (Get projector ready so you can record yourself typing on a keyboard, and show the students in real-time.) Teacher models typing his/her name slowly (finding letters) using the correct placement of hand. For younger students, you can also model using your index finger.
Students Model	Pass out keyboards to pairs/trios of students. Student A practices typing first, while Student B/C makes sure Student A is using the correct placement of their hands. Or if using a worksheet, pass out worksheet to students. Have students first color their name letter by letter in order on the keyboard. Then pencils get put away and students can practice doing correct hand placement on the keyboard worksheet and "pretend" typing their name. Teacher explains and places "Proper Hand Placement" poster near computer workstation area.
Number of Lessons	1 or more depending on class/grade level

LESSON 13	Using the Track Pad
Objective	Students will be able to understand how to click the track pad when using the computer.
Materials	Teacher's laptop, brief online video on how to use the track pad, 2 pictures to put up of teacher sliding finger on track pad and double-clicking

LESSON 13	Using the Track Pad
Time	10 minutes
Procedures Teacher Models	"Previously, we learned the correct way to type our name on the keyboard. Today, you will learn how to use the track pad or mouse on the laptop. Just as with the keyboard, there's a right way and a wrong way to touch the track pad." Teacher gathers students in a circle on rug so every student can see and models wrong way (pressing hard on track pad, clicking hard on the left select and right menu buttons) and right way (sliding finger gently across track pad and pressing gently on the left select and right menu buttons) on their own laptop. *"Is this the correct way or the wrong way? Why?"* *"Why is it important to learn the right way to use the track pad on the keyboard?"* *"What could happen if we used the track pad in the wrong way?"* "You can use the track pad to slide the arrow to where you want it on your screen. You do this by gently sliding your right index finger then picking it up and sliding it again to get to where you want the arrow to be. You can slide right to left or left to right. Let me show you." Teacher models for students. "When we have the arrow on the program that we want to open, we open it by double-clicking on the left select button. We do not need to use the right menu button." *"Show me on your fingers what 'double' means."* (Students show 2 fingers). "So, when I say double click, how many times do we have to click?" (Students say "2 times.") "Not only do we have to click 2 times, but we have to do it fast. Let me show you on my computer." Teacher models opening up a program (Firefox, Internet Explorer) from his/her desktop. "Here's a 5-minute video to show you how to use the track pad on the laptop." (Show video.)
Students Model	"Now it's your turn to try doing the two motions we learned today. (1) Sliding our index finger to move the arrow, and (2) double-clicking using our thumb."

(continued)

LESSON 13	Using the Track Pad
	"Now you try it in the air. First, lift your right index finger in the air and practice sliding it from one side to the other. Now, keep your right hand up with your palm facing down like your hand is resting on the track pad. Now move your right thumb up and down fast 2 times to double-click in the air." Teacher explains and puts up pictures of how to slide finger on track pad and double-clicking in the computer workstation area.
Number of Lessons	1 or more depending on class/grade level 2 pictures of teacher sliding finger on track pad and double-clicking

LESSON 14	Logging In
Objective	Students will be able to access their user account by logging in.
Materials	PowerPoint with mock click account for practice
Time	5 minutes
Procedures Teacher Models	"Your program account is just for you, and no one else should be using it because it's where you will complete all of your work. After selecting the program you will use, you will need to log into YOUR account." (Begin PowerPoint—logging in.) "This is all you will need to do to log into your account. Once you're logged in, you may begin your blended-learning experience." Explain synonyms for log out: close, exit, quit.
Students Model	Invite a student to demo this using the PowerPoint.
Number of Lessons	1

LESSON 15	Logging Out
Objective	Students will be able to end their session by logging out of their account.

LESSON 15	Logging Out
Materials	PowerPoint with mock log-out buttons
Time	5 minutes
Procedures Teacher Models	"Previously, you learned how to log in to your own account. *Well, what happens after your turn at the computer station has ended?*" "*Should we just walk away from the computer? Why/why not?*" "Your account has all of your information and all of your hard work. When your time is up, you need to *log out*. This means that you will close out your account, so that no one else can use your information." (Begin PowerPoint—logging out.) "1) Click on the button that says any of these terms we listed. "2) The next window will most likely say, "Are you sure?" What do you think we'll click? (YES!) "3) And you're done!" "Once you are logged out, you are ready to clean up and prepare the station for the next student."
Students Model	"Recap: 1. Why must we log out of our accounts when we are finished? 2. What are some terms we can expect to see that mean logging out?" (log out, exit, quit, end session) Invite a student to demo this using the PowerPoint.
Number of Lessons	1

LESSON 16	When the Computer Is Loading
Objective	Students will be able to know what it means when the computer is loading.
Materials	PowerPoint with screenshots showing different "loading" images
Time	5 minutes

(*continued*)

LESSON 16	When the Computer Is Loading
Procedures Teacher Models	"When you click on things on the computer, sometimes you have to wait for the computer to respond. During this wait time, we say that the computer is 'loading.'" "When the computer is loading, you do not have to do anything. All you have to do is wait." "However, this is a good time to read, work on your reading or math packet, or complete your progress-monitoring reflection." "You will know that the computer is loading when you see the following types of pictures, or icons, on your screen." Show students the loading icons. "When you are turning on the computer, or when you are logging into your account, you will have to wait for the computer to load." "Now, I will turn on the computer and log in to my account. (Turn on the computer and log in to account.) Shut down the computer, and wait for the computer to turn off."
Students Model	Choose students to turn on the computer, log in, and then turn off the computer.
Number of Lessons	1

LESSON 17	Troubleshooting Problems During Log-In
Objective	Students will be able to know how to troubleshoot problems during log-in.
Materials	PowerPoint with screenshots showing log-in pages, error icons
Time	5 minutes
Procedures Teacher Models	"Sometimes, when you type or click on things on the computer, you might make a mistake, and the computer will not go on to the next screen." "This is called an 'error.'" "You will know that there is a computer error when you see the following types of pictures, or icons, on the screen."

LESSON 17	Troubleshooting Problems During Log-In
	Show the students the error icons. "A common error is typing in the wrong user name or password when logging in to your account. When this happens, just go back, and re-check that you typed in the correct information, and try again." Model typing in the wrong user name (getting the error message), going back and re-checking the information, correcting the error, and then, successfully logging in.
Students Model	Choose students to correct user name and password errors.
Number of Lessons	1

LESSON 18	Closing the Program and Logging In Again
Objective	Students will be able to close a program and practice re-logging into the correct program.
Materials	Computer and projector to model how to close a program and re-log in
Time	5–8 minutes
Procedures Teacher Models	Model the correct typing or clicking into specific program(s). Model correctly logging out for the next group of students to use the laptops. *"Why is this important?"* *"What happens if the person in front of me doesn't log out properly?"*
Students Model	Have a student model logging in and out. Have a student model coming to the laptop and encountering a user who did not log out properly. *"What did we learn today, and how is this going to help us during our station time?"*
Number of Lessons	About 5

LESSON 19	What to Do When There's a Computer Problem
Objective	Students will be able to flip to correct help card when a problem arises with the computer.
Materials	PowerPoint illustrating flip cards, sets of flip cards (My computer is frozen. I can't log onto the computer. I can't do _____. There is a problem. Headphones do not work.)
Time	5–10 minutes, depending on classroom needs
Procedures Teacher Models	"Yesterday, I was using a new program on the computer, and I didn't know what to do!" "By the end of today's lesson, you will be able to flip to the correct help card when a problem arises." (Please write what you want your class to do.) Model for the class each slide with what you want them to do.
Students Model	Have a student that you know can't do this correctly model it for the class. Ask the class what can be changed so that when there is a problem, they know exactly what to do. Have the same student model again with the changes—high-five opportunity!
Number of Lessons	Until mastered (duration will be different for each classroom)

LESSON 20	Adjusting the Volume
Objective	Students will be able to know how to adjust the volume to make it louder or quieter.
Materials	Volume PowerPoint (see notes for slides below), popular song (embedded in PowerPoint)
Time	10 minutes

LESSON 20	Adjusting the Volume
Procedures Teacher Models	Slide 1 (title slide): "Sometimes, when we are listening to something, it is too loud and hurts our ears. Sometimes, the opposite happens. It is too quiet, and we cannot hear what is being said. It is important to find the level that is just right!" Slide 2: "This is what the volume keys look like. They are at the top of the keyboard. (Click again) This first button is what you push when you need to make the volume lower. (Click again) If it is too loud, push that button." Check for understanding (CFU)—"*What does this button do? When would I need to push this button?*" (Click again) "The next button is what you push when you need to make the volume louder. (Click again) If it is too quiet, push that button." CFU-"*What does this button do? When would I need to push this button?*" (Click again) "The next button mutes the sound, or makes it so it is completely silent. (Click again) You probably won't need to use this button, because you need to hear the different stories and directions. But, if you accidentally push it once, just push it a second time to un-mute (hear the sound)." CFU—"*What does this button do? When would I need to push this button?*" Slide 3: While listening to the embedded song, teacher models which buttons he/she is pushing on his/her laptop to raise and lower the volume. Also demonstrate the mute button. Ask, "*It is too quiet. I cannot hear it. What button should I press?*" "*Now it is too loud. What button should I press?*" "*I can't hear it at all! I wonder if I accidentally muted the sound. What button should I press?*"
Students Model	Slide 3: "While asking the following questions, have students come up to solve the volume problems." "*It is too quiet. I cannot hear it. What button should I press?*" "*Now it is too loud. What button should I press?*"

(*continued*)

LESSON 20	Adjusting the Volume
	"I can't hear it at all! I wonder if I accidentally muted the sound. What button should I press?" Teacher selects 5 students to practice raising and lowering the volume on their laptops.
Number of Lessons	1 lesson (this is reviewed in following lesson on headphones)

LESSON 21	Handling Headphones
Objective	Students will be able to know how to carefully handle headphones and solve volume problems when using their headphones.
Materials	Headphone PowerPoint (see notes in lesson below), headphones
Time	7 minutes
Procedures Teacher Models	Slide 1: "Today, we are going to learn how to carefully handle our headphones when we are at the computer. Also, we are going to review how to solve volume problems when we are wearing our headphones." Slide 2: *"What do you notice about these headphones? How do you think they got that way?"* "We need to be careful when handling headphones. If we stretch them too far or play with them, they will break." Model how to gently, without stretching too far, put the headphones on. Have students model after you. Slide 3: "One problem you might have is that the volume is too loud with your headphones on." *"How can you solve your problem?"* Slide 4: "The solution is to lower the volume by pressing the lower volume button."

LESSON 21	Handling Headphones
	Slide 5: "Another problem is that you might not be able to hear the sound, or it is too quiet." *"How can you solve your problem?"* Slide 6: "You can raise the volume." Slide 7: "If that doesn't work, check and make sure that your volume is not muted."
Number of Lessons	1

Acknowledgments

Going blended is the ultimate team sport, and this book was drawn from the participation of a multitude of teams, all of whom I feel honored to work with and for, and whose contributions to this work have influenced blended learning in schools far beyond our own.

The principals, teachers, coaches, blended learning teaching assistants, students, and staffs of Aspire ERES Academy, Aspire Titan Academy, and Aspire Hanley I and II were the Aspire pioneers of going blended and have done the hard work that shows what is truly possible. The teachers and principals at Aspire Tate Academy, Aspire Slauson Academy, Aspire Inskeep Academy, Aspire Gateway Academy, and Aspire Tech Charter Academy have begun to take more students on the blended learning journey and we continue to learn from their work as well. Their handprints are on every page of this book.

In particular, my Aspire colleagues Kim Benaraw, Jhonn Hernandez, the Titan teachers, Margaret Chi, Michael Lumpkin, Brian Sullivan, Chris Florez, Elena Sanina, and Katie Kling all shared key documents, writings, lesson plans, newsletters, and artifacts for this book. Teachers Amy Youngman and Claire Hawley wrote the original blended learning handbooks we provided our teachers; Chris Florez used his incredible expertise, writing, design, and communication skills to take what Claire and Amy created, add in the Titan teacher lesson plans, and make it useful enough that we felt confident to share it out with others, and we shared it across the country. Without them, there'd be no book.

Aspire Leaders Elise Darwish, Heather Kirkpatrick, and James Willcox have supported this work from the very start, even when they weren't sure what it could or would look like, and I'm grateful for their trust and encouragement to get this work off the ground, and then to write the book. My blended learning teammate,

Elena Sanina, has gleefully run up the steepest blended learning curve with the utmost enthusiasm to deepen this work and serve our latest schools going blended so that I could write; her contributions to this work have been crucial to our success in scaling blended throughout Aspire. Mala Batra offered much sage advice that got me through the process of writing my first book and staying sane. My Aspire Home Office colleagues are among the best people in the country to have as colleagues, and their support has made me feel even more lucky to work with all of them. And of course, there'd be no book (or Aspire Public Schools, for that matter) without Don Shalvey, who kicked off the idea of writing a book in the first place.

Outside Aspire, my blended learning friends in the Community of Innovative Practice (CIP) have been among the most professionally fulfilling, collaborative and collegial relationships in my career, and they gave me the courage and encouragement to write the book. The members of this community hail from many impressive charter organizations, schools, and districts: KIPP Foundation, KIPP Los Angeles, Milpitas Public Schools (California), New Classrooms, Touchstone Education (now Matchbook), Summit Public Schools, Rocketship Education, E. L. Haynes Public Charter School, the Alliance College-Ready Public Schools, Cornerstone Charter Schools, Highline Public Schools (Washington), Mastery Charter Schools, FirstLine Schools, New York City's iZone, DaVinci Charter, Achievement First, the Partnership for Los Angeles Schools, and Seaton Partners. I'm also grateful to Scott Benson, who helped us start the group and has let us grow it to include so many others doing this work in charters, districts, and parochial schools across the country.

I'm also deeply grateful to our funders who helped us take the initial steps into going blended, including the Michael and Susan Dell Foundation, the Bill and Melinda Gates Foundation, The Eli and Edythe Broad Foundation, the Next Generation Learning Challenges, the Charter School Growth Fund, an anonymous donor, the Rogers Family Foundation, the Harry Singer Foundation, and the Lovett and Ruth Peters Foundation.

My dear friends and blended learning colleagues Rachel Klein, Chris-Liang Vergara, Jon Deane, Pablo Meija, Meg Evans, Caryn Voskuil, Chris Florez, and Heather Kirkpatrick gave much of their time and all read through the manuscript to give me early feedback and contribute their own ideas and ensure this work rang true with their experiences, too. Bryant Wong saved me from uncertain doom with his numerous and thoughtful contributions to the technology chapter.

Jeanne Chang, Jonathan Tiongco, Robert Pambello, Anirban Bhattacharyya, Nithi Thomas, Mike Teng, and Tom Willis generously shared their perspectives and ideas based on their blended experiences, which also added texture to this work. Rachel Klein ensured there'd be some kind of merit badging experience, and Elena Sanina's creativity combined with Mayra Vega's incredible design talents made the badges come alive. The team at Jossey-Bass has made writing my first book a walk in the park.

My dear friends and former colleagues, Susan Fine and Maddy Hewitt, both told me more than a decade ago that I had a book inside me and encouraged me to write it. And my best neighbor (and attorney) ever, Larry Siskind, offered me helpful legal advice to get me from writer to published author.

My parents have fostered my love of writing from a very early age and have been my biggest champions when it comes to my work and I'm grateful they've given me the confidence and support to always follow my professional passions.

Finally, my rock-star husband, Shawn Antaya, and my truly awesome children deserve my gratitude for making my life outside the confines of the book wonderful enough to allow me the space to even consider writing the book in the first place.

Index

NOTES

NOTES

NOTES

NOTES

NOTES

NOTES